A
COLE PORTER
DISCOGRAPHY

Also by Walter Rimler

Not Fade Away
A Gershwin Companion

A
COLE PORTER
DISCOGRAPHY

WALTER RIMLER

N. CHARLES SYLVAN COMPANY
SAN FRANCISCO
1995

Copyright © 1995 by Walter Rimler

ISBN 1-886385-25-4 (hardcover)
LC 94-069684

Published by N. Charles Sylvan Company
41 Sutter Street #1533 San Francisco, CA 94104
Internet: wlr@crl.com

Printed in the United States of America
First Edition

For Jacob, Jesse and Rose

Sing me the songs I delighted to hear
Long, long ago, long ago.

—T. H. Bayley

INTRODUCTION

Until now, thorough discographies of popular music have always been about performers, not about songwriters. If you wanted to get a complete list of the people who have recorded the songs of Berlin or Porter or Rodgers or Kern or Arlen--writers who did not make a living by performing--you had to either accept the sketchy lists that could sometimes be found in the appendices of biographies, or you had to make a list of your own.

I hope that this book will begin to rectify that situation. It is the most complete listing so far of the artists who have recorded the music of Cole Porter. Included are more than 3,000 recordings by some 1,100 singers and musicians, spanning nearly eighty years of recorded sound.

The book is arranged chronologically, beginning with Porter's first published effort (a 1902 piano piece entitled "Bobolink Waltz") and concluding with songs from his last score, the 1958 television production *Aladdin*. Each song title is followed by the name of the performer who introduced the work and the venue (show, film, nightclub) in which that introduction was made. Then comes an alphabetical list of the recording artists who have released their versions. Each listing is followed by the record label and catalogue number, the format (78's to CD's), the album title, and the year of first release. There are four concluding indexes: compositions, recording artists, album titles, and shows.

Information about recording dates and reissues has not always been available and I have chosen not to make any educated guesses about these things. When it was not clear just when a recording was made, I did not enter a date. When I could not determine if one recording was the reissue of another, I have presented both of them as separate entries. Perhaps at some later stage this information will be more readily available and can be incorporated into a subsequent edition of the book. Valuable as it will then be, it will still be secondary to the main concern, which is to give admirers and students of Porter's work a way to determine who has recorded his songs and where those recordings can be found.

Popular songs differ from concert or "highbrow" music in that they are not set down in any one definitive place or form. They are continually returning to us over the years in new shapes, from new angles, and with new urgency. I hope that this book will be of use to those who want to look into the living history of the songs of Cole Porter, a master craftsman of both words and music.

Works From 1902 Through 1925

1902

Bobolink Waltz
piano piece

> **Orchestra**
> RCA LRL2-5054 (LP): "Cole"

1910

Bingo Eli Yale
Yale football song

> **Lucy Fenwick/Elizabeth Power/Angela Richards/Una Stubbs**
> RCA LRL2-5054 (LP): "Cole"

When the Summer Moon Comes 'Long
written at Yale

> **Ray Cornell/Peter Gale/Bill Kerr/Rod McLennan**
> RCA LRL2-5054 (LP): "Cole"

1911

Bull Dog
Yale football song

Male Chorus
Motion Picture Tracks MPT 6 (LP): soundtrack from the film *Night and Day* 1945

1914

I Want To Row On The Crew
introduced by Newbold Noyes in the Yale show *Paranoia*

Patti LuPone
RCA 7769-2-RC (CD), 7769-4-RC (CS): "Anything Goes"

I've a Shooting Box In Scotland
introduced by Newbold Noyes and Rufus F. King in the Yale show *Paranoia*

Prince's Band/Orchestra
Columbia A-5960 (78) 1917
Joseph C. Smith's Orchestra
Victor 18165 (78) 1917

1916

See America First
introduced by Sam Edwards in *See America First*

> **Julia McKenzie**
> RCA LRL2-5054 (LP): "Cole"

1919

Chelsea
lyrics by Cole Porter, music by Melville Gideon
introduced by Nancy Gibbs and F. Pope Stamper in the English
show *The Eclipse*

> **Garrick Theatre Orchestra**
> English Columbia 783 (78) 1919
> **Nancy Gibbs and F. Pope Stamper**
> English Columbia F-1033 (78) 1919

I Never Realized
lyrics by Cole Porter, music by Melville Gideon
introduced by Nancy Gibbs and F. Pope Stamper in the English
show *The Eclipse*

> **Garrick Theatre Orchestra**
> English Columbia 783 (78) 1919
> **Nancy Gibbs and F. Pope Stamper**
> English Columbia F-1033 (78) 1919

I Introduced
introduced by Raymond Hitchcock in *Hitchy-Koo of 1919*

> **Harold Lang, Kaye Ballard, Carmen Alvarez, Elmarie Wendel**
>> Columbia COS-2810 and CBS Special Products AOS-2810 (LP) "The Decline and Fall of the Entire World as Seen Through the Eyes of Cole Porter" 1965

Peter Piper
introduced by Raymond Hitchcock in *Hitchy-Koo of 1919*

> **Prince's Band/Orchestra**
>> Columbia A-2874 (78) 1919

Old-Fashioned Garden
introduced by Lilian Kemble Cooper in *Hitchy-Koo of 1919*

> **William Bolcom/Joan Morris**
>> Omega Record Classics OCD-3002 (CD): "Night & Day"
>
> **Cary Grant**
>> Motion Picture Tracks MPT 6 (LP): soundtrack from the film *Night and Day* 1945
>
> **Joseph M. Knecht**
>> Emerson 10319 (78) 1920
>
> **Yerkes Jazarimba Band**
>> Paramount 20043 (78) 1920
>
> **Palace Trio**
>> Victor 35696 (78) 1920
>
> **Prince's Band/Orchestra**
>> Columbia A-2874 (78) 1919

That Black and White Baby of Mine
written for but unused in *Hitchy-Koo of 1919*

> **Mabel Mercer and Bobby Short**
> Atlantic 2-604 (LP) "At Town Hall"

1920

Look Around
lyrics by Clifford Grey, music by Cole Porter
introduced by Lily St. John in *A Night Out*

> **Lily St. John and Leslie Henson**
> English Columbia F-1062 (78) 1920

Why Didn't We Meet Before?
lyrics by Clifford Grey, music by Cole Porter
introduced by Lily St. John and Leslie Henson in *A Night Out*

> **Lily St. John and Leslie Henson**
> English Columbia F-1061 (78) 1920

1922

The Bandit Band
introduced by Llora Hoffman in *Hitchy-Koo of 1922*

> **Chorus**
> > Painted Smiles PS-1371 (LP): "Cole Porter Revisited, Volume IV"

1923

Within the Quota
ballet score

> **Richard Rodney Bennett** (playing a two-piano arrangement)
> DRG-6102 (LP)

1924

Two Little Babes In The Wood
introduced by Julia Silvers/Georgie Hale/Rosie and Jennie
Dolly/James Clemons/James Naulty in *Greenwich
Village Follies of 1924*

> **Irene Bordoni/Irving Aaronson and His Commanders**
> Recorded but not released (RCA master number BVE
> 43761)
> **Leslie Hutchinson**
> World SHB-28 (78)
> **Cole Porter**
> Victor 24825 (78) 1934
> **Cole Porter**
> JJA 19732 (LP): "Cole Porter--1924-1944"

I'm In Love Again
introduced by Rosie and Jennie Dolly in *Greenwich Village
Follies of 1924*

> **Tony Bennett/Torrie Zito Orchestra**
> DRG CDMRS-801 (CD), MRSC-801 (CS): "The
> Special Magic of Tony Bennett"

I'm In Love Again (cont.)

> **Georgia Engel**
>> Painted Smiles PS-1370 (LP): "Cole Porter Revisited, Volume III"
>
> **Susannah McCorkle**
>> Stanyan SR-10136 (LP)
>
> **Bobby Short**
>> MCA MCAD-6190 (CD), MCAC-6190 (CS): "Hannah & Her Sisters"
>
> **Bobby Short**
>> Atlantic 82062-2 (CD), 82062-4 (CS): "Bobby, Noel & Cole (Bobby Short Loves Cole Porter/Bobby Short Is Mad About Noel Coward)"
>
> **Bobby Short**
>> Atlantic SD2-606 (LP)
>
> **Keely Smith**
>> Fantasy 5F-9639 (CS), F-9639 (LP): "I'm In Love Again"
>
> **Paul Whiteman**
>> Pro-Arte CDD-437 (CD), PCD-437 (CS): "Paper Moon"
>
> **Jane Wyman**
>> Motion Picture Tracks MPT 6 (LP): soundtrack from the film *Night and Day* 1945

1925

Hot-House Rose
  written for Fanny Brice

> **Bobby Short**
>> Atlantic SD 2-606 (LP): "Bobby Short Loves Cole Porter" 1971

Hot-House Rose (cont.)

Bobby Short
> Atlantic 82062-2 (CD), 82062-4 (CS): "Bobby, Noel & Cole (Bobby Short Loves Cole Porter/Bobby Short Is Mad About Noel Coward)"

Lee Wiley
> Liberty Music Shop L-297 (78) 1940

Lee Wiley
> Audiophile ACD-1 (CD), Monmouth-Evergreen MES-7034 (LP): "Lee Wiley Sings George Gershwin and Cole Porter"

The Laziest Gal In Town
written in 1927
sung by Marlene Dietrich in the 1950 film *Stage Fright*

Adrian
Accent 6004 (LP): "Adrian"
Pearl Bailey
Roulette 42004 (LP): "Pearl Bailey"
Mae Barnes
Atlantic 81817-2 (CD), 81817-4 (CS): "The Erteguns'
New York, New York Cabaret Music"
Marlene Dietrich
Columbia ML-4975 (LP): "Marlene Dietrich at the
Cafe de Paris"
Marlene Dietrich
Columbia MDK-47254 (CD), MDT-47254 (CS):
"Marlene Dietrich Album - Live at the Cafe de Paris"
Marlene Dietrich
DRG DRG-13310 (CD): "Marlene Dietrich in
London"
Nina Simone
Verve 314-518190-2 (CD): "Broadway-Blues-Ballads"
Frankie Trumbauer and His Orchestra/Fredda Gibson
Varsity 8223 (78) 1940
Julie Wilson
DRG CDSL-5208 (CD), SLC-5208 (CS): "Cole Porter
Songbook"

Let's Misbehave
introduced by Irving Aaronson and His Commanders at Les
Ambassadeurs nightclub in Paris

Irving Aaronson and His Commanders
Victor LPV-523 (78) 1928

Let's Misbehave (cont.)

Irving Aaronson and His Commanders
Victor 21260 (78)
Irving Aaronson
Warner Bros. 2HW-3639 (LP): soundtrack from the
film *Pennies From Heaven*
Irving Aaronson
RCA 2258-2-R (CD), 2258-4-R (CS): "Nipper's
Greatest Hits - the 20's"
Ben Bernie
Brunswick 3761 (78) 1927
Banjo Buddy
Brunswick 3865 (78) 1928
The Bluebirds
Vocalion 15652 (78) 1928
Irene Bordoni/Irving Aaronson and His Commanders
RCA DMM4-0407 (LP)
Lou Calabrese and His Hot Shots
Gennett 6421 (78) 1928
Hal Linden/Eileen Rodgers/Barbara Land
Epic EK-15100 (CD), JST-15100 (CS): "Anything
Goes"
Rod McLennan
RCA CRL2-5054 (LP)
Eileen Rodgers/Kenneth Mars
Epic FLM-13100 and FLS-15100 (LP)
Cybill Shepherd
MCA MCAC-25173 (CS), MCA-25173 (LP): "Cybill
Does It...To Cole Porter"
Cybill Shepherd
RCA ABL2-0967 (LP)
Bobby Short
Mobile Fidelity Sound Lab UDCD-589 (CD), Atlantic
2-609 (LP), CS2-609 (CS): "Bobby Short Live at the
Cafe Carlyle"
Billy Stritch
DRG CDSL-5215 (CD), SLC-5215 (CS): "Billy
Stritch"

Quelque-Chose
written for but unused in *Paris*

Patrice Munsel
Painted Smiles PS-1371 (LP): "Cole Porter Revisited, Volume IV"

Weren't We Fools
written for Fanny Brice

Bobby Short
Atlantic SD 2-606 (LP): "Bobby Short Loves Cole Porter" 1971
Bobby Short
Atlantic 82062-2 (CD), 82062-4 (CS): "Bobby, Noel & Cole (Bobby Short Loves Cole Porter/Bobby Short Is Mad About Noel Coward)"

Works From 1928

Lost Liberty Blues
introduced by Evelyn Hoey in the Parisian show *La Revue des Ambassadeurs*

> **Angela Richards**
> RCA LRL2-5054 (LP): "Cole"

Pilot Me
introduced by Muriel Harrisson and Carter Wardell in the Parisian show *La Revue des Ambassadeurs*

> **Bobby Short**
> Atlantic SD 2-606 (LP) "Bobby Short Loves Cole Porter" 1971
> **Bobby Short**
> Atlantic 82062-2 (CD), 82062-4 (CS): "Bobby, Noel & Cole (Bobby Short Loves Cole Porter/Bobby Short Is Mad About Noel Coward)"

Looking At You
introduced by Clifton Webb and Dorothy Dickson with Noble Sissle's Orchestra in *La Revue des Ambassadeurs*

> **Leslie Hutchinson**
> Parlophone F-242 and R-342 (78)
> **Leslie Hutchinson**
> World Records SHB-28 (LP)
> **Jack Hylton and His Orchestra**
> HMV B-5621 (78)
> **Yehudi Menuhin/Stephane Grappelli**
> Angel 4XS-37156 (CS), 37156 (LP): "Fascinating Rhythm (Music of the 30's)"

Looking At You (cont.)

Yehudi Menuhin/Stephane Grappelli
Angel CDM-69219 (CD): "Menuhin & Grappelli Play
Berlin, Kern, Porter & Rodgers & Hart" 1988
Mabel Mercer/Bobby Short
Atlantic 2-604 (LP), CS2-604 (CS): "At Town Hall"
Mabel Mercer
Atlantic 81264-4 (CS): "Mabel Mercer Sings Cole
Porter (With Cy Walter & Stan Freeman)"
Liza Minnelli
Capitol C2-96361 (CD), C4-96361 (CS): "Anything
Goes - Capitol Sings Cole Porter"
Lucy Ann Polk
V.S.O.P. 6 (LP): "Lucky Lucy Ann"
Bobby Short
Atlantic 1321 (LP)
Lee Wiley
Audiophile ACD-1 (CD), Monmouth-Evergreen MES-
7034 (LP): "Lee Wiley Sings George Gershwin and
Cole Porter"
Lee Wiley
Black Lion BLCD-760911 (CD): "Duologue"

Don't Look At Me That Way
introduced by Irene Bordoni in *Paris*

Irene Bordoni and Irving Aaronson's Commanders
Victor 21742 (78) 1928
Irene Bordoni and Irving Aaronson's Commanders
RCA LPV-523 (LP)
Susannah McCorkle
Stanyan SR-10136 (LP)
Sheila M. Sanders
Philips PHM 200-169 (LP)
Jeri Southern
Capitol T-1173 (LP)

Don't Look At Me That Way (cont.)

Sarah Vaughan
Mercury 826327-2 (CD): "Complete Sarah Vaughan
on Mercury, Vol. 2: Sings Great American Songs
(1956-1957)"
Julie Wilson
DRG CDSL-5208 (CD), SLC-5208 (CS): "Cole Porter
Songbook"

Let's Do It, Let's Fall In Love
Introduced by Irene Bordoni and Arthur Margetson in *Paris*

Irving Aaronson and His Commanders
Victor 21745 (78) 1928
Louis Armstrong
Verve 847202-2 (CD), 847202-4 (CS): "Night & Day:
The Cole Porter Songbook"
Carlos Barbosa-Lima
Concord Jazz CCD-42008 (CD), CC-42008 (CS), CC-
42008 (LP): "Barbosa-Lima Plays The Music of Bonfa
& Porter"
Tony Bennett/Marian & Jimmy McPartland
DRG MRSC-910 (CS), MRS-910 (LP): "Tony
Bennett/Marian & Jimmy McPartland & Friends Make
Magnificent Music"
Bunny Berigan
Brunswick 7858 (78) 1937
Bunny Berigan
Columbia 113-33300 (7" single)
Bunny Berigan & His Boys
Sony JLN-3109 (LP): "Take It Bunny"
William Bolcom/Joan Morris
Omega Record Classics OCD-3004 (CD): "Let's Do it
- Bolcom & Morris at Aspen"
William Bolcom/Joan Morris
Omega Record Classics OCD-3002 (CD): "Night &
Day"

Let's Do It, Let's Fall In Love (cont.)

Charlie Byrd
> Riverside OJCCD-262-2 (CD), OJC-5262 (CS), OJC-262 (LP): "Byrd at the Gate"

Elsie Carlisle
> Dominion A-125 (78)

Ian Carmichael/Patricia Routledge/Susannah McCorkle/Elaine Stritch/The Mike Sammes Singers
> Stanyan SR-10136 (LP)

Noel Coward
> Columbia MDK-47253 (CD), MGT-47253 (CS): "Noel Coward Album - Noel Coward Live From Las Vegas & New York"

Bing Crosby
> Biograph BLP-C13 (LP): "Rare Early Recordings (1929-1933)"

Meyer Davis
> Duophone D-4045 (78) 1928

Dial & Oatts
> Digital Music Products CD-495 (CD): "Dial & Oatts Play Cole Porter"

The Dorsey Brothers' Orchestra
> Okeh 41181 (78) 1929

The Dorsey Brothers' Orchestra
> Columbia C3K-52862 (CD), C3T-52862 (CS): "Swing Time! The Fabulous Big Band Era, 1925-1955"

Bobby Dukoff & the Ray Charles Singers
> RCA 547-0427 (45)

Ella Fitzgerald
> Verve 821989-2/821990-2 (CD), 823278-4 (CS), 823278-1 (LP): "Cole Porter Songbook" 1956

Ella Fitzgerald
> Pablo OJCCD-789-2 (CD), PACD-2310-751-2 (CD), 52310-751 (CS), 2310-751 (LP): "Montreux '75"

Ella Fitzgerald/Louis Armstrong
> Verve 825373-2 (CD), 827176-4 (CS): "Ella & Louis"

The Georgians
> Harmony 776-H (78) 1928

Let's Do It, Let's Fall In Love (cont.)

Terry Gibbs
> Verve 840034-2 (CD), 840034-4 (CS): "Jazz-Club Vibraphone"

Benny Goodman
> Okeh 6474 (78) 1941

Benny Goodman/Peggy Lee
> Columbia GT-31547 (CS): "All-Time Greatest Hits"

Benny Goodman/Peggy Lee
> Columbia CK-53422 (CD), CT-53422 (CS): "Best of the Big Bands, Vol. 2"

Benny Goodman/Peggy Lee
> Columbia CK-53422 (CD), CT-53422 (CS): "Benny Goodman Featuring Peggy Lee"

Mary Cleere Haran
> Columbia CK-52403 (CD), CT-52403 (CS): "There's A Small Hotel (Live at the Algonquin)"

Billie Holiday
> Okeh 6134 (78) 1941

Billie Holiday
> Columbia PG-32127 (LP): "Billie Holiday Story, Vol. 3"

Billie Holiday
> Columbia CK-47031 (CD), CT-47031 (CS): "Quintessential Billie Holiday, Vol. 9, 1940-1942"

Billie Holiday
> Columbia C3K-47724 (CD), C3T-47724 (CS): "Billie Holiday: The Legacy Box 1933-1958"

Leslie Hutchinson
> Parlophone F-242 and R-342 (78)

Leslie Hutchinson
> World Records SHB-28 (LP)

Dick Hyman
> Musicmasters 5060-2-C (CD), 5060-4-C (CS): "Cole Porter: All Through the Night"

Hal Kemp and Orchestra
> Victor 26300 (78) 1939

Anita Kerr Singers
> Bainbridge 6228 (LP): "'Round Midnight"

Let's Do It, Let's Fall In Love (cont.)

The Kirby Stone Four
Columbia 4-41229 (45) 1958
Eartha Kitt
MCA MCAC-1554 (CS): "The Best of Eartha Kitt"
Eartha Kitt
RCA 66022-2 (CD), 66022-4 (CS): "'Miss Kitt', To You"
Mundell Lowe
The Jazz Alliance TJA-10011 (CD): "Souvenirs - A Tribute To Nick Ceroli"
Majestic Dance Orchestra (recording as The Detroiters)
Cameo 9005 (78) 1929
Mary Martin
Decca 23148 (78) 1940
Glenn Miller
Everest 4004/5 (LP): "Glenn Miller"
Lee Morse
Columbia 1659-D (78) 1928
Orchestra
Decca DL 8318 (LP): soundtrack from the film *Anything Goes* 1956
Tony Pastor and His Orchestra
Bluebird B-10902 (78) 1940
Oscar Peterson/Duke Ellington/Ella Fitzgerald
Pablo 3PACD-2625-704-2 (CD): "The Greatest Jazz Concert in the World"
Trudy Richards/Billy May
Capitol C2-96361 (CD), C4-96361 (CS): "Anything Goes - Capitol Sings Cole Porter"
B. A. Rolfe and His Palais D'Or Orchestra
Edison Diamond Disk 52505 (78) 1929
Arthur Roseberry and His (Kit-Cat) Dance Band
Parlophone E-6150 (78) 1929
Royal Society Jazz Orchestra
Klavier Records International KC-5022 (CS): "Harlem to Hollywood, Vol. I"
Royal Society Jazz Orchestra/Carla Normand/Don Neely
Klavier KCD-11024 (CD): "Harlem to Hollywood"

Let's Do It, Let's Fall In Love (cont.)

Terry Shand and His Orchestra
Decca 3587 (78) 1940
Adrian Schubert and His Salon Orchestra
Banner 6245 (78) 1928
Cybill Shepherd
MCA MCAC-25173 (CS), MCA-25173 (LP): "Cybill
Does It...To Cole Porter"
Cybill Shepherd
Paramount PAS-1018 (LP)
Simon & Bard Group/Ralph Towner
Flying Fish FF-262 (LP): "Tear it Up"
Frank Sinatra/Shirley MacLaine
Capitol SW 1301 (LP): soundtrack from the film *Can-Can* 1960
Toni Tenille
USA Music Group USACD-596 (CD), USACA-596
(CS), USALP-596 (LP): "Do It Again"
Rudy Vallee and His Connecticut Yankees
Harmony 808-H (78) 1928
George Van Eps
Corinthian COR-121 (LP): "Mellow Guitar"
Ray Ventura
Odeon 165529 (78) 1929
Dinah Washington
Emarcy 826453-2 (CD), 826453-4 (CS): "In the Land
of Hi-Fi"
Paul Whiteman and His Orchestra
Columbia 1701-D (78) 1928
Lee Wiley
Liberty Music Shop L-296 (78) 1940
Lee Wiley
Audiophile ACD-1 (CD), Monmouth-Evergreen MES-7034 (LP): "Lee Wiley Sings George Gershwin and
Cole Porter"
Julie Wilson/William Roy
DRG CDSL-5208 (CD), SLC-5208 (CS): "Cole Porter
Songbook"

Let's Do It, Let's Fall In Love (cont.)

Bill Wirges and His Orchestra
Brunswick 4116 (78) 1928
Jane Wyman
Motion Picture Tracks MPT 6 (LP): soundtrack from
the film *Night and Day* 1945
Arthur Young
Regal Zonophone MR-1861 (78) 1935

The Heaven Hop
introduced by Irving Aaronson and his Commanders in *Paris*

Margery Gray
Epic FLM-13100 and FLS-15100 (LP)
Hal Linden/Eileen Rodgers/Barbara Land
Epic EK-15100 (CD), JST-15100 (CS): "Anything
Goes"

Dizzy Baby
written for but unused in *Paris*

Kenneth Nelson/Rod McLennan
RCA CRL2-5054 (LP)

Which
written for but unused in *Paris*
introduced by Jessie Matthews in *Wake Up and Dream*

William Bolcom/Joan Morris
Omega Record Classics OCD-3002 (CD): "Night &
Day"
Cybill Shepherd/Eileen Brennan
RCA ABL2-0967 (LP)
Jeri Southern
Capitol T-1173 (LP)

Works From 1929

Wake Up And Dream
introduced by Georges Metaxa in *Wake Up and Dream*

> **Nancy Grennan**
> > Painted Smiles PS-1370 (LP): "Cole Porter Revisited, Volume III"
>
> **Georges Metaxa**
> > HMV B-3016 (78)
>
> **Georges Metaxa**
> > World SHB-26 (LP)
>
> **Georges Metaxa**
> > Parlophone PMC-7150 (LP)

I Loved Him But He Didn't Love Me
introduced by Jessie Matthews in *Wake Up and Dream*

> **Kaye Ballard**
> > Columbia OL-6410, OS-2810 and CBS Special Products AOS-2810 (LP): "The Decline and Fall of the Entire World as Seen Through the Eyes of Cole Porter" 1965
>
> **Madeline Kahn/Cybill Shepherd**
> > RCA ABL2-0967 (LP)

The Banjo that Man Joe Plays
introduced by William Stephens in *Wake Up and Dream*

> **Jack Hylton and His Orchestra**
> > HMV B-5622 (78)

What Is This Thing Called Love?
introduced by Elsie Carlisle in *Wake Up and Dream*

Cannonball Adderly
> Landmark LCD-1305-2 (CD), LLP-51305 (CS), LLP-1305 (LP): "Cannonball Adderly Collection, Vol. 5: At the Lighthouse"

Ray Anthony Orchestra
> Hindsight HCD-412 (CD), HSC-412 (CS), HSR-412 (LP): "Young Man With a Horn - 1952-1954"

Ray Anthony
> Aero Space RACD-995 (CD), RACS-995 (CS): "Dancing In The Dark"

Claire Austin
> Contemporary OJCCD-1711-2 (CD): "Claire Austin Sings When Your Lover Has Gone"/"Claire Austin Sings The Blues With Kid Ory"

Patti Austin
> MCA MCAD-10136 (CD), MCAC-10136 (CS): "The Russia House"

Count Basie/Anita O'Day
> EPM Musique 157922 (CD): "Count Basie Featuring Anita O'Day & The Tadd Dameron Trio (1945-1948)"

BBC Swing Band
> Bainbridge BCD-2511 (CD): "The Age of Swing, Vol. 1"

Sidney Bechet
> His Master's Voice JK-2720 (78) 1941

Sidney Bechet
> Bluebird 2402-2-RB35 (CD), 2402-4-RB24 (CS): "Victor Sessions/Master Takes 1932-43"

Richie Beirach/George Coleman
> Triloka 185-2 (CD), 185-4 (CS): "Convergence"

Louie Bellson/Paul Smith/Ray Brown
> Outstanding 009 (LP): "Heavy Jazz, Vol. 1"

Tony Bennett/Torrie Zito Orchestra
> DRG CDMRS-801 (CD), MRSC-801 (CS): "The Special Magic of Tony Bennett"

Robert Russell Bennett
> AEI-2106 (LP)

What Is This Thing Called Love? (cont.)

Ben Bernie
   Brunswick 4708 (78) 1930
Leon Berry
   Audiofidelity Enterprises 5844 (LP): "Giant Wurlitzer
   Pipe Organ, Vol. 3"
Walter Bishop, Jr.
   Red 123251-2 (CD): "Midnight Blue"
William Bolcom/Joan Morris
   Omega Record Classics OCD-3002 (CD): "Night &
   Day"
Dee Dee Bridgewater
   Verve 314-519607-2 (CD): "Keeping Tradition"
Dial & Oatts
   Digital Music Products CD-495 (CD): "Dial & Oatts
   Play Cole Porter"
Alan Broadbent/Gary Foster
   Concord Jazz CCD-4562 (CD): "Concord Duo Series,
   Vol. 4"
Clifford Brown
   Emarcy 81460-2 (CD): "Jam Sessions"
Les Brown & His Band of Renown
   Fantasy FCD-9650-2 (CD), 5F-9650 (CS), F-9650
   (LP): "Digital Swing"
Dave Brubeck
   Musicmasters 65083-2 (CD), 65083-4 (CS): "Once
   When I Was Very Young"
The Dave Brubeck Quartet
   Columbia CK-40455 (CD), CJT-40455 (CS): "Dave
   Brubeck Quartet Plays Music from 'West Side Story'
   & 'Wonderful Town' (Plus Others)"
The Dave Brubeck Octet
   Fantasy OJCCD-101-2 (CD), OJC-5101 (CS), OJC-
   101 (LP): "The Dave Brubeck Octet"
Don Byas
   Prestige P-7598 (LP): "Don Byas in Paris"
Joey Calderazzo
   Blue Note B2-80902 (CD), B4-80902 (CS): "The
   Traveler"

What Is This Thing Called Love? (cont.)

Eddie Cano
> RCA International 3459-2-RL (CD): "Cole Porter, Duke Ellington & Me"

Elsie Carlisle
> Dominion A-125 (78)

Casa Loma Orchestra
> Decca 2144 (78) 1938

Chorus
> RCA LRL2-5054 (LP): "Cole"

Nat King Cole Trio
> Blue Note B2-98288 (CD), B4-98288 (CS): "The Best of Nat King Cole Trio"

Nat King Cole
> Blue Note B2-98931 (CD): "Capitol Jazz 50th Anniversary Collection"

Nat King Cole
> Capitol C2-99777 (CD), C4-99777 (CS): "Nat King Cole"

Cal Collins
> Concord Jazz CJ-119 (LP): "By Myself"

Chris Connor
> Contemporary CCD-14023-2 (CD), 5C-14023 (CS), C-14023 (LP): "Classic"

Connie Crothers
> New Artists NA-1002CD (CD), NA-1002 (LP): "Concert at Cooper Union"

King Curtis
> Prestige P-24033 (LP): "Jazz Groove"

King Curtis
> Prestige P-7833 (LP): "Soul Meeting"

Eddie Lockjaw Davis
> Enja 3097-08 (CD): "Jaws Blues"

Lenny Dee
> Decca ED-2347 (45)

Don & Jerry
> Lifetime 1035 (45)

Tommy Dorsey and His Orchestra
> Victor 27782 (78) 1941

What Is This Thing Called Love? (cont.)

Tommy Dorsey
> RCA PK-5121 (CS): "This is Tommy Dorsey, Vol. 2"

Eddy Duchin
> Columbia 35204 (78) 1939

Nelson Eddy
> Everest 354 (LP): "Love Songs"

Roy Eldridge
> Mercury 830923-2 (CD): "Roy Eldridge & The Swing Trumpets"

David L. Esleck
> Yes Yes SMS1000C (CS), SMS1000 (LP): "Nocturne"

Bill Evans
> Riverside 12RCD-018-2 (CD), R-018 (LP): "The Complete Riverside Recordings"

Bill Evans
> Milestone M-47034 (LP): "Spring Leaves"

Bill Evans
> Milestone 5M-47068 (CS), M-47068 (LP): "Time Remembered"

Bill Evans Trio
> Riverside OJCCD-088-2 (CD), OJC-5088 (CS), OJC-088 (LP): "Portrait in Jazz"

Tal Farlow
> Prestige P-24042 (LP): "Guitar Player"

Carl Fenton and His Orchestra
> Gennett 7104 (78) 1930

Firehouse Five Plus Two
> Good Time Jazz 12014 (LP): "Firehouse Five Plus Two Plays For Lovers"

Ella Fitzgerald
> Verve 821989-2/821990-2 (CD), 823278-4 (CS), 823278-1 (LP): "Cole Porter Songbook" 1956

Andy Fite/Red Mitchell
> New Artists NA-1014CD (CD): "Everybody Got Happy"

Curtis Fuller
> Prestige OJCCD-077-2 (CD), OJC-077 (LP): "New Trombone"

What Is This Thing Called Love? (cont.)

Hal Galper Trio
Concord Jazz CCD-4383 (CD), CJ-383-C (CS):
"Portrait"
Red Garland Trio
Prestige OJCCD-126-2 (CD), OJC-5126 (CS), OJC-
126 (LP): "A Garland of Red"
Erroll Garner
Mercury 824892-4 (CS): "Erroll Garner Plays Misty"
Erroll Garner
Verve 834935-2 (CD): "Dancing on the Ceiling -
Erroll Garner Collection 2"
Ted Giola/Mark Lewis
Quartet QCD-1006 (CD), QTC-1006 (CS): "Tango
Cool"
Dexter Gordon
Blue Note B2-46397 (CD), B4-85135 (CS): "The
Other Side of Round Midnight" 1987
Don Grolnick
Blue Note B2-98689 (CD), B4-98689 (CS):
"Nighttown"
Adelaine Hall
Teldec 75277-2 (CD): "Centennial Gala Concert"
Barry Harris Trio
Riverside OJCCD-486-2 (CD), OJC-5486 (CS), OJC-
486 (LP): "Preminado"
Hampton Hawes
Contemporary OJCCD-316-2 (CD), OJC-316 (LP):
"The Trio: Vol. 1"
Johnny Hodges/Charlie Shavers
Storyville 4073 (LP): "Man & His Music"
Billie Holiday/Ella Fitzgerald
MCA MCAC2-4099 (CS), MCA2-4099 (LP): "Billie
Holiday & Ella Fitzgerald"
Libby Holman
Brunswick 4700 (78) 1930
Lena Horne
Victor 27829 (78) 1941

What Is This Thing Called Love? (cont.)

Lena Horne
Bluebird 2192-2-RB11 (CD), 2192-4-RB6 (CS): "Bluebird Sampler 1990"

Lena Horne
RCA 66021-2 (CD), 66021-4 (CS): "At Long Last Lena"

Hot Club of France
Elektra 60857-2 (CD), 60857-4 (CS): soundtrack from the film *New York Stories*

Leslie Hutchinson
Parlophone F-243 and R-343 (78)

Leslie Hutchinson
World Records SHB-28 (LP)

Harry James
Hindsight HSC-142 (CS), HSR-142 (LP): "The Uncollected Harry James & His Orchestra, Vol. 5 (1943-1953)"

Harry James
Hindsight HCD-406 (CD), HSC-406 (CS), HSR-406 (LP): "Harry James & His Orchestra Play 22 Original Big Band Recordings (1943-1953)"

Jazz at the Philharmonic
Pablo 2PACD-2620-119-2 (CD), 52620-119 (CS), 2620-119 (LP): "Jazz at the Philharmonic in London/1969"

J.J. Johnson
Savoy SJL-2232 (LP): "Mad Bebop"

J.J. Johnson
Columbia CK-44443 (CD), CJT-44443 (CS): "Trombone Master"

J. J. Johnson/Kai Winding
Savoy Jazz SV-0163 (CD): "Jay & Kai"

James P. Johnson (Jimmie Johnson and His Orchestra)
Brunswick 4712 (78) 1930

Hank Jones
Concord Jazz CCD-4502 (CD): "Live at Maybeck Recital Hall, Vol. 16 (Hank Jones at Maybeck)"

What Is This Thing Called Love? (cont.)

Morgana King
>Muse MC-5224 (CS), MR-5224 (LP): "Higher Ground"

Eartha Kitt
>Disques Swing SWC-8410 (CS), SW-8410 (LP): "Eartha Kitt/Doc Cheatham/Bill Coleman with George Duvivier & Co."

L.A. Jazz Choir
>The Jazz Alliance TJA-10006 (CD), Pausa PC-7184 (CS), PR-7184 (LP): "From All Sides"

Sam Lanin and His Orchestra
>Romeo 1244 (78) 1930

Peggy Lee
>Hindsight HCD-220 (CD), HSC-220 (CS), HSR-220 (LP): "The Uncollected Peggy Lee with the David Barbour & Billy May Bands (1948)"

Philip Lewis and His Dance Orchestra
>Decca F-1512 (78) 1929

Enoch Light
>Project 3 PRD2-6013 (CD), PRC2-6013 (CS), 6013/14 (LP): "Big Band Hits of the 30's, 40's & 50's, Vol. 2"

Enoch Light
>Project 3 PRD-5089 (CD), PRC-5089 (CS), 5089 (LP): "Big Band Hits of the 30's, Vol. 2"

Jeff Linsky
>Kamei KR-7001CD (CD), KR-7001C (CSS): "Simpatico"

Julie London
>EMI E2-93455 (CD), E4-93455 (CS): "Julie London Sings Cole Porter"

Julie London
>EMI Records Group North America E2-99804 (CD), E4-99804 (CS): "Julie Is Her Name, Vol. 1 & 2"

Bobby Lyle
>Blue Note B2-89284 (CD), B4-89284 (CS): "The Best of Bobby Lyle"

What Is This Thing Called Love? (cont.)

Tyner McCoy
> Chesky JD51 (CD), JC51 (CS): "New York Reunion"

Howard McGhee/Sonny Criss/Barney Kessell/Trummy Young/Hampton Hawes/Wardell Gray
> Savoy Jazz SV-0166 (CD): "Jazz Concert West Coast, Vol. 3"

Marian McPartland
> Savoy ZDS-4404 (CD), SJK-2248 (CS), SJL-2248 (LP): "At the Hickory House"

Marian McPartland Trio
> Halcyon 103 (LP): "Ambiance"

Carmen McRae
> Concord Jazz CCD-4342 (CD), CJ-342-C (CS): "Fine & Mellow"

Adam Makowicz
> Novus 3006-2 (CD), 3006-4 (CS), 3003-1 (LP): "Moonray"

Bevan Manson
> Iris ICD-1004 (CD), IC-1004 (CS): "Rhythm Chowder"

Guido Manusardi/George Garzone/John Lockwood/Bob Gullotti
> Ram RMCD-4504 (CD): "Colored Passages"

Wynton Marsalis
> Columbia CK-47346 (CD), CT-47346 (CS), CM-47346 (MD)

Mary Martin
> Decca 23150 (78) 1940

Georges Metaxa
> HMV B-3016 (78)

Georges Metaxa
> World SHB-26 (LP)

Helen Merrill
> Inner City 1060 (LP): "Something Special"

Charlie Mingus
> ITI CDP-72961 (CD): "Bop Things & Cool Strings"

What Is This Thing Called Love? (cont.)

Charles Mingus
Debut 12DCD-4402-2 (CD): "The Complete Debut
Recordings"
Gene Montgomery/Wild Bill Moore
Savoy SJL-2242 (LP): "Black California, Vol. 2"
Frank Morgan Quintet
Contemporary CCD-14026-2 (CD), 5C-14026 (CS),
C-14026 (LP): "Bebop Lives!"
Paul Motian
Verve 834430-2 (CD), 834430-1 (LP): "Paul Motian
on Broadway, Vol. 1"
Gerry Mulligan/Ben Webster
Verve 841661-2 (CD): "Gerry Mulligan Meets Ben
Webster"
Naima
Altenburgh NAI-105 (CD), NAI-105C (CS): "So
Much Like Real Life"
Anita O'Day
Glendale 6001 (LP): "Anita O'Day"
Anita O'Day/Billy May
Verve 849266-2 (CD), 849266-4 (CS): "Anita O'Day
Swings Cole Porter"
Orchestra
RCA LRL2-5054 (LP): "Cole"
Charlie Parker
Verve 831553-4 (CS): "Charlie Parker With Strings"
Charlie Parker
Verve 821684-4 (CS): "Verve Years (1950-1951)"
Charlie Parker
Verve 827154-4 (CS), 827154-1 (LP): "Verve Years
(1952-1954)"
Charlie Parker
Verve 823250-2 (CD), 823250-4 (CS): "The Cole
Porter Songbook"
**Charlie Parker/Johnny Hodges/Benny Carter/Oscar
Peterson**
Verve 833564-2 (CD): "Norman Granz Jam Session
(The Charlie Parker Sides)"

What Is This Thing Called Love? (cont.)

Les Paul
> Capitol C2-97654 (CD), C4-97654 (CS): "The Legend & the Legacy, Pts. 1-4"

Art Pepper
> Discovery DSCD-837 (CD), DS-837MC (CS), DS-837 (LP), Contemporary C-7718 (LP): "Among Friends"

Art Pepper
> Blue Note B2-46848 (CD): "Modern Art - The Complete Art Pepper Aladdin Recordings, Vol. II" 1988

Art Pepper
> Pacific Jazz B2-97194 (CD): "The Artistry of Art Pepper"

Art Pepper
> Pacific Jazz B2-89281 (CD): "The Best of Art Pepper"

The Pickens Sisters
> Victor 36085 (78) 1933

The Pied Pipers
> Victor 26364 (78) 1939

Tito Puente
> Bluebird 66148 (CD), 66148 (CS): "Puente Goes Jazz"

Puttin' On The Ritz
> Pausa 7161 (LP): "Steppin' Out"

Casper Reardon and His Group
> Liberty Music Shop L-218 (78) 1937

Leo Reisman and His Orchestra/Lewis Conrad
> Victor 22282 (78) 1930

Leo Reisman and His Orchestra
> Victor 27629 (78) 1941

Leo Reisman and His Orchestra
> RCA LPV-565 (LP)

Fred Rich
> Columbia 2099-D (78) 1930

Angela Richards
> RCA LRL2-5054 and CRL2-5054 (LP)

What Is This Thing Called Love? (cont.)

Max Roach/Clifford Brown
Emarcy 814648-2 (CD): "Clifford Brown & Max Roach at Basin Street"

Marcus Roberts
Novus 63149-2 (CD), 63149-4 (CS): "If I Could Be With You"

Sonny Rollins
Blue Note B2-46518 (CD): "A Night at the Village Vanguard, Vol. II"

Sonny Rollins
Verve 314-511392-2 (CD), 314-511392-4 (CS): "Compact Jazz - Sonny Rollins & Friends"

Arthur Roseberry and His (Kit-Cat) Dance Band
Parlophone R-344 (78) 1929

Doc Severinsen/The Tonight Show Band
Amherst AMH-94405 (CD), AMH-54405 (CS): "Once More...With Feeling!"

Doc Severinsen/Cincinnati Pops Orchestra/Erich Kunzel
Telarc CD-80304 (CD), CS-80304 (CS): "Unforgettably Doc"

Artie Shaw and His Orchestra
Bluebird B-10001 (78) 1938, Bluebird 6274-2-RB (CD), 6274-4-RB (CS), 6274-1-R (LP): "Begin the Beguine"

Artie Shaw
RCA AXK2-5517 (CS): "Complete Artie Shaw, Vol. 1 (1938-1939)"

Artie Shaw and His Orchestra
Hindsight HCD-401 (CD), HSC-401 (CS), HSR -401 (LP): "Artie Shaw & His Orchestra Play 22 Original Big Band Recordings"

Artie Shaw and His Orchestra
Ranwood RC-8218 (CS): "Artie Shaw & His Orchestra"

Artie Shaw
RCA PK-5119 (CS): "This is Artie Shaw, Vol. 2"

What Is This Thing Called Love? (cont.)

Artie Shaw
>Hindsight HCD-139 (CD), HSC-139 (CS): "The Uncollected Artie Shaw & His Orchestra (1938)"

Ginny Simms
>Motion Picture Tracks MPT 6 (LP): soundtrack from the film *Night and Day* 1945

Ginny Simms
>Royale VLP 6055 (LP): "Ginny Simms"

Zoot Sims/Bucky Pizzarelli
>Classic Jazz 21 (LP): "Zoot Sims/Bucky Pizzarelli"

Frank Sinatra
>Capitol EAP-4-581 (45) 1955

Frank Sinatra
>Capitol C2-96826 (CD), C4-96826 (CS): "In the Wee Small Hours"

Frank Sinatra
>Capitol 4N-16110 (CS): "What Is This Thing Called Love"

Frank Sinatra
>Capitol CD-94317 (CD), C4-94317 (CS): "The Capitol Years"

Frank Sinatra
>Capitol C2-96611 (CD), C4-96611 (CS): "Frank Sinatra Sings the Select Cole Porter"

Frank Sinatra
>Capitol C2-94777 (CD), C4-94777 (CS), C1-94777 (LP): "The Capitol Years"

Frank Sinatra
>Capitol C2-99225 (CD), C4-99225 (CS), C5-99225 (DCC), C8-99225 (MD): "The Best of the Capitol Years" - Selections from 'The Capitol Years' Box Set

Frank Sinatra
>Capitol BBX2-99956 (CD), BBX4-99956 (CS): "Concepts"

Frank Sinatra
>Pair PDK-2-1028 (CS): "Timeless"

What Is This Thing Called Love? (cont.)

Jack Six/Francis Thorne
>Composers Recordings 585 (CD): "Porter On My Mind"

Jimmy Smith
>Blue Note B2-46546 (CD), B4-84002 (CS): "Houseparty"

Keely Smith/Nelson Riddle
>Capitol C2-96361 (CD), C4-96361 (CS): "Anything Goes - Capitol Sings Cole Porter"

Paul Smith
>Outstanding 023 (LP): "Jazz Spotlight on Cole Porter & George Gershwin"

Kay Starr
>Modern 106 (45)

Kay Starr
>Crescendo GNPD-2090 (CD), GNP5-2090 (CS), GNPS-2090 (LP): "Back To The Roots"

Kay Starr
>G.N.P. Crescendo 493 (7" single)

Ted Straeter and His Orchestra
>Decca 24053 (78) 1942

Gabor Szabo
>MCA/Impulse MCAD-33117 (CD): "The Sorcerer: Live at Jazz Workshop"

Art Tatum
>Pablo PACD-2405-426-2 (CD): "The Tatum Group Masterpieces, Vol. 3"

Art Tatum
>Pablo PACD-2405-428-2 (CD): "The Tatum Group Masterpieces, Vol. 5"

Art Tatum
>G.N.P. Crescendo GNP-9026 (LP): "Art Tatum at His Piano, Vol. 2"

Mel Torme With the Meltones
>Verve 314-511522-2 (CD), 314-511522-4 (CS): "Back In Town" 1991

What Is This Thing Called Love? (cont.)

Mel Torme
Verve 847202-2 (CD), 847202-4 (CS): "Night & Day:
The Cole Porter Songbook"
George Van Eps
Corinthian COR-121 (LP): "Mellow Guitar"
Sarah Vaughan
Hindsight HCD-601 (CD), HSC-601 (CS): "Soft &
Sassy"
Sarah Vaughan/Kirk Stuart Trio
Mercury 832788-2 (CD): "Sassy Swings the Tivoli"
Dionne Warwick
Arista ARCD-8573 (CD), AC-8573 (CS), AL-8573
(LP): "Dionne Warwick Sings Cole Porter"
Ben Webster
Contemporary OJCCD-390-2 (CD), OJC-5390 (CS),
OJC-390 (LP): "At The Renaissance"
Elisabeth Welch
Koch International 313-752-2 (CD), 213-754-4 (CS):
"The Ultimate Elisabeth Welch - the Collection of Her
Most Popular Songs"
Randy Weston
Riverside 2508 (LP): "Randy Weston Plays Cole
Porter in a Modern Mood" 1954
Paul Whiteman and His Orchestra
Victor 36085 (78) 1933
Bob Wills & His Texas Playboys
Kaleidoscope K-35 (CD), C-35 (CS), F-35 (LP):
"Tiffany Transcriptions, Vol. 9 - In the Mood"
Julie Wilson
DRG CDSL-5208 (CD), SLC-5208 (CS): "Cole Porter
Songbook"
Teddy Wilson
Black Lion BLCD-760166 (CD): "Cole Porter
Classics"
Julie Wintz and His Mayflower Orchestra
Harmony 1099-H (78) 1930
Arthur Young and His Youngsters
Regal Zonophone MR-1861 (78) 1935

What Is This Thing Called Love? (cont.)

Denny Zeitlin
Concord Jazz CCD-4572 (CD): "Live At Maybeck
Recital Hall, Vol. 27 (Denny Zeitlin At Maybeck)"

After All, I'm Only a Schoolgirl
introduced by Jessie Matthews in *Wake Up and Dream*

Alice Playten/Edward Earle
Painted Smiles PS-1358 (LP): "Unpublished Cole
Porter"

I'm A Gigolo
introduced by William Stephens in *Wake Up and Dream*

Peter Gale
RCA LRL2-5054 and CRL2-5054 (LP)
William Hickey
Columbia OL-6410, OS-2810 and CS Special Products
AOS-2810 (LP): "The Decline and Fall of the Entire
World as Seen Through the Eyes of Cole Porter" 1965
Cole Porter
Victor 24843 (78) 1935
Cole Porter
JJA 19732 (LP): "Cole Porter--1924-1944"
Leslie Hutchinson
Parlophone F-243 and R-343 (78)
Leslie Hutchinson
World Records SHB-28 (LP)

I Want To Be Raided By You
introduced by Sonnie Hale in *Wake Up and Dream*

Lynn Redgrave
Painted Smiles PS-1370 (LP): "Cole Porter Revisited,
Volume III"

You Do Something To Me
introduced by William Gaxton and Genevieve Tobin in
Fifty Million Frenchmen

Elly Ameling
Philips 412433-2 (CD), 412433-4 (CS), 412433-1
(LP): "Sentimental Me (Songs by Gershwin, Ellington, Porter)"

Andrews Sisters/Billy May
Capitol C2-96361 (CD), C4-96361 (CS): "Anything Goes - Capitol Sings Cole Porter"

The Avalons
Bim Bam Boom 106 (45) 1958

Maxine Brown
Collectables COL-5116 (CD, CS, LP): "Golden Classics"

Clicquot Club Eskimos
Domino 4464 (78) 1929

John Colianni Trio/Lew Tabackin
Concord Jazz CCD-4367 (CD), CJ-367-C (CS): "Blues-O-Matic"

Ray Conniff & His Orchestra
Columbia CK-8037 (CD): "'S Marvelous"

Ray Conniff
Columbia CK-40214 (CD), CT-40214 (CS): "16 Most Requested Songs"

Meyer Davis
Monmouth-Evergreen MES-6813 (LP): "Meyer Davis Plays Cole Porter"

Sammy Davis, Jr.
Decca ED-2285 (45)

Sammy Davis, Jr.
MCA MCAC2-4109 (CS & LP): "Hey there (It's Sammy Davis, Jr. At His Dynamite Greatest)"

Marlene Dietrich
MCA MCAC-1501 (CS): "Her Complete Decca Recordings"

Tommy Dorsey
RCA 47-3160 (45) 1950

You Do Something To Me (cont.)

Eddy Duchin
Columbia B-105 (45)
Carl Fenton and His Orchestra
Gennett 7104 (78) 1930
Lucy Fenwick/Ray Cornell
RCA LRL2-5054 (LP): "Cole"
George Feyer
Vanguard VSD-93/94 (LP): "Essential Cole Porter"
George Feyer
Vanguard OVC-6014 (CD): "George Feyer Plays Cole Porter"
Ella Fitzgerald
Verve 821989-2/821990-2 (CD), 823278-4 (CS), 823278-1 (LP): "Cole Porter Songbook" 1956
Ella Fitzgerald
Pablo OJCCD-442-2 (CD), OJC-5442 (CS), OJC-442 (LP): "Ella A Nice"
Joao Gilberto
Verve 848507-2 (CD), 848507-4 (CS): "Joao"
Benny Goodman
MCA CHD-31264 (CD), CHC-91552 (CS): "Benny Rides Again"
Marion Harris
Brunswick 4806 (78) 1930
Douglas Henderson
Biograph BLP-1023Q (LP)
Hotel Pennsylvania Music (Jack Albin)
Harmony 1075-H (78) 1929
Lena Horne
RCA 66021-2 (CD), 66021-4 (CS): "At Long Last Lena"
Lena Horne
RCA LPM-1148 (LP)
Etta Jones
Muse MC-5145 (CS), MR-5145 (LP): "My Mother's Eyes"

You Do Something To Me (cont.)

Louis Jourdan
>Capitol SW 1301 (LP): soundtrack from the film *Can-Can* 1960

Andre Kostelanetz
>Columbia CK-40218 (CD), CT-40218 (CS): "16 Most Requested Songs"

Ann Leaf
>New World NW-227-2 (CD), NW-227-4 (CS), 227 (LP): "The Mighty Wurlitzer (Music For Movie-Palace Organs)"

Julie London
>EMI E2-93455 (CD), E4-93455 (CS): "Julie London Sings Cole Porter"

Adam Makowicz
>Sheffield Lab LAB-21 (LP): "The Name is Makowicz"

Adam Makowicz
>Concord Jazz CCD-4541 (CD): "Live At Maybeck Recital Hall, Vol. 24 (Adam Makowicz At Maybeck)"

Sinead O'Connor
>Chrysalis F2-21799 (CD), F4-21799 (CS): "Red Hot & Blue (A Tribute to Cole Porter to Benefit Aids Research & Relief)"

101 Strings Orchestra
>Alshire International ALCD-30 (CD), ALSC-5007 (CS): "Cole Porter"

101 Strings Orchestra
>Alshire International ALCD-50 (CD), ADBL-406 (CS): "The Best of the Great American Composers, Vol. VI"

Ken Peplowski
>Concord Jazz CCD-4419 (CD), CJ-419-C (CS): "Mr. Gentle & Mr. Cool"

Gene Pursell
>Accent 5099 (LP): "Songs For My Friends"

Leo Reisman and His Orchestra
>Victor 22244 (78) 1929

Nelson Riddle & His Orchestra
>Pair PCD-2-1173 (CD): "The Riddle Touch"

You Do Something To Me (cont.)

Sonny Rollins
RCA VLP-2527 (45)
Sonny Rollins/Jim Hall
Bluebird 5634-2-RB (CD), 5634-4-RB (CS), 5634-1-
RB9 (LP): "The Sonny Rollins Quartets"
Sonny Rollins
Bluebird 61061-2 (CD), 61061-4 (CS): "The Bridge"
Jimmy Roselli
M&R CA-1020 (CS), 1020 (LP): "Sold Out (Carnegie
Hall Concert)"
Frank Sinatra
Columbia CGK-40897 (CD), CGT-40897 (CS): "Hello
Young Lovers"
Frank Sinatra
Capitol C2-46573 (CD), C4-46573 (CS): "Sinatra's
Swingin' Session!!!! (& More)"
Frank Sinatra
Capitol C2-91344 (CD): "Frank Sinatra Gift Set"
Frank Sinatra
K-Tel International 662-2 (CD), 662-4 (CS): "Radio
Years"
Frank Sinatra
Intercon OXO-001 (CD): "Original Sessions"
Frank Sinatra
Capitol C2-96611 (CD), C4-96611 (CS): "Frank
Sinatra Sings the Select Cole Porter"
Frank Sinatra
Capitol BBX2-99956 (CD), BBX4-99956 (CS):
"Concepts"
Frank Sinatra
Pair PDK-2-1028 (CS): "Timeless"
Frank Sinatra
Columbia CXK-48673 (CD): "The Columbia Years
(1943-1952) The Complete Recordings"
Jack Six/Francis Thorne
Composers Recordings 585 (CD): "Porter On My
Mind"

You Do Something To Me (cont.)

> **Mary Wells**
>> Motown 37463-5167-2 (CD), MOTD-5167 (CD),
>> 37463-5167-4 (CS), MOTC-5167 (CS): "My Guy"
>
> **Mary Wells**
>> Motown MOTD-8124 (CD): "2 Classic Albums: Two
>> Lovers/My Guy"
>
> **Paul Whiteman and His Orchestra**
>> Victor 36085 (78) 1933
>
> **Lee Wiley**
>> Liberty Music Shop L-294 (78) 1940
>
> **Lee Wiley**
>> Audiophile ACD-1 (CD), Monmouth-Evergreen MES
>> 7034 (LP): "Lee Wiley Sings George Gershwin and
>> Cole Porter"
>
> **Julie Wilson**
>> DRG CDSL-5208 (CD), SLC-5208 (CS): "Cole Porter
>> Songbook"
>
> **Jane Wyman**
>> Motion Picture Tracks MPT 6 (LP): soundtrack from
>> the film *Night and Day* 1945

You've Got That Thing
introduced by Jack Thompson and Betty Compton in
Fifty Million Frenchmen

> **Tommy Bohn Penn-Sirens Orchestra**
>> Okeh 41374 (78) 1930
>
> **Ian Carmichael**
>> Stanyan SR-10136 (LP)
>
> **Clicquot Club Eskimos**
>> Domino 4464 (78) 1929
>
> **Chorus**
>> Motion Picture Tracks MPT 6 (LP): soundtrack from
>> the film *Night and Day* 1945
>
> **Peter Gale**
>> RCA LRL2-5054 (LP): "Cole"

You've Got That Thing (cont.)

Bob Haring
Brunswick 4666 (78) 1929
Ted Lewis and His Band
Columbia 2088-D (78) 1929
Dorothy Provine
Warner W-1419 (LP)
Leo Reisman and His Orchestra
Victor 22244 (78) 1929
Bobby Short
Atlantic SD 2-606 (LP): "Bobby Short Loves Cole
Porter" 1971
Bobby Short
Atlantic 82062-2 (CD), 82062-4 (CS): "Bobby, Noel
& Cole (Bobby Short Loves Cole Porter/Bobby Short
Is Mad About Noel Coward)"
The Tin Pan Paraders
Gennett 7146 (78) 1930
Paul Whiteman and His Orchestra
Victor 36085 (78) 1933
Julie Wilson
DRG CDSL-5208 (CD), SLC-5208 (CS): "Cole Porter
Songbook"
Arthur Young and His Youngsters
Regal Zonophone MR-1861 (78) 1935

Find Me A Primitive Man
introduced by Evelyn Hoey, Billy Reed and Lou Duthers in
Fifty Million Frenchmen

Jan De Gaetani
Columbia M-34533 (LP)
Libby Holman
Brunswick 4666 (78)
Bob Haring
Brunswick 4666 (78) 1929
Madeline Kahn
RCA ABL2-0967 (LP)

Find Me A Primitive Man (cont.)

> **Cybill Shepherd**
>> Paramount PAS-1018 (LP)
>
> **Cybill Shepherd**
>> MCA MCAC-25173 (CS), MCA-25173 (LP): "Cybill Does It...To Cole Porter"
>
> **Elaine Stritch**
>> Painted Smiles PS-1370 (LP): "Cole Porter Revisited, Volume III"
>
> **Lee Wiley**
>> Liberty Music Shop L-296 (78) 1940
>
> **Lee Wiley**
>> Audiophile ACD-1 (CD), Monmouth-Evergreen MES-7034 (LP): "Lee Wiley Sings George Gershwin and Cole Porter"
>
> **Gretchen Wyler**
>> Jubilee JLP-1100 (LP)

Where Would You Get Your Coat?
introduced by Helen Broderick in *Fifty Million Frenchmen*

> **Carmen Alvarez/Laura Kenyon/Alice Playten**
>> Painted Smiles PS-1358 (LP): "Unpublished Cole Porter"

The Tale of the Oyster
introduced by Helen Broderick in *Fifty Million Frenchmen*

> **Kaye Ballard**
>> Painted Smiles PS-1340 (LP): "Cole Porter Revisited"
>
> **William Bolcom/Joan Morris**
>> Omega Record Classics OCD-3002 (CD): "Night & Day"
>
> **Julie Wilson**
>> DRG CDSL-5208 (CD), SLC-5208 (CS): "Cole Porter Songbook"

You Don't Know Paree
introduced by William Gaxton in *Fifty Million Frenchmen*

> **Vicki Benet**
>> MCA MCAC-1562 (CS): "Last Time I Saw Paris"
>
> **Peter Gale**
>> RCA LRL2-5054 (LP): "Cole"
>
> **Bobby Short**
>> Atlantic SD 2-606 (LP): "Bobby Short Loves Cole Porter" 1971
>
> **Bobby Short**
>> Atlantic 82062-2 (CD), 82062-4 (CS): "Bobby, Noel & Cole (Bobby Short Loves Cole Porter/Bobby Short Is Mad About Noel Coward)"
>
> **Julie Wilson**
>> DRG CDSL-5208 (CD), SLC-5208 (CS): "Cole Porter Songbook"

I'm Unlucky At Gambling
introduced by Evelyn Hoey and Larry Ceballos' Hollywood Dancers in *Fifty Million Frenchmen*

> **Eve Arden**
>> Motion Picture Tracks MPT 6 (LP): soundtrack from the film *Night and Day* 1945
>
> **Dolores Gray**
>> Painted Smiles PS-1371 (LP): "Cole Porter Revisited, Volume IV"
>
> **Julie Wilson**
>> DRG CDSL-5208 (CD), SLC-5208 (CS): "Cole Porter Songbook"

Let's Step Out
introduced by Evelyn Hoey and Gertrude McDonald in *Fifty Million Frenchmen*

> **Margery Gray**
>> Epic FLM-13100 (LP)

Let's Step Out (cont.)

Hal Linden/Eileen Rodgers/Barbara Land
Epic EK-15100 (CD), JST-15100 (CS): "Anything Goes"
Mister Tram Associates
Audiophile DAPCD-241 (CD) "Getting Some Fun Out of Life" 1988

The Boy Friend Back Home
introduced by Evelyn Hoey in *Fifty Million Frenchmen*

Patrice Munsel
Painted Smiles PS-1371 (LP): "Cole Porter Revisited, Volume IV"

I Worship You
written for but unused in *Fifty Million Frenchmen*

David Allen
Painted Smiles PS-1340 (LP): "Cole Porter Revisited"
Hildegarde
Decca 23218 (78) 1941
Kenneth Nelson
RCA LRL2-5054 (LP): "Cole"

The Queen of Terre Haute
written for but unused in *Fifty Million Frenchmen*

Katherine Hepburn
Painted Smiles PS-1371 (LP): "Cole Porter Revisited, Volume IV"
Julie Wilson
DRG CDSL-5208 (CD), SLC-5208 (CS): "Cole Porter Songbook"

Why Don't We Try Staying Home?
written for but unused in *Fifty Million Frenchmen*

> **Bobby Short**
>> Atlantic SD 2-606 (LP): "Bobby Short Loves Cole Porter" 1971
>
> **Bobby Short**
>> Atlantic 82062-2 (CD), 82062-4 (CS): "Bobby, Noel & Cole (Bobby Short Loves Cole Porter/Bobby Short Is Mad About Noel Coward)"
>
> **Elaine Stritch**
>> Stanyan SR-10136 (LP)

They All Fall In Love
introduced by Gertrude Lawrence in the film *The Battle of Paris*

> **Will Osborne and His Orchestra**
>> Columbia 2044-D (78) 1929

The Extra Man
written for but unused in *Wake Up and Dream*

> **Arthur Siegel**
>> Painted Smiles PS-1371 (LP): "Cole Porter Revisited, Volume IV"

Where Have You Been?
introduced by Charles King and Hope Williams in
The New Yorkers

> **Emil Coleman and His Orchestra**
> Brunswick 6006 (78) 1930
> **Teddi King**
> RCA Victor LPM 1313 (LP): "To You" 1957
> **Barbara Lea**
> Prestige OJCCD-1713-2 (CD): "Barbara Lea"
> **Andrea Marcovicci**
> DRG 91401 (CD & CS): "What is Love?"
> **Bobby Short**
> Atlantic SD 2-606 (LP): "Bobby Short Loves Cole
> Porter" 1971
> **Bobby Short**
> Atlantic 82062-2 (CD), 82062-4 (CS): "Bobby, Noel
> & Cole (Bobby Short Loves Cole Porter/Bobby Short
> Is Mad About Noel Coward)"
> **Fred Waring's Pennsylvanians/The Three Girlfriends**
> Victor 22598 (78) 1930
> **Fred Waring's Pennsylvanians/The Three Girlfriends**
> JJA 19777 (LP)

I'm Getting Myself Ready For You
introduced by Frances Williams, Barrie Oliver, Ann Pennington and
Maurice Lapue in *The New Yorkers*

> **Blanche Calloway**
> Victor 22659 (78) 1931
> **Emil Coleman and His Orchestra**
> Brunswick 6006 (78) 1930
> **Emil Coleman and His Orchestra**
> JJA 19777 (LP)

Love For Sale
introduced by Kathryn Crawford, June Shafer, Ida Pearson and
Stella Friend in *The New Yorkers*

> **Julian Cannonball Adderly**
> Blue Note B2-46338 (CD), B4-81595 (CS):
> "Somethin' Else"
> **Julian Cannonball Adderly**
> Blue Note B2-95591 (CD), B4-95591 (CS): "Blue
> Porter"
> **Julian Cannonball Adderly**
> Mobile Fidelity Sound Lab UDCD-563 (CD):
> "Somethin' Else"
> **Nat Adderly Quintet**
> Enja 7027-2 (CD): "The Old Country"
> **Ernestine Allen**
> Tru-Sound OBCCD-539-2 (CD), OBC-5539 (CS),
> OBC-539 (LP): "Let It Roll"
> **Ernestine Anderson**
> Concord Jazz CCD-4054 (CD): "Live From Concord
> to London"
> **Ray Anthony**
> Pair PCD-2-1317 (CD), PDK-2-1317 (CS): "Dancing
> & Dreaming"
> **Chet Baker**
> Enja R2-79626 (CD), R4-79626 (CS): "Strollin'"
> **Chet Baker Trio**
> Philology W-55-2 (CD): "Club 21, Paris, Vol. 1"
> **Carlos Barbosa-Lima**
> Concord Jazz CCD-42008 (CD), CC-42008 (CS), CC-
> 42008 (LP): "Barbosa-Lima Plays The Music of Bonfa
> & Porter"
> **Louie Bellson/Paul Smith/Ray Brown**
> Outstanding 011 (LP): "Heavy Jazz, Vol. 2"
> **Ralph Bennett and His Seven Aces**
> Melotone M-12108 (78 1931
> **Tony Bennett**
> Columbia CK-8669 (CD), PCT-00010 (CS): "I Left
> My Heart in San Francisco"

Love For Sale (cont.)

Tony Bennett/Torrie Zito Orchestra
> DRG CDMRS-801 (CD), MRSC-801 (CS): "The Special Magic of Tony Bennett"

George Benson/Earl Klugh
> ITI D2-72980 (CD): "4 For an Afternoon"

William Bolcom/Joan Morris
> Omega Record Classics OCD-3002 (CD): "Night & Day"

Al Bowlly
> Decca F-2404

Ruby Braff and Ellis Larkins
> Vanguard VRS 8019 (LP): "Ruby Braff and Ellis Larkins" 1955

Les Brown
> Bluebird B-10211 (78) 1939

Les Brown
> USA Music Group USACD-685 (CD), USACA-685 (CS): "Anything Goes"

Roy Brown
> Intermedia CQS-5027 (CS), 5027 (LP): "Good Rockin' Tonight"

Kenny Burrell
> Concord Jazz CCD-4121 (CD), CJ-121-C (CS): "Moon & Sand"

Eddie Cano
> RCA International 3459-2-RL (CD): "Cole Porter, Duke Ellington & Me"

Frankie Carle
> RCA EPB-1064 (45)

Benny Carter
> Capitol F15643 (45)

Sonny Criss
> Prestige OJCCD-430-2 (CD), OJC-5430 (CS), OJC-430 (LP): "This is Criss!"

Bobby Darin
> Bainbridge BTC-6220 (CS), 6220 (LP): "Darin at the Copa"

Love For Sale (cont.)

Miles Davis
> Columbia C4K-45000 (CD), C4T-45000 (CS): "Columbia Years 1955-1985"

Miles Davis
> Columbia C2K-46862 (CD), C2T-46862 (CS): "Circle in the Round"

Miles Davis
> Columbia CK-47835 (CD), CT-47835 (CS): "'58 Sessions Featuring Stella By Starlight"

Dorothy Donegan
> Progressive C-7056 (CS), 7056 (LP): "Explosive Dorothy Donegan"

Jimmy Dorsey & His Orchestra
> Laserlight 15768 (CD), 79768 (CS): "Perfidia"

Tommy Dorsey
> RCA 47-3159 (45) 1950

Herb Ellis/Joe Pass/Ray Brown/Jake Hanna
> Concord Jazz CCD-4001 (CD), CCD-6001 (CD): "Jazz/Concord"

Herb Ellis/Joe Pass
> Pablo OJCCD-726-2 (CD): "Two For the Road"

George Feyer
> Vanguard VSD-93/94 (LP): "Essential Cole Porter"

George Feyer
> Vanguard OVC-6014 (CD): "George Feyer Plays Cole Porter"

Fine Young Cannibals
> International Record Syndicate IRS-52760 (7" Single)

Harvey Fierstein
> Polydor 837785-2 (CD), 837785-4 (CS): "Torch Song Trilogy"

Fine Young Cannibals
> Chrysalis F2-21799 (CD), F4-21799 (CS): "Red Hot & Blue (A Tribute to Cole Porter to Benefit Aids Research & Relief)"

Ella Fitzgerald (accompanied by Nelson Riddle and His Orchestra)
> Atlantic SD-1631 (LP): "Ella Loves Cole"

Love For Sale (cont.)

Ella Fitzgerald
Verve 821989-2/821990-2 (CD), 823278-4 (CS),
823278-1 (LP): "Cole Porter Songbook" 1956

Ella Fitzgerald
Pablo PACD-2310-814-2 (CD), 52310-814 (CS),
2310814 (LP): "Dream Dancing"

Ella Fitzgerald
Verve 314-519564-2 (CD), 825670-2 (CD), 825670-4
(CS), 825670-1 (LP): "Mack The Knife - Ella In
Berlin"

Ella Fitzgerald
Verve 314-519804-2 (CD), 314-519804-4 (CS): "The
Best of the Song Books"

Jimmy Forrest
Palo Alto 8021 (LP): "Heart of the Forrest"

Aretha Franklin
Columbia C2K-48515 (CD), C2T-48515 (CS): "Jazz
To Soul"

Red Garland/Ron Carter/Philly Joe Jones
Galaxy OJCCD-472-2 (CD), OJC-5472 (CS), OJC-472
(LP): "Crossings"

Terry Gibbs
Palo Alto 8011 (LP): "Jazz Party - First Time
Together"

Terry Gibbs/Buddy De Franco
Contemporary CCD-14056-2 (CD), 5C-14056 (CS),
C-14056 (LP): "Air Mail Special"

Dexter Gordon
Blue Note B2-46094 (CD): "GO" 1987

Dexter Gordon
Blue Note B2-95591 (CD), B4-95591 (CS): "Blue
Porter"

Dexter Gordon
Black Lion BLCD-760133 (CD): "Take the 'A' Train"

Stephane Grappelli
Concord Jazz CDD-4139 (CD), CJ-139-C (CS): "At
The Winery"

Love For Sale (cont.)

> **Stephane Grappelli**
>> Atlantic 82095-2 (CD), 82095-4 (CS), 82095-1 (LP): "Olympia 1988"
>
> **Stephane Grappelli**
>> Black Lion BLCD-760132 (CD): "Parisian Throughfare"
>
> **The Great Jazz Trio**
>> Inner City C-6003 (CS), 6003 (LP): "Love For Sale"
>
> **Gigi Gryce**
>> Riverside OJCCD-1774-2 (CD), OJC-1774 (LP): "Gigi Gryce & the Jazz Lab Quintet"
>
> **Johnny Guarnieri**
>> Classic Jazz 105 (LP): "Gliss Me Again"
>
> **Eddie Harris**
>> Rhino R2-71514 (CD): "Artist's Choice - The Eddie Harris Anthology"
>
> **Eddie Harris**
>> Rhino R2-71515 (CD): "The In Sound/Mean Greens"
>
> **Paula Hatcher Quartet**
>> Newport Classic NCD-60009 (CD): "Rise & Shine"
>
> **Billie Holiday**
>> Verve 823064-4 (CS), 823064-1 (LP): "First Verve Sessions"
>
> **Billie Holiday**
>> Verve 823233-4 (CS), 8232333-1 (LP): "History of the Real Billie Holiday"
>
> **Billie Holiday**
>> Verve 314-517172-2 (CD), 314-517172-4 (CS): "The Essential Billie Holiday - Songs of Lost Love"
>
> **Billie Holiday**
>> Verve 314-519810-2 (CD): "Solitude"
>
> **Libby Holman**
>> Brunswick 6045 (78) 1931
>
> **Libby Holman**
>> JJA 19777 (LP)
>
> **John Holmquist/Dan Estrem**
>> Projazz CDJ-606 (CD), PCJ-606 (CS): "Still of the Night"

Love For Sale (cont.)

Shirley Horn
Verve 847202-2 (CD), 847202-4 (CS): "Night & Day:
The Cole Porter Songbook"

Shirley Horn
Mercury 843454-2 (CD): "Loads of Love/Shirley
Horn with Horns"

Shirley Horn
Verve 314-515563-2 (CD), 314-515563-4 (CS): "Jazz
Divas - Studio"

Dick Hyman
Command 18 (45)

Dr. John
Warner Bros. 25889-2 (CD), 25889-4 (CS): "In a
Sentimental Mood"

Thad Jones/Mel Lewis Quartet
A&M 75021-0830-2 (CD), 75021-0830-4 (CS): "That
Jones/Mel Lewis Quarter"

Hal Kemp and His Orchestra
Victor 26278 (78) 1939

Hal Kemp
Pro-Arte CDD-553 (CD), PCD-553 (CS): "Got a Date
With an Angel"

Stan Kenton
Mercury 820288-2 (CD): "Live in Europe"

Stan Kenton/Innovations Orchestra
Garland GRZ-006 (CD): "Summer of '51"

Stan Kenton
Creative World ST-1036 (LP): "By Request, Vol. I
(1944-1952)"

Stan Kenton
Creative World ST-1020 (LP): "Road Show, Volume
II"

Stan Kenton
Capitol C2-96328 (CD), C4-96328 (CS): "Road
Show"

Stan Kenton
Blue Note B2-97350 (CD): "Retrospective - The
Capitol Years, Vol. 1"

Love For Sale (cont.)

Stan Kenton
> Laserlight 15770 (CD), 79770 (CS): "Stan Kenton & His Innovations Orchestra"

Stan Kenton
> Pair PCD-2-1227 (CD), PDK-2-1227 (CS): "The Very Best of Stan Kenton"

L.A. Four
> Concord Jazz CCD-4199 (CD), CJ-199-C (CS): "Just Friends"

Lester Lanin
> Epic EG-7184 (45)

Julie London
> EMI E2-93455 (CD), E4-93455 (CS): "Julie London Sings Cole Porter"

Arthur Lyman
> HiFi 5066 (45) 1963

Les McCann
> Rhino R2-71281 (CD), R4-71281 (CS): "Much Les"

Marian McPartland
> Bainbridge BCD-1045 (CD), BTC-1045 (CS): "Bossa Nova & Soul"

Adam Makowicz
> Concord Jazz CCD-4541 (CD): "Live At Maybeck Recital Hall, Vol. 24 (Adam Makowicz At Maybeck)"

The Manhattan Transfer
> Rhino R2-71053 (CD), R4-71053 (CS): "The Manhattan Transfer Anthology - Down in Birdland"

Ellis Marsalis
> Columbia CK-47509 (CD), CT-47509 (CS), C-47509 (LP): "Heart of Gold"

Ellis Marsalis
> Columbia CK-57295 (CD): "I Like Jazz Two!"

Dick Meldonian/Sonny Igoe
> Statiras SC-7058 (CS), SLP-7058 (LP): "Jersey Swing Records"

Buddy Merrill
> Accent ACS5-5030 (CS), ACS-5030 (LP): "The Best of Buddy Merrill"

Love For Sale (cont.)

Buddy Merrill
Accent C-5024 (CS), 5024 (LP): "Sounds of Love"
Hal Mooney
Bainbridge BTC-1008 (CS), 1008 (LP): "Big Band & Voices"
Oscar Moore Quartet/Carl Perkins
V.S.O.P. 34 (LP): "Oscar Moore Quartet With Carl Perkins"
Phineas Newborn Trio
Contemporary C-57648 (CS), C-7648 (LP): "Back Home"
Ruby Newman and His Orchestra
Decca 23619 (78) 1939
Red Norvo
V.S.O.P. 35 (LP): "Norvo...Naturally"
Anita O'Day
Glendale 6000 (LP): "Once Upon a Summertime"
Anita O'Day
Emily 42181 (LP): "Anita O'Day Live at the City (the Second Best)"
Anita O'Day/Billy May
Verve 849266-2 (CD), 849266-4 (CS): "Anita O'Day Swings Cole Porter"
101 Strings Orchestra
Alshire International ALCD-7 (CD): "Love Songs"
Marty Paich Band
Discovery DS-829MC (CS), DS-829 (LP): "I Get a Boot Out of You"
Charlie Parker
Verve 827154-4 (CS), 827154-1 (LP): "Verve Years (1952-1954)"
Charlie Parker
Verve 823250-2 (CD), 823250-4 (CS): "The Cole Porter Songbook"
Joe Pass/Ella Fitzgerald
Pablo PACD-2310-921-2 (CD), 52310-92 (CS), 2310-921 (LP): "Easy Living"

Love For Sale (cont.)

Joe Pass
>Pablo 52310-877 (CS), 2310-877 (LP):"Eximious"

Oscar Peterson
>Verve 821987-2 (CD), 821987-4 (CS): "Oscar Peterson Plays the Cole Porter Songbook"

Jimmy Raney
>Biograph BLP-12060 (LP): "Too Marvelous For Words"

Dianne Reeves
>Blue Note B2-90264 (CD), B4-90264 (CS): "I Remember"

Buddy Rich
>Pacific Jazz L4N-10090 (CS): "Big Swing Face"

Fred Rich and His Orchestra
>Odeon ONY-36816 (78) 1931

Lisas Rich/Clare Fischer Quartet
>Trend TRCD-541 (CD): "Touch of the Rare"

Frank Rosolino
>Specialty OJCCD-1763-2 (CD), SPC-2161 (CS), SPS-2161 (LP): "Free For All"

Saint Louis Brass
>Summit DCD-140 (CD), DCC-140 (CS): "Pops"

Schuur, Diane
>GRP GRD-2006 (CD), GRC-2006 (CS): "In Tribute"

Ben Selvin and His Orchestra
>Columbia 2400-D (78) 1931

Doc Severinsen
>MCA MCAC2-4168 (CS): "The Best of Doc Severinsen"

Artie Shaw
>Thesaurus 487 (78) 1937

George Shearing
>Jazz 45711 (45)

George Shearing/Brian Torff
>Concord Jazz CCD-4132 (CD), CJ-132-C (CS): "On a Clear Day"

Love For Sale (cont.)

George Shearing/Montgomery Brothers
Riverside OJCCD-040-2 (CD), OJC-5040 (CS), OJC-040 (LP): "George Shearing & The Montgomery Brothers"

George Shearing/Marian McPartland
Savoy Jazz SV-0160 (CD): "Great Britain's Marian McPartland & George Shearing"

Travis Shook
Columbia CK-53138 (CD), CT-53138 (CS): "Travis Shook"

Andy Simpkins
Discovery DSCD-958 (CD): "Calamba"

Andy Simpkins Quintet
Discovery DS-892 (LP): "Summer Strut"

Derek Smith
Progressive 7002 (LP): "Love For Sale"

Jo Stafford
Corinthian COR-112 (LP): "Jo Plus Broadway"

Jude Swift
Nova 8917-2 (CD), 8917-4 (CS): "Music For Your Neighborhood"

Art Tatum
Pablo PACD-2405-418-2 (CD), 52405-418 (CS), 2405-418 (LP): "The Best of Art Tatum"

Art Tatum
Pablo PACD-2405-427-2 (CD): "The Tatum Group Masterpieces, Vol. 4"

Art Tatum
Pablo PACD-2405-429-2 (CD): "The Tatum Group Masterpieces, Vol. 6"

Art Tatum
Pablo PACD-2405-432-2 (CD): "The Art Tatum Solo Masterpieces, Vol. 1"

Art Tatum
Pablo 7PACD-4404-2 (CD): "The Complete Pablo Solo Masterpieces"

Love For Sale (cont.)

Art Tatum/Lionel Hampton/Buddy Rich
Pablo 52310-775 (CS), 2310-775 (LP): "Tatum-Hampton-Rich...Again"
Billy Taylor Trio/Candido
Prestige OJCCD-015-2 (CD), OJC-5015 (CS), OJC-015 (LP): "Billy Taylor Trio with Candido"
Jack Teagarden
Varsity 8202 (78) 1940
Jack Teagarden
Savoy SJK-1162 (CS), SJL-1162 (LP): "Varsity Sides"
The Three Sounds
Blue Note 4044 (45)
Cal Tjader Quintet
Fantasy OJC-279 (LP): "Concert on the Campus"
Turtle Island String Quartet/Billy Taylor Trio
Windham Hill 10132-2 (CD), 10132-4 (CS)" On the Town"
Turtle Island String Quartet
Windham Hill 10136-2 (CD), 10136-4 (CS): "Commotion 2"
Frank Vignola
Concord Jazz CCD-4576 (CD): "Appel Direct"
Fred Waring's Pennsylvanians/The Three Girl Friends
Victor 22598 (78) 1930
Fred Waring's Pennsylvanians/The Three Girl Friends
RCA LPV-554 and JJA 19777 (LP)
Dinah Washington
Mercury 30114 (45)
Dinah Washington
Pair PDK-2-1138 (CS): "Classic Dinah"
Elisabeth Welch
Teldec 75277-2 (CD): "Centennial Gala Concert"
Elisabeth Welch
World SH-233 (LP)
Elisabeth Welch
Koch International 313-752-2 (CD), 213-754-4 (CS): "The Ultimate Elisabeth Welch - the Collection of Her Most Popular Songs"

Love For Sale (cont.)

> **Gerald Wiggins Trio**
> > V.S.O.P. 28 (LP): "Gerald Wiggins Trio"
>
> **Gerald Wilson Orchestra**
> > Discovery 75005-2 (CD), 75005-4 (CS): "Malibu
> > Sunset"
>
> **Teddy Wilson**
> > Black Lion BLCD-760166 (CD): "Cole Porter
> > Classics"
>
> **Sam Wooding and His Orchestra**
> > Brunswick A-500097 (78) 1931
>
> **Arthur Young**
> > Regal Zonophone MR-1861 (78) 1935
>
> **Denny Zeitlin/Charlie Haden**
> > ECM 837020-2 (CD): "Time Remembers One Time
> > Once"
>
> **Denny Zeitlin**
> > Concord Jazz CCD-4572 (CD): "Live At Maybeck
> > Recital Hall, Vol. 27 (Denny Zeitlin At Maybeck)"

The Great Indoors
Introduced by Frances Williams in *The New Yorkers*

> **Martha Wright**
> > Jubilee 1028 (LP)

Take Me Back to Manhattan
introduced by Frances Williams in *The New Yorkers*

> **Eileen Rodgers**
> > Epic FLM-13100 (LP)
>
> **Hal Linden/Eileen Rodgers/Barbara Land**
> > Epic EK-15100 (CD), JST-15100 (CS): "Anything
> > Goes"

Let's Fly Away
introduced by Charles King and Hope Williams in
The New Yorkers

Bobby Short
Atlantic SD 2-606 (LP): "Bobby Short Loves Cole
Porter" 1971
Bobby Short
Atlantic 82062-2 (CD), 82062-4 (CS): "Bobby, Noel
& Cole (Bobby Short Loves Cole Porter/Bobby Short
Is Mad About Noel Coward)"
Lee Wiley
Liberty Music Shop L-296 (78) 1940
Lee Wiley
Audiophile ACD-1 (CD), Monmouth-Evergreen MES
7034 (LP): "Lee Wiley Sings George Gershwin and
Cole Porter"

I Happen To Like New York
introduced by Oscar Ragland in *The New Yorkers*

John Barrowman
Teldec 75277-2 (CD): "Centennial Gala Concert"
William Bolcom/Joan Morris
Omega Record Classics OCD-3002 (CD): "Night &
Day"
Judy Garland
Capitol 94407 (LP): "Judy in London" 1960
Judy Garland
Capitol C2-96361 (CD), C4-96361 (CS): "Anything
Goes - Capitol Sings Cole Porter"
Judy Garland
Capitol C2-96600 (CD), C4-96600 (CS): "The One &
Only"
Judy Garland
Capitol C2-99618 (CD), C4-99618 (CS): "The Best of
the Capitol Masters - Selections From 'The One &
Only' Box Set (The London Sessions)"

I Happen To Like New York (cont.)

Harold Lang
    Columbia OL-6410, COS-2810 and CBS Special
    Products AOS-2810 (LP) "The Decline and Fall of the
    Entire World as Seen Through the Eyes of Cole
    Porter" 1965
Liza Minnelli
    Telar CD-85502 (CD), CS-35502 (CS): "Liza Minnelli
    at Carnegie Hall"
Bobby Short
    Mobile Fidelity Sound Lab UDCD-589 (CD), Atlantic
    2-609 (LP), CS2-609 (CS): "Bobby Short At The Cafe
    Carlyle"
Jack Six/Francis Thorne
    Composers Recordings 585 (CD): "Porter On My
    Mind"

Works From 1932

After You, Who?
introduced by Fred Astaire in *Gay Divorce*

Ambrose Orchestra
G.N.P. Crescendo GNP-9004 (LP): "Ambrose Tribute to Cole Porter"
Fred Astaire
English Columbia DB-1215 and FB-1255 (78) 1933
Fred Astaire
World SHB-26, SH-124, Monmouth-Evergreen MES-7036, JJA-19779
Lorna Dallas
Teldec 75277-2 (CD): "Centennial Gala Concert"
Tommy Dorsey
RCA AXK2-5573 (CS): "Complete Tommy Dorsey, Vol. 5 (1937)"
Eddy Duchin
Brunswick 6445 (78) 1932
Eddy Duchin/Lew Sherwood
Columbia CK-46150 (CD), CT-46150 (CS): "Best of the Big Bands"
Bill Evans
Warner Bros. M5 3177 (LP): "New Conversations--Monologue, Dialogue, Trialogue" 1978
Ella Fitzgerald
Pablo PACD-2310-814-2 (CD), 52310-814 (CS), 2310814 (LP): "Dream Dancing"
Stan Kenton/The Pastels
Creative World ST-1062 (LP): "By Request, Vol. III (1943-1951)"
Stan Kenton/The Four Freshman
Creative World STD-1059 (CD), 1059 (CS), ST-1059 (LP): "The Four Freshman Live at Butler University with Stan Kenton & His Orchestra"

After You, Who? (cont.)

Dorothy Loudon
> DRG CDSL-5203 (CD), SLC-5203 (CS), SL-5203
> (LP): "Broadway Baby"

Andrea Marcovicci
> DRG 91401 (CD & CS): "What is Love?"

Mabel Mercer
> Atlantic 81264-4 (CS): "Mabel Mercer Sings Cole
> Porter (With Cy Walter & Stan Freeman)"

Helen Merrill
> Mercury 826340-2 (CD): "Complete Helen Merrill on
> Mercury (1954-1958)"

Helen Merrill
> Verve CD 314-511-070-2 (CD): "The Cole Porter
> Songbook, Vol. II"

George Shearing/Barry Tuckwell
> Concord Jazz CCD-42010 (CD), CC-2010-C (CS):
> "George Shearing & Barry Tuckwell Play the Music
> of Cole Porter"

Bobby Short
> Telarc CD83311 (CD), CS-33311 (CS): "Late Night at
> the Cafe Carlyle"

Sylvia Syms
> DRG 91402 (CD & CS) "Then Along Came Bill, A
> Tribute to Bill Evans" 1989

Jody Watley
> Chrysalis F2-21799 (CD), F4-21799 (CS): "Red Hot
> & Blue (A Tribute to Cole Porter to Benefit Aids
> Research & Relief)"

Julie Wilson
> DRG CDSL-5208 (CD), SLC-5208 (CS): "Cole Porter
> Songbook"

Why Marry Them?
introduced by Betty Starbuck in *Gay Divorce*

> **Lynn Redgrave**
> Painted Smiles PS-1370 (LP): "Cole Porter Revisited, Volume III"

Night And Day
introduced by Fred Astaire (danced by Fred Astaire and Claire Luce) in *Gay Divorce*

> **Larry Adler**
> Columbia FB-1776 (78) 1938
> **Larry Adler**
> Audiofidelity Enterprises 6193 (LP): "Larry Adler Again"
> **Howard Alden/George Van Eps**
> Concord Jazz CCD-4584 (CD): "Seven & Seven"
> **Ambrose Orchestra**
> G.N.P. Crescendo GNP-9004 (LP): "Ambrose Tribute to Cole Porter"
> **Franco Ambrosetti**
> Enja R279670 (CD): "Music For Symphony & Jazz Band"
> **Elly Ameling**
> Philips 412433-2 (CD), 412433-4 (CS), 412433-1 (LP): "Sentimental Me (Songs by Gershwin, Ellington, Porter)"
> **Van Alexander and His Orchestra**
> Bluebird B-10073 (78) 1938
> **Fred Astaire**
> EMI EMTC 101 & Soundtrak STK-105 & EMI Pathe Marconi 2C184-95807/8 (LP): soundtrack from the film *Gay Divorcee* 1934
> **Fred Astaire with Leo Reisman and His Orchestra**
> Victor 24193 (78) 1932
> **Fred Astaire**
> English Columbia DB-1215 and FB-1255 (78) 1933

Night and Day (cont.)

Fred Astaire
ASV Living Era 5021-2 (CD): "Crazy Feet!"
Fred Astaire
RCA 66099-2 (CD), 66099-4 (CS): "Hurray For Hollywood"
Fred Astaire
Pro-Arte CDD-431 (CD), PCD-431 (CS): "Cheek to Cheek"
Carlos Barbosa-Lima
Concord Jazz CCD-42008 (CD), CC-42008 (CS), CC-42008 (LP): "Barbosa-Lima Plays The Music of Bonfa & Porter"
George Barnes
Concord Jazz CJ-67 (LP): "Plays So Good"
Charlie Barnet and His Orchestra
Bluebird B-10888 (78) 1940
Charlie Barnet
RCA AXK2-5587 (CS): "Complete Charlie Barnet, Vol. 5 (1940-1941)"
Steve Barton
Teldec 75277-2 (CD): "Centennial Gala Concert"
Gerry Beaudoin/Boston Jazz Ensemble
North Star NS0039/CD (CD), NS0039/CS (CS): "In a Sentimental Mood"
Tony Bennett/Torrie Zito Orchestra
DRG CDMRS-801 (CD), MRSC-801 (CS): "The Special Magic of Tony Bennett"
Tony Bennett
Columbia CK-52965 (CD), CT-52965 (CS), CM-52965 (MD): "Perfectly Frank" 1992
Jerry Bergonzi
Blue Note B2-96256 (CD): "Standard Gonz"
Carver Blanchard/Nel Moore/Glen Saunders
Albany TROY-083-2 (CD): "Lute Unleashed"
William Bolcom/Joan Morris
Omega Record Classics OCD-3002 (CD): "Night & Day"

Night and Day (cont.)

Earl Bostic
Gusto GT4-2143 (7" single)
Al Bowlly
Decca F-3695
The Brass Connection
The Jazz Alliance TJA-10014 (CD): "Standards"
Don Byas
Emarcy 833405-2 (CD): "On Blue Star"
Carmen Cavallaro
Decca 25401 (45)
Frank Chacksfield and His Orchestra
London SP-44185 (LP): "The Music of Cole Porter"
Clebanoff
Mercury SR-613 (45)
Ray Conniff & His Orchestra & Chorus
Columbia CK-8282 (CD): "Say It With Music"
Sammy Davis, Jr.
MCA MCAC2-4109 (CS & LP): "Hey there (It's
Sammy Davis, Jr. At His Dynamite Greatest)"
Doris Day/Frank De Vol Orchestra
Columbia CK-8066 (CD) and Sony XPT-5 (CS) and
AC2-5 (LP): "Hooray For Hollywood, Vol. I"
Tommy Dorsey and His Orchestra
Victor 25657 (78) 1937
Tommy Dorsey
RCA AXK2-5573 (CS): "Complete Tommy Dorsey,
Vol. 5 (1937)"
Tommy Dorsey
RCA PK-5121 (CS): "This is Tommy Dorsey, Vol. 2"
Tommy Dorsey/Frank Sinatra
RCA 2269-2-R (CD), 2269-4-R (CS): "All-Time
Greatest Hits, Vol. 4 (& the Historic Stordahl
Session)"
Eddy Duchin
Brunswick 6445 (78) 1932
Eddy Duchin/Lew Sherwood
Columbia CK-46150 (CD), CT-46150 (CS): "Best of
the Big Bands"

Night and Day (cont.)

Ray Elis and Johnny Douglas conducting the Ray Elis Strings
RCA CAS-2522 (LP): "The Great Hits of Cole Porter"

Duke Ellington
Columbia CK-44444 (CD), CJT-44444 (CS), PCT-8053 (CS): "Ellington Indigos"

Empire Brass/Richard Jensen/Andy Kubiszewski/Robert Leidhecker
Telarc 80303 (CD), 30303 (CS): "Empire Brass On Broadway"

Bill Evans
Riverside 12RCD-018-2 (CD), R-018 (LP): "The Complete Riverside Recordings"

Bill Evans
Fantasy OJCCD-718-2 (CD), 5F-9568 (CS): "Crosscurrents"

Bill Evans
Riverside OJCCD-068-2 (CD), OJC-5068 (CS), OJC-068 (LP): "Everybody Digs Bill Evans"

Bill Evans/Hank Jones/Red Mitchell
Evidence Music ECD-22072-2 (CD): "Moods Unlimited"

Frances Faye
G.N.P. Crescendo GNPD-41 (CD), GNPS-41 (LP): "Caught in the Act"

Frederick Fennell/Eastman-Rochester Pops Orchestra
Mercury 43427-2 (CD): "Fennell Conducts Porter & Gershwin"

George Feyer
Vanguard VSD-93/94 (LP): "Essential Cole Porter"

George Feyer
Vanguard OVC-6014 (CD): "George Feyer Plays Cole Porter"

Ella Fitzgerald
Verve 821989-2/821990-2 (CD), 823278-4 (CS), 823278-1 (LP): "Cole Porter Songbook" 1956

Night and Day (cont.)

Ella Fitzgerald
Pablo OJCCD-442-2 (CD), OJC-5442 (CS), OJC-442 (LP): "Ella A Nice"
Ella Fitzgerald
Pablo 2PACD-2620-117-2 (CD), 52620-117 (CS), 2620-117 (LP): "J.A.T.P. - Return To Happiness, Tokyo 1983"
Ella Fitzgerald
Verve 847202-2 (CD), 847202-4 (CS): "Night & Day: The Cole Porter Songbook"
Ella Fitzgerald
Verve 314-515563-2 (CD), 314-515563-4 (CS): "Jazz Divas - Studio"
Dave Frishberg
Palo Alto 8028 (LP): "Bill Evans - A Tribute"
Lowell Fulsom
Aladdin 45-3104 (45) 1951
Erroll Garner
Pickwick Entertainment PJFD-15003 (CD), PJFT-15003 (CS): "Masters of the Black & Whites"
Erroll Garner
Mercury 834909-2 (CD), 834909-4 (CS): "Mambo Moves Garner"
The Geezinslaws
Step One SOR-0056 (CD, CS, LP): "World Tour"
Stan Getz
Roost EP-302 (45)
Stan Getz/Bill Evans
Verve 833802-2 (CD): "Stan Getz & Bill Evans"
Stan Getz/Chick Corea/Bill Evans
Verve 823242-4 (CS), 823242-1 (LP): "Chick Corea/Bill Evans - Sessions"
Stan Getz/Bill Evans/Ron Carter/Elvin Jones
Verve 835317-2 (CD), 835317-4 (CS): "Compact Jazz - Getz & Friends"
Stan Getz/Kenny Barron
Verve 314-510823-2 (CD), 314-510823-4 (CS): "People Time"

Night and Day (cont.)

Dizzy Gillespie
Bulldog CBDS-2006 (CS), 2006 (LP): "20 Golden
Pieces of Dizzy Gillespie"

Dizzy Gillespie
Everest 237 (LP): "Dizzy Gillespie"

Benny Goodman
Columbia 35410 (78) 1939

Benny Goodman
Columbia CK-40588 (CD), CJT-40588 (CS): "Roll
'Em"

Cary Grant
Motion Picture Tracks MPT 6 (LP): soundtrack from
the film *Night and Day* 1945

Stephane Grappelli/Django Reinhardt
Verve 820591-2 (CD): "Souvenirs"

Jerry Gray
Hindsight HSC-212 (CS), HSR-212 (LP): "The
Uncollected Jerry Gray & His Orchestra (1952)"

Joe Henderson
Blue Note B2-95591 (CD), B4-95591 (CS): "Blue
Porter"

Joe Henderson
Blue Note B2-84189 (CD): "Inner Urge"

Billie Holiday
Columbia CK-47030 (CD), CT-47030 (CS):
"Quintessential Billie Holiday, Vol. 8, 1939-1940"

Billie Holiday
Columbia C3K-47724 (CD), C3T-47724 (CS): "Billie
Holiday: The Legacy Box 1933-1958"

Lena Horne
DRG CDMRS-510 (CD), MRSC-510 (CS), MRS-510
(LP): "Lena Goes Latin & Sings Your Requests"

Dick Hyman
Musicmasters 5060-2-C (CD), 5060-4-C (CS): "Cole
Porter: All Through the Night"

Shigeaki Ikeno & His Quintet
Denon DC-8506 (CD): "Music To Dream By"

Night and Day (cont.)

The King's Singers
Angel CDC-47677 (CD), 4XS-47677 (CS): "Tribute to the Comedian Harmonists"
Ron McClure Trio
Ken KEN-015 (CD): "Inspiration"
Yehudi Menuhin/Stephane Grappelli
Angel CDM-69219 (CD): "Menuhin & Grappelli Play Berlin, Kern, Porter & Rodgers & Hart" 1988
Billie Holiday
Vocalion/Okeh 5377 (78) 1939
Billie Holiday
Columbia PG-32127 (LP): "Billie Holiday Story, Vol. 3"
John Holmquist/Dan Estrem
Projazz CDJ-606 (CD), PCJ-606 (CS): "Still of the Night"
Lena Horne
Bulldog CBDL-2000 (CS), 2000 (LP): "20 Golden Pieces of Lena Horne"
Lena Horne
DCC Compact Classics DZS-016 (CD): "The Lady"
Julio Iglesias
Columbia C2K-39570 (CD), K2T-39570 (CS): "In Concert"
Irving Joseph
Bainbridge BTC-1014 (CS), 1014 (LP): "Heritage of Broadway - Music of Cole Porter"
Dick Jurgens and His Orchestra
Okeh 6022 (78) 1941
Swing and Sway With Sammy Kaye
Vocalion 3932 (78) 1937
Earl Klugh Trio
Warner Bros. 26750-2 (CD), 26750-4 (CS): "Earl Klugh Trio, Vol. 1"
Frances Langford
Decca 1831 (78) 1938
Mario Lanza
RCA 549-5127 (45)

Night and Day (cont.)

Mario Lanza
        RCA EPA-5047 (45)
L.A. Salsa Society
        Rampart 3308-2 (CD), 3308-4 (CS): "Night & Day"
Adam Makowicz
        Concord Jazz CCD-4541 (CD): "Live At Maybeck
        Recital Hall, Vol. 24 (Adam Makowicz At Maybeck)"
Henry Mancini
        RCA 60795-2 (CD), 60795-4 (CS): "Top Hat: Music
        from the Films of Astaire & Rogers"
Shelly Manne
        Doctor Jazz FW-38728 (LP): "Shelly Manne & His
        Friends"
Marjorie-Jean
        Carmel MJ-10001 (CD, CS, LP): "Losing My Mind"
Frank Marocco
        Discovery DS-979 (LP): "Jazz Accordion"
Freddie Martin and His Orchestra
        Banner 32663 (78) 1933
Sergio Mendes
        A&M 853 (45) 1967
Sergio Mendes
        A&M 8520 (45) 1968
Sergio Mendes & Brasil '66
        A&M AM-8520 (7" single)
Yehudi Menuhin/Stephane Grappelli
        Angel 4XT-36968 (CS), 36968 (LP): "Jalousie -
        Music of the 30's"
Roy Milton
        Specialty 438 (45) 1952
Frank Minion
        Bethlehem 45-11090 (45) 1962
Hugo Montenegro
        Bainbridge BCD-1002 (CD), BTC-1002 (CS), BT-
        1002 (LP): "Overture: American Musical Theatre,
        Vol. One 1924-1935"
Peter Nero/Rochester Philharmonic Orchestra
        Pro-Arte CDS-576 (CD): "Classic Connections"

Night and Day (cont.)

Ruby Newman and His Orchestra
Decca 23618 (78) 1939
Red Norvo Trio
Savoy SJL-2212 (LP): "Red Norvo Trio with Tal
Farlow & Charles Mingus - The Savoy Sessions"
Anita O'Day
Glendale 6000 (LP): "Once Upon a Summertime"
Anita O'Day/Billy May
Verve 849266-2 (CD), 849266-4 (CS): "Anita O'Day
Swings Cole Porter"
101 Strings Orchestra
Alshire International ALCD-30 (CD), ALSC-5007
(CS): "Cole Porter"
101 Strings Orchestra
Alshire International ALCD-45 (CD), ADBL-401
(CS): "The Best of the Great American Composers,
Vol. I"
101 Strings Orchestra
Alshire International ALSC-5035 (CS): "Million Seller
Hit Songs of the 30's"
Orchestra
RCA LRL2-5054 (LP): "Cole"
Charlie Parker
Verve 827154-4 (CS), 827154-1 (LP): "Verve Years
(1952-1954)"
Charlie Parker
Verve 823250-2 (CD), 823250-4 (CS): "The Cole
Porter Songbook"
Charlie Parker
Verve 833288-2 (CD), 833288-4 (CS): "Compact -
Charlie Parker"
Joe Pass
Pablo 52310-877 (CS), 2310-877 (LP): "Eximious"
Joe Pass
Pablo PACD-2310-708-2 (CD), 52310-708 (CS):
"Virtuoso"

Night and Day (cont.)

Joe Pass
> Rhino R2-70722 (CD), R4-70722 (CS): "Legends of Jazz Guitar, Vol. 2"

Joe Pass
> Blue Note B2-96581 (CD), B4-96581 (CS): "Blue Guitar"

Joe Pass
> Pablo PACD-2310-931-2 (CD), 52310-931 (CS), 2310-931 (LP): "Blues For Fred"

Art Pepper Quartet/Sonny Clark Trio
> Time Is TI-9805 (CD): "Art Pepper Quartet, Vol. 1, With the Sonny Clark Trio"

Oscar Peterson
> Verve 821987-2 (CD), 821987-4 (CS): "Oscar Peterson Plays the Cole Porter Songbook"

Michel Petrucciani
> Blue Note B2-26295 (CD): "Pianism" 1986

The Pickens Sisters (with Phil Dewey)
> Victor 36085 (78) 1933

Quintette of the Hot Club of France
> Decca F-6616 (78) 1938

Samuel Ramey/Metropolitan Opera Orchestra
> RCA 61508-2 (CD): "A Salute To American Music"

Jimmy Raney
> Biograph BLP-12060 (LP): "Too Marvelous For Words"

Quintet of the Hot Club of France/Django Reinhardt
> G.N.P. Crescendo GNP-9001 (LP): "Quintet of the Hot Club of France"

The Razor's Edge
> POW 103 (45)

Red Raider Band
> Fidelity 1278 (LP): "Texas Tech. University"

Django Reinhardt
> ITI CDP-72961 (CD): "Bop Things & Cool Strings"

Django Reinhardt
> Rhino R2-70722 (CD), R4-70722 (CS): "Legends of Jazz Guitar, Vol. 2"

Night and Day (cont.)

Dick Robertson and His Orchestra
Crown 3428 (78) 1932
Red Rodney/Ira Sullivan
Muse MR-5274 (LP): "Night & Day"
Ginger Rogers
EMI/Odeon ODN-1002 (LP)
David Rose Orchestra
MCA MCAC2-4176 (CS): "Music of the 1930's"
Jimmy Roselli
M & R CA-1027 (CS), 1027 (LP): "More I See You"
David Schnitter
Muse MR-5153 (LP): "Goliath"
Loren Schoenberg & His Jazz Orchestra
Musicmasters 5039-2-C (CD), 5039-4-C (CS): "Just
A-Settin' & A-Rockin'"
Artie Shaw
Brunswick 7914 (78) 1937
Artie Shaw
Columbia 13-33316 (45)
Artie Shaw
Portrait RK-44090 (CD), RJT-44090 (CS): "Free For
All"
Artie Shaw
Columbia PCT-32031 (CS): "Best of the Big Bands"
Shigeaki & His Quintet
Denon DC-8506 (CD): "Music to Dream By"
Bobby Short
Telarc CD83311 (CD), CS-33311 (CS): "Late Night at
the Cafe Carlyle"
Frank Sinatra/Tommy Dorsey
RCA AFK1-4741 (CS): "Dorsey/Sinatra Radio Years
1940-42"
Frank Sinatra/Axel Stordahl & Orchestra
Rhino R2-71249 (CD), R4-71249 (CS): "Sentimental
Journey: Pop Vocal Classics Vol. 1 (1942-1946)"
Frank Sinatra
Bluebird B-11463 (78) 1942

Night and Day (cont.)

Frank Sinatra
        Reprise 1386 (45) 1956
Frank Sinatra
        K-Tel International 662-2 (CD), 662-4 (CS): "Radio
        Years"
Frank Sinatra
        Capitol 803-4 (45) 1956
Frank Sinatra
        Capitol 6195 (45) 1956
Frank Sinatra
        Capitol 6915 (7" single)
Frank Sinatra
        Capitol 4XBB-11357 (CS), SABB-11357 (LP): "Round
        No. 1"
Frank Sinatra
        Reprise 1016-2 (CD), J5-1016 (CS): "Sinatra - A Man
        & His Music"
Frank Sinatra
        Intercon OXO-001 (CD): "Original Sessions"
Frank Sinatra
        Capitol CD-94317 (CD), C4-94317 (CS): "The
        Capitol Years"
Frank Sinatra
        Reprise 26340-2 (CD), 26340-4 (CS): "The Reprise
        Collection"
Frank Sinatra
        Reprise 26501-2 (CD), 26501-4 (CS): "Sinatra Reprise
        - The Very Good Years"
Frank Sinatra
        RCA 9855-2-R (CD), 9855-4-R (CS): "Nipper's
        Greatest Hits - the 40's, Vol. 1"
Frank Sinatra
        Capitol C2-94518 (CD), C4-94518 (CS): "A Swingin'
        Affair!"
Frank Sinatra
        Capitol C2-96611 (CD), C4-96611 (CS): "Frank
        Sinatra Sings the Select Cole Porter"

Night and Day (cont.)

Frank Sinatra
Reprise 27020-2 (CD), 27020-4 (CS): "Sinatra & Strings"
Frank Sinatra
Capitol C2-94777 (CD), C4-94777 (CS), C1-94777 (LP): "The Capitol Years"
Frank Sinatra
Capitol C2-99225 (CD), C4-99225 (CS), C5-99225 (DCC), C8-99225 (MD): "The Best of the Capitol Years" - Selections from 'The Capitol Years' Box Set
Frank Sinatra
Capitol BBX2-99956 (CD), BBX4-99956 (CS): "Concepts"
Frank Sinatra
Pair PDK-2-1028 (CS): "Timeless"
Frank Sinatra
Columbia CXK-48673 (CD): "The Columbia Years (1943-1952) The Complete Recordings"
Jack Six/Francis Thorne
Composers Recordings 585 (CD): "Porter On My Mind"
Paul Smith
Outstanding 023 (LP): "Jazz Spotlight on Cole Porter & George Gershwin"
Tommy Smith
Blue Note B2-96452 (CD): "Standards"
Maxine Sullivan
Victor 26132 (78) 1938
Billy Stritch
DRG CDSL-5215 (CD), SLC-5215 (CS): "Billy Stritch"
Jo Stafford
Corinthian COR-118 (LP): "Broadway Revisited"
Art Tatum
Armed Forces Radio Service (AFRS) P-545 1946
Art Tatum
Pablo PACD-2405-418-2 (CD), 52405-418 (CS), 2405-418 (LP): "The Best of Art Tatum"

Night and Day (cont.)

Art Tatum
Pablo PACD-2405-425-2 (CD): "The Tatum Group
Masterpieces, Vol. 2"

Art Tatum
Pablo PACD-2405-437-2 (CD): "The Art Tatum Solo
Masterpieces, Vol. 6"

Art Tatum
Pablo PACD-2405-431-2 (CD): "The Tatum Group
Masterpieces, Vol. 8"

Art Tatum
Pablo 7PACD-4404-2 (CD): "The Complete Pablo
Solo Masterpieces"

Claude Thornhill and His Orchestra
Columbia 37055 (78) 1942

Sumi Tonooka
Candid CCD-79502 (CD): "Taking Time"

Mel Torme
Discovery 70002-2 (CD): "The Best of Musicraft
Jazz"

U2
Chrysalis F2-21799 (CD), F4-21799 (CS): "Red Hot
& Blue (A Tribute to Cole Porter to Benefit Aids
Research & Relief)"

Fred Waring and His Pennsylvanians
MCA MCAC2-4008 (CS): "The Best of Fred Waring
& His Pennsylvanians"

Dionne Warwick/Grover Washington, Jr./Stanley Jordan
Arista ARCD-8573 (CD), AC-8573 (CS), AL-8573
(LP): "Dionne Warwick Sings Cole Porter"

Lawrence Welk
Ranwood RC-4101 (CS), RLP-4101 (LP): "On Tour
With Lawrence Welk, Vol. 2"

Randy Weston
Riverside 2508 (LP): "Randy Weston Plays Cole
Porter in a Modern Mood" 1954

Paul Whiteman and His Orchestra
Victor 36085 (78) 1933

Night and Day (cont.)

John Williams
> Sony Classical SK-47435 (CD), ST-47435 (CS), SM-47435 (MD): "Night & Day"

Julie Wilson
> DRG CDSL-5208 (CD), SLC-5208 (CS): "Cole Porter Songbook"

Teddy Wilson
> Commodore CCD-7014 (CD), CCK-7014 (CD), CCL-7014 (LP): "Teddy Wilson"

Arthur Young
> Regal Zonophone MR-1861 (78) 1935

How's Your Romance?
introduced by Erik Rhodes in *Gay Divorce*

Bobby Short
> Atlantic SD 2-606 (LP): "Bobby Short Loves Cole Porter" 1971

Bobby Short
> Atlantic 82062-2 (CD), 82062-4 (CS): "Bobby, Noel & Cole (Bobby Short Loves Cole Porter/Bobby Short Is Mad About Noel Coward)"

I've Got You On My Mind
introduced by Fred Astaire and Claire Luce in *Gay Divorce*

Ambrose and His Orchestra
> Brunswick (English) 01623 (78) 1933, G.N.P. Crescendo GNP-9004 (LP): "Ambrose Tribute to Cole Porter"

Fred Astaire with Leo Reisman and His Orchestra
> Victor 24193 (78) 1932

Fred Astaire
> RCA 2337-2-R (CD), 2337-4-R (CS): "Fred Astaire Rarities (with Adele Astaire & Ginger Rogers)"

I've Got You On My Mind (cont.)

Bobby Short
Atlantic SD 2-606 (LP): "Bobby Short Loves Cole Porter" 1971
Bobby Short
Atlantic 82062-2 (CD), 82062-4 (CS): "Bobby, Noel & Cole (Bobby Short Loves Cole Porter/Bobby Short Is Mad About Noel Coward)"
Jack Six/Francis Thorne
Composers Recordings 585 (CD): "Porter On My Mind"

Mister And Missus Fitch
introduced by Luella Gear in *Gay Divorce*

Pearl Bailey
Roulette 42004 (LP): "Pearl Bailey"
Bobby Short
Mobile Fidelity Sound Lab UDCD-589 (CD), Atlantic 2-609 (LP), CS2-609 (CS): "Bobby Short Live at the Cafe Carlyle"
Gwen Verdon
RCA LPM-1152 (LP)
Julie Wilson/William Roy
DRG CDSL-5208 (CD), SLC-5208 (CS): "Cole Porter Songbook"

You're In Love
introduced by Fred Astaire, Claire Luce and Erik Rhodes in *Gay Divorce*

Georgia Engel
Painted Smiles PS-1370 (LP): "Cole Porter Revisited, Volume III"

Experiment

introduced by Moya Nugent, reprised by Gertrude Lawrence in *Nymph Errant*

> **Tony Bennett**
> > Improv 7112 (LP): "Life Is Beautiful"
>
> **Tony Bennett/Torrie Zito Orchestra**
> > DRG CDMRS-801 (CD), MRSC-801 (CS): "The Special Magic of Tony Bennett"
>
> **Al Bowlly**
> > HMV B-6408
>
> **Irene Kral**
> > CLT 7625 (LP): "Kral Space"
>
> **Gertrude Lawrence**
> > HMV B-8029 and Victor 25224 (78) 1933
>
> **Gertrude Lawrence**
> > Victor LRT-7001 (LP)
>
> **Gertrude Lawrence**
> > Monmouth-Evergreen MES-7043 (LP)
>
> **Mabel Mercer**
> > Atlantic 1213 (LP) "Mabel Mercer Sings Cole Porter" 1954
>
> **Mabel Mercer**
> > Atlantic 81264-4 (CS): "Mabel Mercer Sings Cole Porter (With Cy Walter & Stan Freeman)"
>
> **Julie Wilson**
> > DRG CDSL-5208 (CD), SLC-5208 (CS): "Cole Porter Songbook"

It's Bad For Me

introduced by Gertrude Lawrence in *Nymph Errant*

> **Al Bowlly**
> > HMV B-6396

It's Bad For Me (cont.)

> **Ruby Braff Trio**
> > Concord Jazz CCD-4423 (CD), CJ-423-C (CS):
> > "Bravura Eloquence"
> **Rosemary Clooney**
> > Columbia B-2107 (45)
> **Rosemary Clooney and the Benny Goodman Sextet**
> > Columbia 54293 (78) 1955
> **Jan De Gaetani**
> > Columbia M-34533 (LP)
> **Judy Holliday/G. Mulligan**
> > DRG CDSL-5191 (CD), SLC-5191 (CS), SL-5191
> > (LP): "Holiday With Mulligan"
> **Gertrude Lawrence**
> > HMV B-8030 and Victor 25225 (78) 1933
> **Gertrude Lawrence**
> > Victor LRT-7001 (LP)
> **Gertrude Lawrence**
> > Monmouth-Evergreen MES-7043 (LP)
> **Roches**
> > Warner Bros. BSK-3475 (LP), 3475-2 (CD), M5-3475
> > (CS): "Nurds"
> **Bobby Short**
> > Atlantic 81715-2 (CD), 81715-4 (CS): "50 By Bobby
> > Short"
> **Jeri Southern**
> > Capitol T-1173 (LP)
> **Julie Wilson**
> > DRG CDSL-5208 (CD), SLC-5208 (CS): "Cole Porter
> > Songbook"

How Could We Be Wrong?
introduced by Gertrude Lawrence in *Nymph Errant*

> **Al Bowlly**
> > HMV B-6396, Decca F-3734
> **Gertrude Lawrence**
> > HMV B-8030 and Victor 25225 (78) 1933

How Could We Be Wrong? (cont.)

Gertrude Lawrence
Victor LRT-7001 (LP)
Gertrude Lawrence
Monmouth-Evergreen MES-7043 (LP)
Bobby Short
Atlantic SD 2-606 (LP): "Bobby Short Loves Cole
Porter" 1971
Bobby Short
Atlantic 82062-2 (CD), 82062-4 (CS): "Bobby, Noel
& Cole (Bobby Short Loves Cole Porter/Bobby Short
Is Mad About Noel Coward)"
Jack Six/Francis Thorne
Composers Recordings 585 (CD): "Porter On My
Mind"

Nymph Errant
introduced by Gertrude Lawrence in *Nymph Errant*

Gertrude Lawrence
HMB B-8031 and Victor 25226 (78) 1933
Gertrude Lawrence
Victor LRT-7001 (LP)
Gertrude Lawrence
Monmouth-Evergreen MES-7043 (LP)

The Physician
introduced by Gertrude Lawrence in *Nymph Errant*

Julie Andrews/Twentieth Century Fox Orchestra
Fox 11009-2 (CD), 11009-4 (CS): soundtrack from the
film *Star!* 1968
William Bolcom/Joan Morris
Omega Record Classics OCD-3002 (CD): "Night &
Day"
Blossom Dearie
DRG DARC 1105 (LP): "Blossoms of Broadway"

The Physician (cont.)

Blossom Dearie
Verve MGV MGV6 S-2133 (LP)
Gertrude Lawrence
HMV B-8029 and Victor 25224 (78) 1933
Gertrude Lawrence
Victor LRT-7001 (LP)
Gertrude Lawrence
Monmouth-Evergreen MES-7043 (LP)
Joan Morris/William Bolcom
Omega OCD 3002 (CD): "Night and Day, The Cole Porter Album" 1988
Cole Porter
Victor 24859 (78) 1935
Cole Porter
JJA 19732 (LP): "Cole Porter--1924-1944"

The Cocotte
introduced by Queenie Leonard in *Nymph Errant*

Cole Porter
Victor 24859 (78) 1935
Cole Porter
JJA 19732 (LP): "Cole Porter--1924-1944"

Solomon
introduced by Elizabeth Welch in *Nymph Errant*

Bibi Osterwald
Painted Smiles PS-1340 (LP): "Cole Porter Revisited"
Elisabeth Welch
His Master's Voice B-8031 and Victor 25226 (78) 1933
Elisabeth Welch
Koch International 313-752-2 (CD), 213-754-4 (CS): "the Ultimate Elisabeth Welch - the Collection of Her Most Popular Songs"

Solomon (cont.)

> **Elisabeth Welch**
>> Monmouth-Evergreen MES-7043 (LP)

You're Too Far Away
  written for but unused in *Nymph Errant*

> **David Allen/Kaye Ballard**
>> Painted Smiles PS-1340 (LP): "Cole Porter Revisited"
> **Dolores Gray**
>> Painted Smiles PS-1370 (LP): "Cole Porter Revisited, Volume III"

Sweet Nudity
  written for but unused in *Nymph Errant*

> **Chorus**
>> Painted Smiles PS-1358 (LP): "Unpublished Cole Porter"

Si Vous Aimez Les Poitrines
  introduced by Iris Ashley in *Nymph Errant*

> **Alice Playten**
>> Painted Smiles PS-1358 (LP): "Unpublished Cole Porter"

When Love Comes Your Way
  written for but not used in *Nymph Errant*
  introduced by Derek Williams and Margaret Adams
  in *Jubilee*

> **Jimmy Dorsey and His Orchestra**
>> Decca 570 (78) 1935

When Love Comes Your Way (cont.)

> **Johnny Green and His Orchestra**
>> Brunswick 7522 (78) 1935
> **Mabel Mercer**
>> Atlantic 81264-4 (CS): "Mabel Mercer Sings Cole
>> Porter (With Cy Walter & Stan Freeman)"
> **Cole Porter**
>> Columbia KS-31456 (LP) from a demo made in 1935
> **Paul Whiteman and His Orchestra**
>> Victor 25134 (78) 1935 and Victor 36175 (78) 1935

Once Upon a Time
written for but unused in the unproduced show *Once
Upon a Time*

> **Bobby Short**
>> Atlantic SD 2-606 (LP): "Bobby Short Loves Cole
>> Porter" 1971
> **Bobby Short**
>> Atlantic 82062-2 (CD), 82062-4 (CS): "Bobby, Noel
>> & Cole (Bobby Short Loves Cole Porter/Bobby Short
>> Is Mad About Noel Coward)"

Waltz Down The Aisle
written for but unused in the unproduced dhow *Once
Upon a Time*
rewritten as "Wunderbar" for *Kiss Me Kate*

> **Ray Charles Singers**
>> Decca DL-8787 (LP)
> **Xavier Cugat and His Waldorf-Astoria Orchestra**
>> Victor 25133 (78) 1935
> **Paul Whiteman and His Orchestra**
>> Victor 36141 (78) 1934
> **Paul Whiteman and His Orchestra**
>> RCA LPV-555 (LP): "Paul Whiteman - Volume I"

Works From 1934

Miss Otis Regrets
introduced by Douglas Byng in the English show *Hi Diddle Diddle*

Adrian
Accent 6004 (LP): "Adrian"
Fred Astaire
DRG CDAR-1107 (CD), DARC-1C-1107 (CS), S3L-5181 (LP): "Three Evenings With Fred Astaire"
William Bolcom/Joan Morris
Omega Record Classics OCD-3002 (CD): "Night & Day"
Douglas Byng
English Decca F-5249 (78) 1934
Cab Calloway and His Orchestra
Brunswick 7504 (78) 1935
Rosemary Clooney
Concord Jazz CCD-4496 (CD), CJ-496-C (CS): "Girl Singer"
Nat King Cole
Capitol C2-93786 (C), C4-93786 (CS): "At the Sands"
Anita Day
Brunswick A-500474 (78) 1934
Marlene Dietrich
Columbia PCT-1275 (CS) and Sony CCL-1275 (LP): "Lili Marlene" (sung in German)
Marlene Dietrich
Columbia CK-53209 (CD), CT-53209 (CS): "The Cosmopolitan Marlene Dietrich"
Francis Faye
Capitol C2-96361 (CD), C4-96361 (CS): "Anything Goes - Capitol Sings Cole Porter"
George Feyer
Vanguard VSD-93/94 (LP): "Essential Cole Porter"
George Feyer
Vanguard OVC-6014 (CD): "George Feyer Plays Cole Porter"

Miss Otis Regrets (cont.)

Ella Fitzgerald
Verve 821989-2/821990-2 (CD), 823278-4 (CS),
823278-1 (LP): "Cole Porter Songbook" 1956
Ella Fitzgerald
Verve 314-519804-2 (CD), 314-519804-4 (CS): "The
Best of the Song Books"
Four Blackbirds
Columbia C2K-52454 (CD), C2T-52454 (CS): "A
Tribute to Black Entertainers"
Art Hodes/Milt Hinton
Muse MR-5279 (CS): "Just the Two of Us"
Alberta Hunter
DRG CDSL-5195 (CD), SLC-5195 (CS), SL-5195
(LP): "Legendary Alberta Hunter (London Sessions)"
Jack Jackson and His Orchestra
His Master's Voice B-6525 (78) 1934
James P. Johnson
MCA MCAC-1332 (CS): "Jazz Heritage - Piano in
Style (1926-1930)"
Peggy Johnson and Her Orchestra
Victor 24691 (78) 1934
King Singers
Hindsight HSC-168 (CS), HSR-168 (LP): "The
Uncollected King Singers (1947)"
Jimmie Lunceford
Decca 130 (78) 1934
Jimmie Lunceford
MCA MCAC-1320 (CS): "Jazz Heritage - Jimmie's
Legacy (1934-1937)"
Kirsty MacColl/The Pogues
Chrysalis F2-21799 (CD), F4-21799 (CS): "Red Hot
& Blue (A Tribute to Cole Porter to Benefit Aids
Research & Relief)"
Junior Mance
Inner City 6018 (LP): "Holy Mama"

Miss Otis Regrets (cont.)

Bette Midler
Atlantic 82129-2 (CD), 82129-4 (CS), 82129-1 (LP):
"Some People's Lives"
Bette Midler
Atlantic 82497-2 (CD), 82497-4 (CS): "Experience
The Divine (Greatest Hits)"
The Mills Brothers
Decca 166 (78) 1934
Patrick et Son Orchestre
Pathe Actuelle PA-537 (78) 1935
Jean Sablon
Columbia DF-1672 (78) 1935
Bobby Short
Mobile Fidelity Sound Lab UDCD-589 (CD), Atlantic
2-609 (LP), CS2-609 (CS): "Bobby Short Live at the
Cafe Carlyle"
Ethel Waters
Decca 140 (78) 1934
Josh White
Stinson 14 (LP): "Josh White Sings, Vol. 2"
Julie Wilson
DRG CDSL-5208 (CD), SLC-5208 (CS): "Cole Porter
Songbook"
Monty Woolley
Motion Picture Tracks MPT 6 (LP): soundtrack from
the film *Night and Day* 1945

Thank You So Much, Mrs. Lowsborough-Goodby
an independently published song

Ambrose Orchestra
Crescendo GNP-9004 (LP): "Ambrose Tribute to Cole
Porter"
Cole Porter
Victor 24766 (78) 1934
Cole Porter
JJA 19732 (LP): "Cole Porter--1924-1944"

Thank You So Much, Mrs. Lowsborough-Goodby (cont.)

Julia McKenzie
RCA LRL2-5054 (LP): "Cole"

I Get A Kick Out Of You
introduced by Ethel Merman in *Anything Goes*

Elly Ameling
Philips 412433-2 (CD), 412433-4 (CS), 412433-1
(LP): "Sentimental Me (Songs by Gershwin, Ellington,
Porter)"
Ambrose Orchestra
G.N.P. Crescendo GNP-9004 (LP): "Ambrose Tribute
to Cole Porter"
Ray Anthony
Capitol 292 (45)
Ray Anthony
Hindsight HCD-412 (CD), HSC-412 (Cs), HSR-412
(LP): "Young Man With a Horn - 1952-1954"
Ray Anthony
Aero Space RACD-995 (CD), RACS-995 (CS):
"Dancing In The Dark"
Louis Armstrong
Verve CD 314-511-070-2 (CD): "The Cole Porter
Songbook, Vol. II"
Jeanne Aubert/The Four Admirals
Columbia DX-697 (78)
Tony Bennett
Columbia C4K-46843 (CD), C4T-46843 (CS): "Forty
Years: The Artistry of Tony Bennett"
Art Blakey & The Jazz Messengers
Soul Note 121155-2 (CD), 121155-4 (CS), 121155-1
(LP): "I Get A Kick Out Of You"
William Bolcom/Joan Morris
Omega Record Classics OCD-3002 (CD): "Night &
Day"

I Get A Kick Out Of You (cont.)

Clifford Brown/Max Roach/Harold Land
Verve 842933-2 (CD): "Compact Jazz - Clifford Brown"

Dave Brubeck
Columbia C4K-52945 (CD), C4T-52945 (CS): "Time Signatures: A Career Retrospective"

Eddie Cano
RCA International 3459-2-RL (CD): "Cole Porter, Duke Ellington & Me"

Frankie Carle
RCA EPB-1064 (45)

Benny Carter
Verve 314-515392-2 (CD), 314-515392-4 (CS): "Jazz 'Round Midnight - The George Gershwin & Cole Porter Songbook"

Bob Causer and his Cornellians
Banner 33292 (78, 1934

Rosemary Clooney
Concord Jazz CJ-185 (LP), CCD-4185 (CD), CJ-185-C (CS): "Rosemary Clooney Sings the Music of Cole Porter" 1982

Nat King Cole
Blue Note B2-81203 (CD), B4-81203 (CS): "The Piano Stylings of Nat King Cole"

Ray Conniff & His Orchestra
Columbia CK-925 (CD): "'S Wonderful"

Chris Connor
Atlantic 81817-2 (CD), 81817-4 (CS): "The Erteguns' New York, New York Cabaret Music"

Chris Connor
Creative World ST-1028 (LP): "Fabulous Alumni of Stan Kenton"

Chris Connor/Stan Kenton
Capitol C2-96361 (CD), C4-96361 (CS): "Anything Goes - Capitol Sings Cole Porter"

Meyer Davis
Monmouth-Evergreen MES-6813 (LP): "Meyer Davis Plays Cole Porter"

I Get A Kick Out Of You (cont.)

Paul Desmond
Discovery 75005-2 (CD), 75005-4 (CS): "Malibu Sunset"

Paul Desmond Quartet
Discovery DSCD-840 (CD), DS-840MC (CS), DS-840 (LP): "East of the Sun"

The Dorsey Brothers' Orchestra
Decca 319 (78) 1934

Tommy Dorsey
RCA PK-5121 (CS): "This is Tommy Dorsey, Vol. 2"

Tommy Dorsey
Bluebird 66156-2 (CD), 66156-4 (CS): "The Post-War Era"

Ray Elis and Johnny Douglas conducting the Ray Elis Strings
RCA CAS-2522 (LP): "The Great Hits of Cole Porter"

George Feyer
Vanguard VSD-93/94 (LP): "Essential Cole Porter"

George Feyer
Vanguard OVC-6014 (CD): "George Feyer Plays Cole Porter"

Ella Fitzgerald (accompanied by Nelson Riddle and His Orchestra)
Atlantic SD-1631 (LP): "Ella Loves Cole"

Ella Fitzgerald
Verve 821989-2/821990-2 (CD), 823278-4 (CS), 823278-1 (LP): "Cole Porter Songbook" 1956

Ella Fitzgerald
Pablo PACD-2310-814-2 (CD), 52310-814 (CS), 2310814 (LP): "Dream Dancing"

Forbidden Broadway, Vol. 2
DRG CDSBL-12599 (CD), SBLC-12599 (CS)

Mike Garson
Reference RR-53CD (CD), RR-53 (LP): "The Oxnard Sessions, Vol. II"

I Get A Kick Out Of You (cont.)

Bob Grant and His Orchestra
Decca 24070 (78) 1942
Stephane Grappelli/Martin Taylor
Angel CDM-69172 (CD): "Just One of Those Things"
Stephane Grappelli/Joe Pass/Niels-Henning/Orsted
Pedersen
Pablo OJCCD-441-2 (CD), OJC-5441 (CS), OJC-441
(LP): "Tivoli Gardens"
Stephane Grappelli
Atlantic 82095-2 (CD), 82095-4 (CS), 82095-1 (LP):
"Olympia 1988"
George Hall
Bluebird B-5765 (78) 1934
Ernie Henry Quartet
Riverside OJCCD-1722-2 (CD), OJC-1722 (LP):
"Seven Standards & A Blues"
Robert Hicks
Velocity VCD-82863 (CD): "New Standards"
Billie Holiday
Clef 369 (45)
Billie Holiday
Verve 827160-4 (CS), 827160-1 (LP): "All Or
Nothing At All"
Billie Holiday
Verve 831371-2 (CD), 831371-4 (CS): "Compact Jazz
- Billie Holiday"
Billie Holiday
Verve 314-515392-2 (CD), 314-515392-4 (CS): "Jazz
'Round Midnight - The George Gershwin & Cole
Porter Songbook"
John Holmquist/Dan Estrem
Projazz CDJ-606 (CD), PCJ-606 (CS): "Still of the
Night"
Jack Hylton and His Orchestra
HMV C-2757 (78)
Jeanmaire
Decca DL 8318 (LP): soundtrack from the film
Anything Goes 1956

I Get A Kick Out Of You (cont.)

Jungle Brothers
Chrysalis F2-21799 (CD), F4-21799 (CS): "Red Hot
& Blue (A Tribute to Cole Porter to Benefit Aids
Research & Relief)"
Patti LuPone
RCA 61797-2 (CD): "Patti LuPone Live"
Patti LuPone
RCA 61834-2 (CD), 61834-4 (CS): "Patti LuPone
Live (Highlights)"
McGill Swing Band
McGill 750040-2 (CD): "Late Late Show"
Morgana King
Muse MCD-5326 (CD), MC-5326 (CS), MR-5326
(LP): "Simply Eloquent"
Andre Kostelanetz
Columbia CK-40218 (CD), CT-40218 (CS): "16 Most
Requested Songs"
Enoch Light
Command 56 (45)
Hal Linden/Eileen Rodgers/Barbara Land
Epic EK-15100 (CD), JST-15100 (CS): "Anything
Goes"
Patti LuPone
RCA 7769-2-RC (CD), 7769-4-RC (CS): "Anything
Goes"
Susannah McCorkle
Pausa PC-7208 (CS), 7208 (LP): "Dream"
Carmen McRae
GRP GRD-631 (CD), GRC-631 (CS): "Carmen
McRae Sings Great American Songwriters"
Adam Makowicz
Concord Jazz CCD-4541 (CD): "Live At Maybeck
Recital Hall, Vol. 24 (Adam Makowicz At Maybeck)"
Freddy Martin & His Orchestra
Hindsight HSC-169 (CS), HSR-169 (LP): "The
Uncollected Freddy Martin & His Orchestra, Vol. 2
(1944-1946)"

I Get A Kick Out Of You (cont.)

Mary Martin
Decca 23149 (78) 1940
Mary Martin
Columbia CK-53777 (CD), CT-53777 (CS): "16 Most
Requested Songs"
Mary Martin/Noel Coward
DRG CDXP-1103 (CD), DARC-2-1103 (LP):
"Together With Music"
Yehudi Menuhin/Stephane Grappelli
Angel 4XS-37156 (CS), 37156 (LP): "Fascinating
Rhythm (Music of the 30's)"
Yehudi Menuhin/Stephane Grappelli
Angel CDM-69219 (CD): "Menuhin & Grappelli Play
Berlin, Kern, Porter & Rodgers & Hart" 1988
Ethel Merman
Brunswick 7342 (78) 1934
Ethel Merman
Decca 24451 (78)
Ethel Merman
JJA-19767 (LP): soundtrack from the film *Anything
Goes* 1936
Ethel Merman/Mary Martin
Decca DL-7027 (LP) 1953
Ethel Merman
London XPS-901 (LP) 1972
Ethel Merman
A&M SP-4775 (LP) 1979
Ethel Merman
Columbia KS-31456 (LP): "Cole"
Ethel Merman
Columbia CK-57111 (CD), CT-57111: "This Is Art
Deco"
Vaughn Monroe
RCA 47-4172 (45) 1951
Ruby Newman and His Orchestra
Decca 23617 (78) 1938

I Get A Kick Out Of You (cont.)

Red Norvo Trio
Savoy SJL-2212 (LP): "Red Norvo Trio with Tal
Farlow & Charles Mingus - The Savoy Sessions"
Red Norvo
Musicmasters 65090-2 (CD), 65090-4 (CS): "Red
Norvo Orchestra Live From the Blue Gardens"
Red Norvo
Savoy Jazz SV-0168 (CD): "Move!"
Anita O'Day
Glendale 6001 (LP): "Anita O'Day"
Anita O'Day
Emily 9578 (LP): "Anita O'Day Live in Tokyo, 1975"
Anita O'Day
Emily 83084 (LP): "Song For You"
Anita O'Day
Evidence Music ECD-22054-2 (CD): "I Get A Kick
Out Of You"
Anita O'Day/Billy May
Verve 849266-2 (CD), 849266-4 (CS): "Anita O'Day
Swings Cole Porter"
Charlie Parker
Verve 827154-4 (CS), 827154-1 (LP): "Verve Years
(1952-1954)"
Patrick et Son Orchestre
Pathe Actuelle PA-669 (78) 1935
Oscar Peterson Trio
Verve 825769-2 (CD), 825769-4 (CS): "A Jazz
Portrait of Frank Sinatra"
Joe Reichman
Camden CAE-146 (45)
Leo Reisman and His Orchestra
Brunswick 7332 (78) 1934
Max Roach/Clifford Brown
Crescendo GNPD-18 (CD), GNP5-18 (CS), GNPS-18
(LP): "The Best of Max Roach & Clifford Brown in
Concert"

I Get A Kick Out Of You (cont.)

Max Roach/Clifford Brown
> Emarcy 814644-2 (CD): "Brown & Roach
> Incorporated"

Saint Louis Brass
> Summit DCD-140 (CD), DCC-140 (CS): "Pops"

Arturo Sandoval
> GRP GRD-9668 (CD), GRC-9668 (CS): "I Remember
> Clifford"

Artie Shaw
> MCA MCAC2-4081 (CS): "The Best of Artie Shaw"

Artie Shaw
> MCA MCAC-27094 (CS): "Best of the Big Bands"

Cybill Shepherd
> RCA ABL2-0967 (LP)

Bobby Short
> Mobile Fidelity Sound Lab UDCD-589 (CD), Atlantic
> 2-609 (LP), CS2-609 (CS): "Bobby Short Live at the
> Cafe Carlyle"

Bobby Short
> Telarc CD83311 (CD), CS-33311 (CS): "Late Night at
> the Cafe Carlyle"

Ginny Simms
> Motion Picture Tracks MPT 6 (LP): soundtrack from
> the film *Night and Day* 1945

Ginny Simms
> Royale VLP 6055 (LP): "Ginny Simms"

Frank Sinatra
> Capitol EBF-488 (45) 1953

Frank Sinatra
> Capitol 4N-16112 (CS): "My One & Only Love"

Frank Sinatra
> Capitol 4XBB-11357 (CS), SABB-11357 (LP): "Round
> No. 1"

Frank Sinatra
> Capitol C2-48470 (CD), C4-48470 (CS): "Songs For
> Young Lovers & Swing Easy"

Frank Sinatra
> Capitol C2-91344 (CD): "Frank Sinatra Gift Set"

I Get A Kick Out Of You (cont.)

Frank Sinatra
        Capitol CD-94317 (CD), C4-94317 (CS): "The
        Capitol Years"
Frank Sinatra
        Reprise 26340-2 (CD), 26340-4 (CS): "The Reprise
        Collection"
Frank Sinatra
        Reprise 26501-2 (CD), 26501-4 (CS): "Sinatra Reprise
        - The Very Good Years"
Frank Sinatra
        Capitol C2-96611 (CD), C4-96611 (CS): "Frank
        Sinatra Sings the Select Cole Porter"
Frank Sinatra
        Capitol C2-94777 (CD), C4-94777 (CS), C1-94777
        (LP): "The Capitol Years"
Frank Sinatra
        Capitol C2-99225 (CD), C4-99225 (CS), C5-99225
        (DCC), C8-99225 (MD): "The Best of the Capitol
        Years" - Selections from 'The Capitol Years' Box Set
Frank Sinatra
        Reprise 27021-2 (CD), 27021-4 (CS), FS-1005 (LP):
        "Sinatra & Swingin' Brass"
Frank Sinatra
        Capitol BBX2-99956 (CD), BBX4-99956 (CS):
        "Concepts"
Frank Sinatra
        Pair PDK-2-1028 (CS): "Timeless"
Jack Six/Francis Thorne
        Composers Recordings 585 (CD): "Porter On My
        Mind"
Paul Smith
        Outstanding 007 (LP): "Art Tatum Touch, Vol. 2"
Dick Twardzik
        New Artists NA-1006CD (CD): "1954 Improvisations"
Dionne Warwick
        Arista ARCD-8573 (CD), AC-8573 (CS), AL-8573
        (LP): "Dionne Warwick Sings Cole Porter"

I Get A Kick Out Of You (cont.)

Dinah Washington
Verve 847202-2 (CD), 847202-4 (CS): "Night & Day: The Cole Porter Songbook"

Dinah Washington
Verve 314-512905-2 (CD), 314-512905-4 (CS): "The Essential Dinah Washington: The Great Songs"

Mae West
Sony BT-2751 (CS), ACL-2751 (LP): "Merman-Roberti-West"

Randy Weston
Riverside 2508 (LP): "Randy Weston Plays Cole Porter in a Modern Mood" 1954

Lenny White/Nancy Wilson/Stanley Clarke/Chick Corea/Joe Henderson/ Freddie Hubbard
Elektra 60165-4 (CS): "Echoes of an Era - The Concert"

Paul Whiteman and His Orchestra
Victor 36141 (78) 1934

Paul Whiteman and His Orchestra
RCA LPV-555 (LP): "Paul Whiteman - Volume I"

Margaret Whiting
Teldec 75277-2 (CD): "Centennial Gala Concert"

John Williams
Sony Classical SK-47435 (CD), ST-47435 (CS), SM-47435 (MD): "Night & Day"

Roger Williams
Kapp 346 (45) 1960

Teddy Wilson
Black Lion BLCD-760166 (CD): "Cole Porter Classics"

Bon Voyage
introduced by the ensemble in *Anything Goes*

Hal Linden/Eileen Rodgers/Barbara Land
Epic EK-15100 (CD), JST-15100 (CS): "Anything Goes"

Bon Voyage (cont.)

Patti LuPone
RCA 7769-2-RC (CD), 7769-4-RC (CS): "Anything Goes"

All Through The Night
introduced by Bettina Hall and William Gaxton in *Anything Goes*

Bing Crosby
Decca DL 8318 (LP): soundtrack from the film *Anything Goes* 1956
Paul Desmond
Bluebird 2306-2-RB (CD), 2306-4-RB (CS): "Easy Living"
The Dorsey Brothers' Orchestra
Decca 318 (78) 1934
Tommy Dorsey and His Orchestra
Victor 25866 (78) 1938
Tommy Dorsey
Victor AXM2-5582 (LP), RCA AXK2-5582 (CS): "Complete Tommy Dorsey, Vol. 7 (1938)"
Percy Faith
Royale EP-198 (45)
Ella Fitzgerald
Verve 821989-2/821990-2 (CD), 823278-4 (CS), 823278-1 (LP): "Cole Porter Songbook" 1956
Johnny Griffin
Antilles 314-512604-2 (CD), 314-512604-4 (CS): "Dance of Passion"
Johnny Griffin
Who's Who in Jazz CD-21036 (CD), C-21036 (CS): "Take My Hand"

All Through The Night (cont.)

Scott Hamilton Quintet
Concord Jazz CCD-4311 (CD), CJ-311-C (CS): "The Right Time"

Jack Hylton and His Orchestra
HMV C-2757 (78)

Dick Hyman
Musicmasters 5060-2-C (CD), 5060-4-C (CS): "Cole Porter: All Through the Night"

Hal Kemp and His Orchestra
Brunswick 7322 (78) 1934

Anita Kerr
Sesac AD-56 (45)

Barbara Lea, with Bucky Pizzarelli
Audiophile ACD 252 (CD): "You're the Cats!" 1989

Hal Linden/Eileen Rodgers/Barbara Land
Epic EK-15100 (CD), JST-15100 (CS): "Anything Goes"

Julie London
EMI E2-93455 (CD), E4-93455 (CS): "Julie London Sings Cole Porter"

Patti LuPone
RCA 7769-2-RC (CD), 7769-4-RC (CS): "Anything Goes Original Lincoln Center Cast"

Yo-Yo Ma
Columbia MK-45574 (CD), FMT-45574 (CS): "Anything Goes - Music of Cole Porter"

Russell Malone
Columbia CK-53912 (CD), CT-53912 (CS): "Black Butterfly"

Johnny Mathis
Columbia B-10281 (45)

Mary Martin
Columbia CK-57111 (CD), CT-57111 (CS): "This is Art Deco"

Tony Martin
RCA 47-3250 (45) 1950

All Through The Night (cont.)

Orchestra
> Decca DL 8318 (LP): soundtrack from the film
> *Anything Goes* 1956

101 Strings Orchestra
> Alshire International SC-5026 (CS): "Quiet Hours,
> Vol. 1"

Bill Perkins Quartet
> Contemporary C-14011 (LP): "Journey To The East"

Paul Robeson
> His Master's Voice B-8668 (78) 1937

Paul Robeson
> Angel CDC-47839 (CD): "Paul Robeson Sings 'Ol'
> Man River' & Other Favorites" 1987

Paul Robeson
> Omega Record Classics OCD-3007 (CD), COM-3007
> (CS): "The Odyssey of Paul Robeson"

Harry Rosenthal and His Orchestra
> Columbia 2986-D (78) 1934

George Shearing/Marian McPartland
> Concord Jazz 1171 (LP), CCD-4171 (CD), CJ-171-C
> (CS): "Alone Together"

George Shearing/Barry Tuckwell
> Concord Jazz CCD-42010 (CD), CC-2010-C (CS):
> "George Shearing & Barry Tuckwell Play the Music
> of Cole Porter"

Warren Vache
> Concord Jazz CCD-4392 (CD), CJ-392-C (CS):
> "Warm Evenings"

Paul Whiteman and His Orchestra
> Victor 36141 (78) 1934

Paul Whiteman and His Orchestra
> RCA LPV-555 (LP): "Paul Whiteman - Volume I"

Jack Whiting
> Columbia DX-698 (78) 1935

Jack Whiting
> Monmouth-Evergreen MES-7049 (LP)

All Through The Night (cont.)

> **Jack Whiting**
>> Smithsonian R-007 and RCA DPM1-0284 (LP):
>> "Anything Goes"
>
> **Dave Willets/Claire Moore**
>> Teldec 75277-2 (CD): "Centennial Gala Concert"

There'll Always Be A Lady Fair
introduced by The Foursome Quartet (Marshall Smith,
Ray Johnson, Dwight Snyder and Del Porter) in
Anything Goes

> **The Anything Goes Foursome**
>> Victor 24817 (78) 1934
>
> **The Anything Goes Foursome**
>> JJA 19732 (LP): "Cole Porter--1924-1944"
>
> **Bing Crosby**
>> JJA-19767 (LP): soundtrack from the film *Anything Goes* 1936

You're The Top
introduced by Ethel Merman and William Gaxton in
Anything Goes

> **Ambrose Orchestra**
>> G.N.P. Crescendo GNP-9004 (LP): "Ambrose Tribute to Cole Porter"
>
> **Louis Armstrong**
>> Verve MGV 4035 (LP): "I've Got the World on a String" 1957
>
> **William Bolcom/Joan Morris**
>> Omega Record Classics OCD-3002 (CD): "Night & Day"
>
> **Les Brown**
>> Coral 9-60607 (45) 1951
>
> **Sammy Cahn**
>> Teldec 75277-2 (CD): "Centennial Gala Concert"

You're The Top (cont.)

Bob Causer and his Cornellians
Banner 33292 (78) 1934
Rosemary Clooney
Concord Jazz CJ-185 (LP), CCD-4185 (CD), CJ-185-
C (CS): "Rosemary Clooney Sings the Music of Cole
Porter" 1982
Bing Crosby/Frank Sinatra/Bob Hope
Laserlight 15413 (CD), 79413 (CS): "Mail Call"
Bing Crosby/Mitzi Gaynor
Decca DL 8318 (LP): soundtrack from the film
Anything Goes 1956
Decca All-Star Review (Bob Crosby Kay Weber, Johnnie Davis)
Decca 345 (78) 1935
Decca All-Star Review (Pee Wee Hunt, the Tune Twisters
Bob Howard), Decca 345 (78) 1935
The Dorsey Brothers' Orchestra
Decca 319 (78) 1934
Alice Faye
Teldec 75277-2 (CD): "Centennial Gala Concert"
George Feyer
Vanguard VSD-93/94 (LP): "Essential Cole Porter"
George Feyer
Vanguard OVC-6014 (CD): "George Feyer Plays Cole
Porter"
Ella Fitzgerald
Verve 821989-2/821990-2 (CD), 823278-4 (CS),
823278-1 (LP): "Cole Porter Songbook" 1956
William Gaxton
Startone ST-203 (LP)
William Gaxton/Dolores Gray
TVT TVT-9436-2 (CD), TVT-9436-4 (CS): "The
Sullivan Years - The Best of Broadway"
Mitzi Gaynor
Decca DL 8318 (LP): soundtrack from the film
Anything Goes 1956

You're The Top (cont.)

Bob Grant and His Orchestra
Decca 24070 (78) 1942
George Hall
Bluebird B-5765 (78) 1934
Jack Hylton and His Orchestra
HMV C-2757 (78)
Irving Joseph
Bainbridge BTC-1014 (CS), 1014 (LP): "Heritage of
Broadway - Music of Cole Porter"
Hal Kemp and His Orchestra
Brunswick 7322 (78) 1934
Hal Kemp
Columbia CK-45346 (CD), CT-45346 (CS): "Best of
the Big Bands"
Stan Kenton/Jean Turner
Creative World ST-1046 (LP): "Stan Kenton/Jean
Turner"
Stan Kenton/Jean Turner
Capitol C2-96361 (CD), C4-96361 (CS): "Anything
Goes - Capitol Sings Cole Porter"
Hal Linden/Eileen Rodgers/Barbara Land
Epic EK-15100 (CD), JST-15100 (CS): "Anything
Goes"
Patti LuPone
RCA 7769-2-RC (CD), 7769-4-RC (CS): "Anything
Goes"
Billy May & His Orchestra
Creative World ST-1051 (LP): "Sorta May"
Ethel Merman
Brunswick 7342 (78) 1934
Ethel Merman
Decca 24451 (78)
Ethel Merman/Bing Crosby
Encore ST 101 (LP): "Merman At The Movies"
soundtrack from the film *Anything Goes* 1936
Ethel Merman/Bing Crosby/Charles Ruggles
JJA-19767 (LP): soundtrack from the film *Anything
Goes* 1936

You're The Top (cont.)

Ethel Merman
Columbia KS-31456 (LP): "Cole"
Ethel Merman
Sony BT-2751 (CS), ACL-2751 (LP): "Merman-Roberti-West"
Ethel Merman
London XPS-901 (LP): 1972
Anita O'Day/Billy May
Verve 849266-2 (CD), 849266-4 (CS): "Anita O'Day Swings Cole Porter"
Cole Porter
Victor 24766 (78) 1934
Cole Porter
RCA LPV-560 and RCA DMM4-0407 (LP)
Cole Porter
JJA 19732 (LP): "Cole Porter--1924-1944"
Cole Porter
RCA 9971-2-R (CD), 9971-4-R (CS): "Nipper's Greatest Hits - the 30's, Vol. 1"
Burt Reynolds/Madeline Kahn/Duilio Del Prete/Cybill Shepherd
RCA ABL2-0967 (LP)
Harry Rosenthal and His Orchestra
Columbia 2986-D (78) 1934
Sonny Schuyler (with Loretta Lee)
Bluebird B-5765 (78) 1934
Ginny Simms/Cary Grant
Motion Picture Tracks MPT 6 (LP): soundtrack from the film *Night and Day* 1945
Ginny Simms
Royale VLP 6055 (LP): "Ginny Simms"
Frank Sinatra
Intermedia CQS-5001 (CS), 5001 (LP): "Tenderly"
Frank Sinatra
Intercon OXO-001 (CD): "Original Sessions"
Frank Sinatra
Pilz America 449335-2 (CD): "A Good Man Is Hard To Find"

You're The Top (cont.)

Barbra Streisand
Columbia C4K-44111 (CD), C4T-44111 (CS): "Barbra
Streisand...Just For The Record"
Barbra Streisand/Ryan O'Neal
Columbia CK-52849 (CD), CT-52849 (CS):
"Highlights from 'Just For The Record'"
Thomas "Fats" Waller
Victor LPT-6001 (78) 1935
Dionne Warwick
Arista ARCD-8573 (CD), AC-8573 (CS), AL-8573
(LP): "Dionne Warwick Sings Cole Porter"
Paul Whiteman and His Orchestra
Victor 36141 (78) 1934
Paul Whiteman and His Orchestra
RCA LPV-555 (LP): "Paul Whiteman - Volume I"
Jack Whiting/Jeanne Aubert
Columbia DX-697 (78) 1935
Jack Whiting/Jeanne Aubert
Monmouth Evergreen MES-7049 (LP)
Jack Whiting/Jeanne Aubert
Smithsonian R-007 and RCA DPM1-0284 (LP):
"Anything Goes"

Anything Goes
introduced by Ethel Merman in *Anything Goes*

Ambrose Orchestra
G.N.P. Crescendo GNP-9004 (LP): "Ambrose Tribute
to Cole Porter"
Jeanne Aubert/The Four Admirals
Columbia DX-697 (78)
Tony Bennett/Count Basie
Intermedia CQS-5016 (CS), 5016 (LP): "Big Band
Bash"
Tony Bennett/Count Basie
DCC Compact Classics DZS-004 (CD): "Chicago"

Anything Goes (cont.)

Tony Bennett/Count Basie
Roulette B2-93899 (CD), B4-93899 (CS): "Basie
Swings, Bennett Sings"

Tony Bennett/Count Basie
Capitol C2-96361 (CD), C4-96361 (CS): "Anything
Goes - Capitol Sings Cole Porter"

Tony Bennett/County Basie
Pair PCD-2-1237 (CD): "Some Pair"

Les Brown
USA Music Group USACD-685 (CD), USACA-685
(CS): "Anything Goes"

Rosemary Clooney
Concord Jazz CJ-185 (LP), CCD-4185 (CD), CJ-185-
C (CS): "Rosemary Clooney Sings the Music of Cole
Porter" 1982

Ray Conniff
Columbia AK-53140 (CD), AT-53140 (CS): "'S
Always Conniff"

The Dorsey Brothers' Orchestra
Decca 318 (78) 1934

Tal Farlow
Verve 829580-2 (CD): "Tal"

Frederick Fennell/Eastman-Rochester Pops Orchestra
Mercury 43427-2 (CD): "Fennell Conducts Porter &
Gershwin"

George Feyer
Vanguard VSD-93/94 (LP): "Essential Cole Porter"

George Feyer
Vanguard OVC-6014 (CD): "George Feyer Plays Cole
Porter"

**Ella Fitzgerald (accompanied by Nelson Riddle and His
Orchestra)**
Atlantic SD-1631 (LP): "Ella Loves Cole"

Ella Fitzgerald
Verve 821989-2/821990-2 (CD), 823278-4 (CS),
823278-1 (LP): "Cole Porter Songbook" 1956

Anything Goes (cont.)

Ella Fitzgerald
Pablo PACD-2310-814-2 (CD), 52310-814 (CS),
2310814 (LP): "Dream Dancing"
Ella Fitzgerald
Verve 847202-2 (CD), 847202-4 (CS): "Night & Day:
The Cole Porter Songbook"
Forbidden Broadway, Vol. 2
DRG CDSBL-12599 (CD), SBLC-12599 (CS)
Mitzi Gaynor
Decca DL 8318 (LP): soundtrack from the film
Anything Goes 1956
Stan Getz/Gerry Mulligan
Verve 849392-2 (CD): "Getz Meets Mulligan in Hi-
Fi"
Benny Goodman
NBC Thesaurus 127 (78) 1935
Stephane Grappelli
Accord 139004 (CD): "Stephane Grappelli Plays
George Gershwin & Cole Porter"
Stephane Grappelli
Who's Who In Jazz 21035 (CD): "Stephane Grappelli"
Harpers Bizarre
Warner Brothers 7063 (45) 1967
Jack Hylton and His Orchestra
HMV C-2757 (78)
Irving Joseph
Bainbridge BTC-1014 (CS), 1014 (LP): "Heritage of
Broadway - Music of Cole Porter"
Hal Linden/Eileen Rodgers/Barbara Land
Epic EK-15100 (CD), JST-15100 (CS): "Anything
Goes"
Patti LuPone
RCA 7769-2-RC (CD), 7769-4-RC (CS): "Anything
Goes"
Patti LuPone
RCA 61797-2 (CD): "Patti LuPone Live"

Anything Goes (cont.)

Patti LuPone
RCA 61834-2 (CD), 61834-4 (CS): "Patti LuPone
Live (Highlights)"
Mary Martin
Columbia A-967 (45) 1950
Mary Martin
Columbia CK-53777 (CD), CT-53777 (CS): "16 Most
Requested Songs"
Ethel Merman
Capitol C2-46076 (CD), C4-46076 (CS): soundtrack
from the film *Terms of Endearment*
Helen Merrill
Mercury 826340-2 (CD): "Complete Helen Merrill on
Mercury (1954-1958)"
Hugo Montenegro
Bainbridge BCD-1002 (CD), BTC-1002 (CS), BT-
1002 (LP): "Overture: American Musical Theatre,
Vol. One 1924-1935"
Orchestra
Motion Picture Tracks MPT 6 (LP): soundtrack from
the film *Night and Day* 1945
Patrick et Son Orchestre
Pathe Actuelle PA-669 (78) 1935
Sid Phillips
Parlophone F-1683 (78) 1940
Cole Porter
Victor 24825 (78) 1934
Cole Porter
New World NW-272 (LP)
Cole Porter
Pelican LP-120 (LP)
Cole Porter
JJA 19732 (LP): "Cole Porter--1924-1944"
Andre Previn
RCA 2431-2-R11 (CD), 2431-4-R6 (CS): "Piano
Stylings of Andre Previn"
Estelle Reiner
Iti 4XT-72955 (CS), ST-72955 (LP): "Just in Time"

Anything Goes (cont.)

Leo Reisman and His Orchestra
Brunswick 7332 (78) 1934
Debbie Shapiro
Teldec 75277-2 (CD): "Centennial Gala Concert"
Cybill Shepherd
MCA MCAC-25173 (CS), MCA-25173 (LP): "Cybill
Does It...To Cole Porter"
Cybill Shepherd
Paramount PAS-1018 (LP)
Frank Sinatra
Capitol EAP-1-653 (45) and DV-653 (45) 1956
Frank Sinatra/Nelson Riddle Orchestra
Capitol C2-46570 (CD): "Songs For Swingin' Lovers"
Frank Sinatra
Capitol C2-91344 (CD): "Frank Sinatra Gift Set"
Frank Sinatra
Capitol C2-96611 (CD), C4-96611 (CS): "Frank
Sinatra Sings the Select Cole Porter"
Frank Sinatra
Mobile Fidelity Sound Lab UDCD-538 (CD): "Songs
For Swingin' Lovers"
Frank Sinatra
Capitol BBX2-99956 (CD), BBX4-99956 (CS):
"Concepts"
Frank Sinatra
Pair PDK-2-1028 (CS): "Timeless"
Jo Stafford
Corinthian COR-112 (LP): "Jo Plus Broadway"
The Starsound Orchestra
Dominion Entertainment 3170-2 (CD): "45 Broadway
Showstoppers"
Mel Torme
Atlantic 81817-2 (CD), 81817-4 (CS): "The Erteguns'
New York, New York Cabaret Music"
Dionne Warwick
Arista ARCD-8573 (CD), AC-8573 (CS), AL-8573
(LP): "Dionne Warwick Sings Cole Porter"

Anything Goes (cont.)

Paul Whiteman and His Orchestra
Victor 36141 (78) 1934
Paul Whiteman and His Orchestra
RCA LPV-555 (LP): "Paul Whiteman - Volume I"
John Williams
Polydor 821592-4 (CS): "Indiana Jones & the Temple
of Doom"

Public Enemy Number One
introduced by the ensemble in *Anything Goes*

Hal Linden/Eileen Rodgers/Barbara Land
Epic EK-15100 (CD), JST-15100 (CS): "Anything
Goes"
Patti LuPone
RCA 7769-2-RC (CD), 7769-4-RC (CS): "Anything
Goes"

Blow, Gabriel, Blow
introduced by Ethel Merman in *Anything Goes*

Jeanne Aubert/The Four Admirals
Columbia DX-698 (78)
Jeanne Aubert/The Four Admirals
Smithsonian R-007 and RCA DPM1-0284 (LP):
"Anything Goes"
Bon Bon and His Buddies
Decca 8567 (78) 1941
Frank Chacksfield and His Orchestra
London SP-44185 (LP): "The Music of Cole Porter"
Al Cohn
Concord Jazz CJ-194 (LP): "Overtones"
Bing Crosby/Donald O'Connor/Mitzi Gaynor/Jeanmaire
Decca DL 8318 (LP): soundtrack from the film
Anything Goes 1956

Blow, Gabriel, Blow (cont.)

Rev. Gary Davis/Pink Anderson
Riverside OBCCD-524-2 (CD), OBC-524 (LP):
"Gospel, Blues & Street Songs"
Frederick Fennell and the Eastman Rochester Pops
Mercury 75110 (LP): "Music of Cole Porter"
Frederick Fennell/Eastman-Rochester Pops Orchestra
Mercury 43427-2 (CD): "Fennell Conducts Porter &
Gershwin"
Nat Gonella
Parlophone F-193 (78) 1935
Jack Hylton and His Orchestra
HMV C-2757 (78)
Hal Linden/Eileen Rodgers/Barbara Land
Epic EK-15100 (CD), JST-15100 (CS): "Anything
Goes"
Patti LuPone
RCA 7769-2-RC (CD), 7769-4-RC (CS): "Anything
Goes"
Lorna Luft
Teldec 75277-2 (CD): "Centennial Gala Concert"
Enric Madriguera and His Hotel Weylin Orchestra
Victor 24818 (78) 1934
Ethel Merman
Decca 24453 (78) 1947
Ethel Merman
Reprise R-6032 and Stanyan SR-10070 (LP) 1962
Ethel Merman
London XPS-901 (LP) 1972
Martha Tilton
Capitol C2-96361 (CD), C4-96361 (CS): "Anything
Goes - Capitol Sings Cole Porter"

Buddie Beware
introduced by Ethel Merman in *Anything Goes*

> **Helen Gallagher**
>> Painted Smiles PS-1371 (LP): "Cole Porter Revisited, Volume IV"
>
> **Patti LuPone**
>> RCA 7769-2-RC (CD), 7769-4-RC (CS): "Anything Goes"

Be Like the Bluebird
introduced by Victor Moore in *Anything Goes*

> **Cole Porter**
>> Victor 24843 (78) 1935
>
> **Cole Porter**
>> JJA 19732 (LP): "Cole Porter--1924-1944"
>
> **Hal Linden/Eileen Rodgers/Barbara Land**
>> Epic EK-15100 (CD), JST-15100 (CS): "Anything Goes"
>
> **Patti LuPone**
>> RCA 7769-2-RC (CD), 7769-4-RC (CS): "Anything Goes"
>
> **Jack Whiting/Sydney Howard**
>> Columbia DX-698 (78) 1935
>
> **Jack Whiting/Sydney Howard**
>> Smithsonian R-007 and RCA DPM1-0284 (LP): "Anything Goes"

The Gypsy In Me
introduced by Bettina Hall in *Anything Goes*

> **The Anything Goes Foursome**
>> Victor 24817 (78) 1934
>
> **The Anything Goes Foursome**
>> JJA 19732 (LP): "Cole Porter--1924-1944"
>
> **Jack Hylton and His Orchestra**
>> HMV C-2757 (78)

The Gypsy In Me (cont.)

> **Patti LuPone**
> > RCA 7769-2-RC (CD), 7769-4-RC (CS): "Anything
> > Goes"

Kate the Great
  written for but unused in *Anything Goes*

> **Karen Morrow**
> > Painted Smiles PS-1358 (LP): "Unpublished Cole
> > Porter"
> **Cybill Shepherd**
> > MCA MCAC-25173 (CS), MCA-25173 (LP): "Cybill
> > Does It...To Cole Porter"
> **Cybill Shepherd**
> > Paramount PAS-1018 (LP)

There's No Cure Like Travel
  written for but unused in *Anything Goes*

> **Patti LuPone**
> > RCA 7769-2-RC (CD), 7769-4-RC (CS): "Anything
> > Goes"

Why Shouldn't I?
introduced by Margaret Adams in *Jubilee*

Chet Baker
Sony JCL-549 (LP): "Chet Baker & Strings"
Chet Baker
Columbia CK-46174 (CD), CT-46174 (CS): "Chet Baker: With Strings"
Laverne Butler
Chesky JD-91 (CD), JC-91 (CS): "No Looking Back"
Louise Carlyle
Walden 301 (LP)
Rosemary Clooney
Concord Jazz CCD-4282 (CD), CJ-282-C (CS): "Rosemary Clooney Sings Ballads"
Paul Desmond
CBS Associated ZK-40806 (CD), FZT-40806 (CS): "Pure Desmond"
Jimmy Dorsey and His Orchestra
Decca 571 (78) 1935
Tal Farlow
Concord Jazz CJ-204 (LP): "Cookin' on All Burners"
Johnny Green and His Orchestra
Brunswick 7522 (78) 1935
Joe Haymes and His Orchestra
Thesaurus 184 (78) 1935
Mary Martin
Decca 23148 (78) 1940
Anita O'Day
Emily 11279 (LP): "My Ship"
Anita O'Day/Billy May
Verve 849266-2 (CD), 849266-4 (CS): "Anita O'Day Swings Cole Porter"
Betty Roche
Prestige OJCCD-1802-2 (CD): "Lightly & Politely"

Why Shouldn't I? (cont.)

Shorty Rogers
Time Is TI-9804 (CD): "Big Band, Vol. 1"
Artie Shaw and His Orchestra
Victor 27499 (78) 1941
Artie Shaw
RCA AXK2-5576 (CS): "Complete Artie Shaw, Vol. 5 (1941-1942)"
Hamilton Scott/Warren Vache
Concord Jazz CJ-111 (LP): "Skyscrapers"
Bobby Short
Atlantic SD 2-606 (LP): "Bobby Short Loves Cole Porter" 1971
Bobby Short
Atlantic 82062-2 (CD), 82062-4 (CS): "Bobby, Noel & Cole (Bobby Short Loves Cole Porter/Bobby Short Is Mad About Noel Coward)"
Frank Sinatra
Columbia CK-44236 (CD), FCT-44326 (CS): "Sinatra Rarities - The Columbia Years"
Frank Sinatra
Columbia CXK-48673 (CD): "The Columbia Years (1943-1952) The Complete Recordings"
Jack Six/Francis Thorne
Composers Recordings 585 (CD): "Porter On My Mind"
Jeri Southern
Capitol T-1173 (LP)
Ocie Stockard and the Wanderers
Bluebird B-7296 (78) 1937
Warren Vache
Concord Jazz CJ-98 (LP): "Polished Brass"
Paul Whiteman and His Orchestra
Victor 25134 (78) 1935
Paul Whiteman and His Orchestra
Victor 36175 (78) 1935
Margaret Whiting
Capitol C2-96361 (CD), C4-96361 (CS): "Anything Goes - Capitol Sings Cole Porter"

Why Shouldn't I? (cont.)

> **Lee Wiley**
>> Liberty Music Shop L-295 (78) 1940
>
> **Lee Wiley**
>> Audiophile ACD-1 (CD), Monmouth-Evergreen MES
>> 7034 (LP): "Lee Wiley Sings George Gershwin and
>> Cole Porter"
>
> **Teddy Wilson**
>> Black Lion BLCD-760166 (CD): "Cole Porter
>> Classics"

What a Nice Municipal Park
  introduced by Jack Whitney in *Jubilee*

> **Cole Porter**
>> Columbia KS-31456 (LP) from a demo made in 1935

When Me, Mowgli, Love
  introduced by Mark Plant in *Jubilee*

> **Cole Porter**
>> Columbia KS-31456 (LP) from a demo made in 1935

Entrance of Eric
  introduced by the ensemble in *Jubilee*

> **Cole Porter**
>> Columbia KS-31456 (LP) from a demo made in 1935

The Kling-Kling Bird On The Divi-Divi Tree
  introduced by Derek Williams in *Jubilee*

> **Cole Porter**
>> Columbia KS-31456 (LP) from a demo made in 1935

The Kling-Kling Bird On The Divi-Divi Tree (cont.)

Burl Ives
Decca DL7-8886 (LP)

Begin The Beguine
introduced by June Knight in *Jubilee*

All Star Orchestra Plus Pipe Organ
Alshire International ALCD-16 (CD): "Golden Age of the Dance Bands"
Ambrose Orchestra/Anne Shelton
G.N.P. Crescendo GNP-9004 (LP): "Ambrose Tribute to Cole Porter"
Elly Ameling
Philips 412433-2 (CD), 412433-4 (CS), 412433-1 (LP): "Sentimental Me (Songs by Gershwin, Ellington, Porter)"
Tuck Andress
Windham Hill WD-0124 (CD), WT-0124 (CS): "Reckless Precision"
The Andrews Sisters
Capitol/Curb D2-77400 (CD), D4-77400 (CS): "Greatest Hits"
The Andrews Sisters
MCA MCAD-10093 (CD): "The Andrews Sisters 50th Anniversary Collection, Vol. II"
The Andrews Sisters
Pair PCD-2-1159 (CD), PDK-2-1159 (CS): "At Their Very Best"
The Andrews Sisters
MCA MCAC-20259 (CS): "Beat Me Daddy Eight to the Bar"
The Andrews Sisters
Decca 2290 (78) and Decca ED-2041 (45)
The Andrews Sisters
Capitol C2-94078 (CD), C4-94078 (CS): "Capitol Collectors Series"

Begin The Beguine (cont.)

Ray Anthony
   Capitol 292 (45)
Ray Anthony
   Aero Space RACD-995 (CD), RACS-995 (CS):
   "Dancing In The Dark"
Ray Anthony
   Aero Space RACD-1012 (CD), RACS-1012 (CS):
   "Tribute"
Desi Arnaz Orchestra
   Laserlight 15767 (CD), 79767 (CS): "The Big Bands
   of Hollywood"
Arturo and His Cuban Rhythm (Angeli Ilardi)
   Victor 27732 (78) 1941
Pierre Allier et Son Orchestre
   Swing 89 (78) 1940
Mildred Bailey
   Vocalion 4619 (78) 1939
Carlos Barbosa-Lima
   Concord Jazz CCD-42008 (CD), CC-42008 (CS), CC-
   42008 (LP): "Barbosa-Lima Plays The Music of Bonfa
   & Porter"
Charlie Barnet
   Everest 333 (LP): "Charlie Barnet, Vol. 2"
BBC Swing Band
   Bainbridge BCD-2511 (CD): "The Age of Swing, Vol.
   1"
Louie Bellson
   Musicmasters 5038-2-C (CD), 5038-4-C (CS):
   "Airmail Special: A Salute to the Big Band Masters"
Tony Bennett
   Columbia C4K-46843 (CD), C4T-46843 (CS): "Forty
   Years: The Artistry of Tony Bennett"
Tony Bennett
   Columbia CK-53153 (CD), CT-53153 (CS): "The
   Consummate Collection: Classic Songs From the
   Tony Bennett Boxed Set"
Stanley Black
   London 1720 (45) 1956

Begin The Beguine (cont.)

Carver Blanchard/Nel Moore/Glen Saunders
Albany TROY-083-2 (CD): "Lute Unleashed"
William Bolcom/Joan Morris
Omega Record Classics OCD-3002 (CD): "Night &
Day"
Boston Pops Orchestra/John Williams
Phillips 412626-2 (CD), 412626-4 (CS), 412626-1
(LP): "Swing, Swing, Swing"
Boston Pops Orchestra/John Williams
Sony SK-53380 (CD), ST-53380 (CS), SM-53380
(MD): "Unforgettable"
Connee Boswell
Decca 9-27945 (45) 1952
Nat Brandywynne and His Orchestra
Decca 24074 (78) 1942
Nino Bravo
Capitol/EMI Latin H2-42828 (CD), H4-42828 (CS):
"Mis Mejores Canciones - 17 Super Exitos"
Les Brown
Hindsight HCD-408 (CD), HSC-408 (CS): "Les
Brown & His Orchestra Play 22 Original Big Band
Recordings (1957)"
Les Brown
USA Music Group USACD-685 (CD), USACA-685
(CS): "Anything Goes"
Henry Busse and His Orchestra
Decca 2107 (78) 1938
Frank Chacksfield and His Orchestra
London SP-44185 (LP): "The Music of Cole Porter"
Buddy Cole
Alshire SC-5289 (CS): "Golden Age of the Dance
Bands"
Columbia Ballroom Orchestra
Denon DC-8522 (CD): "Let's Dance, Vol. 2 -
Invitation to Dance Party (I Kiss Your Little Hand,
Madame)"

Begin The Beguine (cont.)

Perry Como
> RCA 66098-2 (CD), 66098-4 (CS): "Yesterday &
> Today - A Celebration in Song"

Ray Conniff & His Orchestra
> Columbia CK-925 (CD): "'S Wonderful"

Gal Costa
> RCA International 2214-2-RL (CD), 2214-4-RL (CS):
> "Plural"

Johnny Costa
> Savoy ZDS-1190 (CD), SJK-1190 (CS), SJL-1190
> (LP): "Neighborhood"

Noel Coward
> Columbia MDK-47253 (CD), MGT-47253 (CS):
> "Noel Coward Album - Noel Coward Live From Las
> Vegas & New York"

Bob Crosby
> Decca 2290 (78) 1939

Xavier Cugat and His Waldorf-Astoria Orchestra
> Victor 25133 (78) 1935

Xavier Cugat
> Pro-Arte CDD-3406 (CD), PCD-3406 (CS): "Adios
> Muchachos"

Joe Daniels and His Hot Shots in "Drumnasticks"
> Parlophone F-1488 (78) 1939

Sammy Davis, Jr.
> MCA MCAC2-4109 (CS & LP): "Hey there (It's
> Sammy Davis, Jr. At His Dynamite Greatest)"

Sammy Davis, Jr.
> MCA Special Products MCAC-20189 (CS): "That Old
> Black Magic"

Sammy Davis, Jr.
> Reprise R9-6051 (LP)

Wild Bill Davison
> Dixieland Jubilee DJS-508 (LP): "Wild Bill Davison
> Plays the Greatest of the Greats"

Jimmy Dorsey & His Orchestra
> Ranwood RC-8219 (CS): "Jimmy Dorsey & His
> Orchestra"

Begin The Beguine (cont.)

Jimmy Dorsey
>Hindsight HSC-153 (CS), HSR-153 (LP): "The Uncollected Jimmy Dorsey & His Orchestra, Vol. 2"

Les & Larry Elgart
>Columbia PCT-38341 (CS): "Swingtime"

Ray Elis and Johnny Douglas conducting the Ray Elis Strings,
>RCA CAS-2522 (LP): "The Great Hits of Cole Porter"

The Exotic Guitars
>Ranwood RC-7014 (CS), RLP-7014 (LP): "22 Great Guitar Favorites"

Frederick Fennell/Eastman-Rochester Pops Orchestra
>Mercury 43427-2 (CD): "Fennell Conducts Porter & Gershwin"

George Feyer
>Vanguard VSD-93/94 (LP): "Essential Cole Porter"

George Feyer
>Vanguard OVC-6014 (CD): "George Feyer Plays Cole Porter"

Ella Fitzgerald
>Verve 821989-2/821990-2 (CD), 823278-4 (CS), 823278-1 (LP): "Cole Porter Songbook" 1956

Erroll Garner
>Mercury 834909-2 (CD), 834909-4 (CS): "Mambo Moves Garner"

Terry Gibbs Dream Band
>Contemporary CCD-7647-2 (CD), C-57647 (CS), C-7647 (LP): "Terry Gibbs Dream Band, Vol. 1"

Dizzy Gillespie
>Verve 314-513875-2 (CD), 314-513875-4 (CS): "Dizzy's Diamonds (The Best of the Verve Years)"

Robert Guillaume
>Teldec 75277-2 (CD): "Centennial Gala Concert"

Adelaide Hall
>ASV CD-AJA-5098 (CD), CS-AJA-5098 (CS): "Hall of Fame"

Begin The Beguine (cont.)

Jim Hall
    Musicmasters 5050-2-C (CD), 5050-4-C (CS): "Jim
    Hall & Friends, Vol. 1 - Live at Town Hall"
Count Red Hastings/Danny Turner/Eddie Woodland
    Collectables COL-5323 (CD, CS, LP): "Count Red
    Hastings/Danny Turner/Eddie Woodland"
Joe Haymes and His Orchestra
    Thesaurus 184 (78) 1935
Horace Heidt
    Hindsight HSC-194 (CS), HSR-194 (LP): "The
    Uncollected Horace Heidt & His Musical Knights
    (1939)"
Eddie Heywood & His Orchestra/Edmond Hall
    Commodore CCD-7010 (CD), CCK-7010 (CS), CCL-
    7010 (LP): "Jazz At Cafe Society, New York in the
    40's"
Eddie Heywood Orchestra
    Commodore CCD-7000 (CD): "The Commodore Jazz
    Sampler"
Lois Hodnett
    Classic International Filmusicals CIF 3002 (LP):
    soundtrack from the film *Broadway Melody of 1940*
    1939
Houston Symphony Orchestra/Newton Wayland
    Pro-Arte CDD-420 (CD), CSD-420 (CS): "Stompin'
    At The Savoy"
Dick Hyman
    Musicmasters 5060-2-C (CD), 5060-4-C (CS): "Cole
    Porter: All Through the Night"
Julio Iglesias
    Columbia C2K-39570 (CD), K2T-39570 (CS): "In
    Concert"
Julio Iglesias
    Columbia CD-38640 (CD), DIC-50333 (CS), DJL-
    50333 (LP): "Julio"
Indios Tabajaras
    RCA 7367-2-RL (CD): "Grandes Exitos de los Indios
    Tabajaras"

Begin The Beguine (cont.)

Irving Joseph
Bainbridge BTC-1014 (CS), 1014 (LP): "Heritage of Broadway - Music of Cole Porter"

Stan Kenton
Hindsight HCD-136 (CD), HSR-136 (LP): "The Uncollected Stan Kenton & His Orchestra, Vol. 3 (1943-1944)"

Stan Kenton
Hindsight HCD-157 (CD), HSC-157 (CS), HSR-157 (LP): "The Uncollected Stan Kenton & His Orchestra, Vol. 5 (1945-1947)"

Leigh Kaplan/Lincoln Mayorga
Cambria 1019 (LP): "Dizzy Fingers"

Swing and Sway with Sammy Kaye
Victor 27725 (78) 1941

Salif Keita
Chrysalis F2-21799 (CD), F4-21799 (CS): "Red Hot & Blue (A Tribute to Cole Porter to Benefit Aids Research & Relief)"

Stan Kenton
Creative World 1025 (LP): "Adventures in Standards"

Stan Kenton
Creative World ST-1041 (LP): "Sketches on Standards"

Max Kortlander
Biograph BLP-1023Q (LP) from a piano roll

Gene Krupa
Verve 845153-2 (CD), 845153-4 (CS): "Jazz-Club Mainstream - Big Bands"

Mario Lanza
RCA 549-5127 (45) and RCA EPA-5047 (45)

Tom Lellis
Inner City 1090 (LP): "Tomo Lellis"

Liberace
Columbia CK-44405 (CD), CT-44405 (CS): "16 Most Requested Songs"

Begin The Beguine (cont.)

Liberace
> Capitol/Curb D2-77516 (CD), D4-77516 (CS): "The
> Golden Age of Television"

Dave Liebman Trio
> Red 123236-2 (CD): "Dave Liebman Trio Plays Cole
> Porter"

Enoch Light
> Project 3 PRD2-6005 (CD), PRC2-6005 (CS), 6005/6
> (LP): "Big Band Hits of the 30's, 40's & 50's"

Enoch Light
> Project Three PR-5049 (45), PRD-5049 (CD), PRC-
> 5049 (CS), 5049 (LP): "Big Band Hits of the 30's"

The Limeliters
> G.N.P. Crescendo GNPD-2206 (CD), GNP5-2206
> (CS): "Singing For the Fun"

Big Tiny Little
> G.N.P. Crescendo GNPD-2113 (CD), GNPS-2113
> (LP): "Golden Piano Hits"

Joe Loco Quintet
> Columbia 4-40636 (45) 1956

Los Tres Diamantes
> RCA International 6410-4-RL (CS): "15 Exitos De
> Los Tres Diamantes - Versiones Originales"

Gordon MacRae
> Capitol C2-96361 (CD), C4-96361 (CS): "Anything
> Goes - Capitol Sings Cole Porter"

Adam Makowicz
> Concord Jazz CCD-4541 (CD): "Live At Maybeck
> Recital Hall, Vol. 24 (Adam Makowicz At Maybeck)"

Richard Maltby ("Begin the Beguine March")
> X 4X-0094 (45) 1955

Mantovani
> Bainbridge BTC-6239 (CS), 6239 (LP): "Flamingo"

Tony Martin
> Decca 2375 (78) 1939

Tony Martin
> Dot ED 605 (LP): "Tony Martin Sings" 1954

Begin The Beguine (cont.)

Tony Martin
Dot 45-159 (45) 1961
Tony Martin
MCA MCAC-1515 (CS): "Tony Martin"
Johnny Mathis
Columbia 3-11001 (45) 1979, Columbia CK-35649
(CD), PCT-35649 (CS): "The Best Days of My Life"
Johnny Mathis
Columbia CGT-37440 (CS): "The First 25 Years
(Silver Anniversary Album)"
Johnny Mathis
Columbia CK-38699 (CD), PCT-38699 (CS): "Live"
Johnny Mathis
Columbia 44K-07837 (CD3)
Buddy Merrill
Accent C-5018 (CS), 5018 (LP): "Latin Festival"
David Matthews Orchestra
G.N.P. Crescendo GNP5-2162 (CS), GNPS-2162
(LP): "Grand Connection"
Michegan State University Steel Band
Smithsonian Folkways 3835 (CS): "Bamboushay Steel
Band"
Glenn Miller
RCA 447-0030 (45)
Glenn Miller
Pair PDC-2-1118 (CD): "Original Recordings, Vol.
3 - Army Air Force Band"
Hugo Montenegro
Bainbridge BTC-1009 (CS), 1009 (LP): "Big Band
Boogie"
Hugo Montenegro
Bainbridge BCD-1002 (CD), BTC-1002 (CS), BT-
1002 (LP): "Overture: American Musical Theatre,
Vol. One 1924-1935"
Michael Nesmith
Pacific Arts Audio PAAD-5000 (CD), PAAC-5000
(CS): "Tropical Campfire's"

Begin The Beguine (cont.)

Ohio State University Marching Band
Fidelity FSRC-1335 (CS), 1335 (LP): "Pride of the Buckeyes"

101 Strings Orchestra
Alshire ALCD-3 (CD), ALSC-5373 (CS): "Best of the 101 Strings"

101 Strings Orchestra
Alshire International ALCD-30 (CD), ALSC-5007 (CS): "Cole Porter"

101 Strings Orchestra
Alshire SC-5305 (CS): "Big Band Hits, Vol. 2"

101 Strings Orchestra
Alshire SC-5391 (CS): "Salute to the Big Bands"

101 Strings Orchestra
Alshire International ALSC-5396 (CS): "101 Strings Salute Julio Iglesias"

101 Strings Orchestra
Alshire International ALSC-5035 (CS): "Million Seller Hit Songs of the 30's"

101 Strings Orchestra
Alshire International ALSC-5391 (CS): "Salute To The Big Bands"

Charlie Parker
Verve 827154-4 (CS), 827154-1 (LP): "Verve Years (1952-1954)"

Art Pepper
V.S.O.P. 30 (LP): "Art of Pepper"

Art Pepper
Blue Note B2-46848 (CD): "Modern Art - The Complete Art Pepper Aladdin Recordings, Vol. II" 1988

Art Pepper
Blue Note B2-46853 (CD): "The Art of Pepper - Complete Art Pepper Aladdin Recordings, Vol. 3" 1988

Charlie Parker
Verve 823250-2 (CD), 823250-4 (CS): "The Cole Porter Songbook"

Begin The Beguine (cont.)

Johnny Puleo
Audiofidelity Enterprises 6130 (LP): "Johnny Puleo &
His Harmonica Gang"
Frankie Questa
Cub 9037 (45) 1959
Carlos Ramirez
Motion Picture Tracks MPT 6 (LP): soundtrack from
the film *Night and Day* 1945
Carlos Ramirez
SMC 2512 (78)
The Ravens
Mercury 5800X45 (45) 1952
Leo Reisman and His Orchestra
Brunswick 7575 (78) 1935
Rochester Pops Orchestra/Erich Kunzel
Pro-Arte CCD-385 (CD), PCD-385 (CS): "Gotta
Dance - A Tribute to Fred Astaire"
Meldora Hardin
Hollywood 61117-2 (CD), 61117-4 (CS): soundtrack
from the film *The Rocketeer* 1991
David Rose Orchestra
MCA MCAC2-4176 (CS): "Music of the 1930's"
**Frank Rosolino/Hal McKusick/Stan Levy/Terry
Gibbs/Barry Harris/That Jones/Billy Mitchell**
Savoy Jazz SV-0188 (CD): "Swing Not Spring"
Saint Louis Brass
Summit DCD-140 (CD), DCC-140 (CS): "Pops"
Mike Sammes Singers
Stanyan SR-10136 (LP)
Jan Savitt
Thesaurus 621 (78) 1939
Doc Severinsen/The Tonight Show Band
Amherst AMH-93311 (CD), AMH-53311 (CS), AMH-
3311 (LP): "The Tonight Show Band with Doc
Severinsen"

Begin The Beguine (cont.)

Doc Severinsen/Ray Brown/Dave Brubeck/Cincinnati Pops/Erich Kunzel
Telarc CD-80177 (CD), CS-30177 (CS): "Big Band Hit Parade"

Artie Shaw
Bluebird B-7746 (78) 1938

Artie Shaw
RCA EPA-5033 (45)

Artie Shaw
Bluebird 6274-2-RB (CD), 6274-4-RB (CS), 6274-1-R (LP): "Begin the Beguine"

Artie Shaw
RCA AXK2-5517 (CS) "Complete Artie Shaw, Vol. 1 (1938-1939)"

Artie Shaw
Everest CD-41 (CD): "Big Bands of the Swinging Years"

Artie Shaw
Capitol C2-90591 (CD): "Swing's the Thing"

Artie Shaw
Bluebird PK-5096 (CS): "This is Artie Shaw"

Artie Shaw
Bluebird PK-5099 (CS): "This Is The Big Band Era"

Artie Shaw
RCA 9972-2-R (CD), 9972-4-R (CS): "Nipper's Greatest Hits - the 30's, Vol. 2"

Artie Shaw
RCA 447-0052 (7" single)

Artie Shaw
Collectables COL-5096 (CD, CS): "Big Bands of the Swinging Years, Vol. I"

Artie Shaw
Bluebird 61064-2 (CD), 61064-4 (CS): "Frenesi, Featuring Begin the Beguine"

Artie Shaw
Pro-Arte CCD-3405 (CD), PCD-3405 (CS): "Begin the Beguine"

Begin The Beguine (cont.)

Artie Shaw
Musicmasters 65101-2 (CD): "More Last Recordings"
Frank Sinatra
K-Tel International 662-2 (CD), 662-4 (CS): "Radio Years"
Frank Sinatra
Sony A2-20709 (CD), XPT-6 (CS), CC2-6 (LP): "Frank Sinatra Story in Music"
Frank Sinatra
Intercon OXO-001 (CD): "Original Sessions"
Frank Sinatra
Columbia CXK-48673 (CD): "The Columbia Years (1943-1952) The Complete Recordings"
Derek Smith Trio
Eastwind CWIND-711 (CS), EWIND-711 (LP): "Dark Eyes"
Keely Smith
Atlantic 45-2429 (45) 1967
Skip Soder Band
Arteen 801 (45) and Arteen 1019 (45)
The Starsound Orchestra
Dominion Entertainment 3079-2 (CD): "Best of the Big Bands"
Gladys Swarthout
Victor 10-1036 (78) 1942
Art Tatum
Decca 8502 (78) 1940
Art Tatum
Pablo PACD-2405-434-2 (CD): "The Art Tatum Solo Masterpieces, Vol. 3"
Art Tatum
Pablo PACD-2405-439-2 (CD): "The Art Tatum Solo Masterpieces, Vol. 8"
Art Tatum
MCA MCAC2-4019 (CS): "Art Tatum Masterpieces"
Art Tatum
MCA MCAD-42327 (CD), MCAC-42327 (CS), MCA 42327 (LP): "Solos (1940)"

Begin The Beguine (cont.)

Art Tatum
Pablo 7PACD-4404-2 (CD): "The Complete Pablo
Solo Masterpieces"
Art Tatum
Black Lion BLCD-760143 (CD): "Standards"
Art Tatum
Black Lion BLCD-760114 (CD): "The V-Discs"
Cal Tjader/Terry Gibbs
Savoy ZDS-1207 (CD), SJK-1207 (CS), SJL-1207
(LP): "Good Vibes"
Pete Townshend
Atco 90539-2 (CD), 90539-4 (CS): "Another Scoop"
Bo Thorpe
Hindsight HCD-247 (CD), HSC-247 (CS): "Swinging
& Sentimental"
University of Notre Dame Band
Fidelity 1256 (LP): "Songs of the Fighting Irish"
Dionne Warwick
Arista ARCD-8573 (CD), AC-8573 (CS), AL-8573
(LP): "Dionne Warwick Sings Cole Porter"
Lawrence Welk
Ranwood RCD-7023 (CD), RC-7023 (CS), RLP-7023
(LP): "22 All Time Big Band Favorites"
Lawrence Welk
Ranwood RCD-7009 (CD), RC-7009 (CS): "22 Great
Songs For Dancing"
Lawrence Welk
Ranwood RBD-3007 (CD), RBC-3007 (CS):
"Lawrence Welk Salutes the Big Bands"
Paul Whiteman and His Orchestra
Victor 36175 (78) 1935
Billy Williams
Coral 9-62230 (45) 1960

A Picture Of Me Without You
introduced by June Knight and Charles Walters in *Jubilee*

> **Cole Porter**
>> Columbia KS-31456 (LP) from a demo made in 1935
>
> **Jimmy Dorsey and His Orchestra**
>> Decca 571 (78) 1935
>
> **Johnny Green and His Orchestra**
>> Brunswick 7521 (78) 1935
>
> **George Hall**
>> Bluebird B-6127 (78) 1935
>
> **Joe Haymes and His Orchestra**
>> Thesaurus 184 (78) 1935
>
> **Burt Reynolds/Cybill Shepherd/Madeline Kahn/Duilio Del Prete**
>> RCA ABL2-0967 (LP)
>
> **Sonny Schuyler**
>> Bluebird B-6127 (78) 1935
>
> **Jack Six/Francis Thorne**
>> Composers Recordings 585 (CD): "Porter On My Mind"
>
> **Paul Whiteman and His Orchestra**
>> Victor 25135 (78) 1935 and Victor 36175 (78) 1935

Ev'rybod-ee Who's Anybod-ee
introduced by the ensemble in *Jubilee*

> **Cole Porter**
>> Columbia KS-31456 (LP) from a demo made in 1935

Sunday Morning, Breakfast Time
introduced by the ensemble in *Jubilee*

> **Cole Porter**
>> Columbia KS-31456 (LP) from a demo made in 1935

Me And Marie
introduced by Mary Boland and Melville Cooper in *Jubilee*

Jimmy Dorsey and His Orchestra
Decca 570 (78) 1935
Johnny Green and His Orchestra
Brunswick 7521 (78) 1935
Joe Haymes and His Orchestra
Thesaurus 184 (78) 1935
Cole Porter
Columbia KS-31456 (LP) from a demo made in 1935
Paul Whiteman and His Orchestra
Victor 25135 (78) 1935 and Victor 36175 (78) 1935

Just One Of Those Things
introduced by June Knight and Charles Walters in *Jubilee*

Cannonball Adderly/Milt Jackson
Riverside OJCCD-032-2 (CD), OJC-5032 (CS), OJC-032 (LP): "Things Are Getting Better"
Ambrose Orchestra/Sam Browne
G.N.P. Crescendo GNP-9004 (LP): "Ambrose Tribute to Cole Porter"
Ray Anthony
Pair PCD-2-1317 (CD), PDK-2-1317 (CS): "Dancing & Dreaming"
Louis Armstrong
Verve MGV 8322 (LP) 1957, 825713-2 (CD), 825713-4 (CS): "Louis Armstrong Meets Oscar Peterson"
Louis Armstrong
Verve 847202-2 (CD), 847202-4 (CS): "Night & Day: The Cole Porter Songbook"
Louis Armstrong/The Oscar Peterson Quartet
Verve 845151-2 (CD), 845151-4 (CS): "Jazz-Club Mainstream - Trumpet"
Tony Bennett
Columbia CGK-40424 (CD), CGT-40424 (CS): "Jazz"

Just One Of Those Things (cont.)

Tony Bennett
Pair PDK-2-1102 (CS): "All-Time Favorites"
Art Blakey & The Jazz Messengers
Blue Note B2-46522 (CD), B4-81508 (CS): "At The
Cafe Bohemia, Vol. 2" 1987
William Bolcom/Joan Morris
Omega Record Classics OCD-3002 (CD): "Night &
Day"
Claude Bolling/Stephane Grappelli
Milan 35633-2 (CD), 35633-4 (CS): "First Class"
Joanne Brackeen Trio
Concord Jazz CCD-4280 (CD), CJ-280-C (CS):
"Havin' Fun"
Nat Brandywynne and His (Stork Club) Orchestra
American Record Company 6-02-13 (78) 1935
Dee Dee Bridgewater
Verve 314-519607-2 (CD): "Keeping Tradition"
Gordon Brisker Big Band
Discovery DSCD-938 (CD): "New Beginning"
Les Brown
Columbia CK-45344 (CD), CT-45344 (CS): "Best of
the Big Bands"
Dave Brubeck Quartet
Fantasy FCD-24728-2 (CD), 5F-24728 (CS), F-24728
(LP): "Stardust"
Don Byas
G.N.P. Crescendo GNP-9027 (LP): "Don Byas"
John Campbell
Contemporary CCD-14053-2 (CD), 5C-14053 (CS),
C-14053 (LP): "After Hours"
Frank Chacksfield and His Orchestra
London SP-44185 (LP): "The Music of Cole Porter"
Maurice Chevalier
Capitol SW 1301 (LP): soundtrack from the film *Can-
Can* 1960

Just One Of Those Things (cont.)

Rosemary Clooney
> Concord Jazz CJ-185 (LP), CCD-4185 (CD), CJ-185-
> C (CS): "Rosemary Clooney Sings the Music of Cole
> Porter" 1982

Rosemary Clooney
> DRG CDSL-5190 (CD), SLC-5190 (CS): "Close
> Enough For Love"

Nat King Cole
> Capitol C2-46649 (CD), C4-46649 (CS): "Just One of
> Those Things (& More)"

Nat King Cole
> Capitol C2-96361 (CD), C4-96361 (CS): "Anything
> Goes - Capitol Sings Cole Porter"

Nat King Cole
> Pair PDK-2-1128 (CS): "Tenderly"

Ray Conniff & His Orchestra & Chorus
> Columbia CK-8282 (CD): "Say It With Music"

J. Lawrence Cook
> Biograph BLP-1023Q (LP) from a piano roll

Johnny Costa
> Savoy ZDS-1190 (CD), SJK-1190 (CS), SJL-1190
> (LP): "Neighborhood"

Eddie Lockjaw Davis
> Muse MR-5202 (LP): "The Heavy Hitter"

Meyer Davis
> Monmouth-Evergreen MES-6813 (LP): "Meyer Davis
> Plays Cole Porter"

Walter Davis, Jr.
> Denon DC-8553 (CD): "Illumination"

Tommy Dorsey
> RCA 47-3159 (45) 1950

Don Ellis
> Candid CCD-79032 (CD): "Out of Nowhere"

Gil Evans/Tadd Dameron
> Prestige P-24049 (LP): "Arrangers' Touch"

Gil Evans & Ten
> Prestige OJCCD-346-2 (CD), OJC-5346 (CS), OJC-
> 346 (LP): "Gil Evans & Ten"

Just One Of Those Things (cont.)

George Feyer
Vanguard VSD-93/94 (LP): "Essential Cole Porter"
George Feyer
Vanguard OVC-6014 (CD): "George Feyer Plays Cole Porter"
Ted Fiorito
Decca 678 (78) 1936
Ella Fitzgerald
Verve 821989-2/821990-2 (CD), 823278-4 (CS), 823278-1 (LP): "Cole Porter Songbook" 1956
Ella Fitzgerald (accompanied by Nelson Riddle and His Orchestra)
Atlantic SD-1631 (LP): "Ella Loves Cole"
Ella Fitzgerald
Pablo PACD-2310-814-2 (CD), 52310-814 (CS), 2310814 (LP): "Dream Dancing"
Ella Fitzgerald
Verve 835454-2 (CD), 835454-4 (CS), 835454-1 (LP): "Ella In Rome - The Birthday Concert"
Ella Fitzgerald
Verve 314-519564-2 (CD), 825670-2 (CD), 825670-4 (CS), 825670-1 (LP): "Mack The Knife - Ella In Berlin"
Pete Fountain
MCA MCAC2-4095 (CS): "The Best of Pete Fountain, Vol. 2"
Russ Freeman Trio/Richard Twardzik Trio
Pacific Jazz B2-46861 (CD): "Trio"
Laura Fygi
Verve/Forecast 314-514724-2 (CD), 314-514724-2 (Cs): "Bewitched"
Stan Getz
Columbia CK-33703 (CD), PCT-33703 (CS): "The Best of Two Worlds"
Dizzy Gillespie
Verve 314-513875-2 (CD), 314-513875-4 (CS): "Dizzy's Diamonds (The Best of the Verve Years)"

Just One Of Those Things (cont.)

Benny Goodman Sextet
> Columbia CK-44292 (CD), CJT-44292 (CS): "Slipped
> Disc, 1945-46"

Stephane Grappelli
> Denon CY-77130 (CD), 81757-9130-4 (CS): "In
> Tokyo"

Stephane Grappelli
> Denon CY-77130 (CD): "Stephane Grappelli in
> Tokyo"

Stephane Grappelli/Martin Taylor
> Angel CDM-69172 (CD): "Just One of Those Things"

Bud Greeman and Bob Wilber
> Monmouth-Evergreen 7022 (LP): "The Compleat Bud
> Freeman" 1969

Al Haig
> Prestige P-7841 (LP): "Al Haig Trio & Quintet"

Lionel Hampton
> Audiofidelity Enterprises, Inc. 5849 (LP): "Lionel"

Susan Hayward
> DRG DARC2-2100 (LP)

Richard Himber
> Victor 25161 (78) 1935

Lena Horne
> QWest 205-3597 (CS): "Live on Broadway (Lena
> Horne: The Lady & Her Music)"

Lena Horne
> RCA 66021-2 (CD), 66021-4 (CS): "At Long Last
> Lena"

Lena Horne
> Sony AK-47838 (CD), AT-47838 (CS): "Cole Porter
> in Hollywood - The MGM Years"

Geoff Keezer
> Blue Note B2-96691 (CD): "Here & Now"

Lady BJ/Ellis Marsalis Quartet
> Rounder CD-2067 (CD), C-2067 (CS), 2067(LP):
> "The New New Orleans Music: Vocal Jazz"

Just One Of Those Things (cont.)

Lester Lanin
> Epic EK-46149 (CD), ET-46149 (CS): "Best of the Big Bands"

Lester Lanin
> Epic EK-53134 (CD), ET-53134 (CS): "This Is Society Dance Music"

Peggy Lee
> Hindsight HCD-220 (CD), HSC-220 (CS), HSR-220 (LP): "The Uncollected Peggy Lee with the David Barbour & Billy May Bands (1948)"

Guy Lombardo
> Decca ED-565 (45)

Jimmy Lyon
> Atlantic 81817-2 (CD), 81817-4 (CS): "The Erteguns' New York, New York Cabaret Music"

Rob McConnell & The Boss Brass/Phil Woods
> MCA/Impulse MCAD-5982 (CD): "Boss Brass & Woods"

Adam Makowicz
> Concord Jazz CCD-4541 (CD): "Live At Maybeck Recital Hall, Vol. 24 (Adam Makowicz At Maybeck)"

Branford Marsalis
> Columbia CKX-44204 (CD), CTX-44204 (CS): "Perspectives: The Columbia Jazz Sampler"

Branford Marsalis
> Columbia CK-40711 (CD), FCT-40711 (CS): "Renaissance"

Freddie Martin and His Orchestra
> Brunswick 7579 (78) 1935

Billy May
> Capitol EAP-3-562 (45)

Billy May & His Orchestra
> Creative World ST-1051 (LP): "Sorta May"

Yehudi Menuhin/Stephane Grappelli
> Angel 4XS-37156 (CS), 37156 (LP): "Fascinating Rhythm (Music of the 30's)"

Just One Of Those Things (cont.)

Yehudi Menuhin/Stephane Grappelli
Angel CDM-69219 (CD): "Menuhin & Grappelli Play
Berlin, Kern, Porter & Rodgers & Hart" 1988
Mabel Mercer
Atlantic SD2-602 (LP): "Art of Mabel Mercer"
Mabel Mercer
Atlantic 81817-2 (CD), 81817-4 (CS): "The Erteguns'
New York, New York Cabaret Music"
Pete Minger Quartet
The Jazz Alliance TJA-10005 (CD): "Minger
Painting"
Lee Morgan
Blue Note B2-95591 (CD), B4-95591 (CS): "Blue
Porter"
Paul Motian
Jazz Music Today 422-849157-2 (CD): "On
Broadway, Vol. III"
Ruby Newman and His Orchestra
Decca 23618 (78) 1939
Red Norvo Trio
Prestige P-24108 (LP): "The Red Norvo Trios"
Red Norvo Trio
Fantasy OJCCD-641-2 (CD), OJC-5641 (CS), OJC-
641 (LP): "Red Norvo Trio"
Anita O'Day/Billy May
Verve 849266-2 (CD), 849266-4 (CS): "Anita O'Day
Swings Cole Porter"
Charlie Parker
Verve 827154-4 (CS), 827154-1 (LP): "Verve Years
(1952-1954)"
Charlie Parker
Verve 823250-2 (CD), 823250-4 (CS): "The Cole
Porter Songbook"
Patachou/Jo Basile
Audiofidelity Enterprises 5814 (LP): "Patachou - With
Jo Basile"

Just One Of Those Things (cont.)

Les Paul
> Capitol C2-97654 (CD), C4-97654 (CS): "The Legend
> & the Legacy, Pts. 1-4"

Ken Peplowski/Howard Alden
> Concord Jazz CCD-4556 (CD): "Concord Duo Series,
> Vol. 3"

Oscar Peterson
> Verve 821987-2 (CD), 821987-4 (CS): "Oscar
> Peterson Plays the Cole Porter Songbook"

Sian Phillips
> Teldec 75277-2 (CD): "Centennial Gala Concert"

Bud Powell
> Verve 827901-2 (CD), 821690-1 (LP): "Genius of Bud
> Powell"

Elizabeth Power/Bill Kerr
> RCA LRL2-5054 (LP): "Cole"

Andre Previn
> RCA 2431-2-R11 (CD), 2431-4-R6 (CS): "Piano
> Stylings of Andre Previn"

Django Reinhardt
> G.N.P. Crescendo GNP5-9038 (CS), GNPS-9038
> (LP): "Immortal Django Reinhardt"

Art Resnick Trio
> Capri 75015-1 (LP): "A Gift"

Burt Reynolds/Cybill Shepherd/Dullio Del Prete
> RCA ABL2-0967 (LP)

Nelson Riddle & His Orchestra
> Pair PCD-2-1173 (CD): "The Riddle Touch"

Max Roach
> Emarcy 822673-2 (CD): "Max Roach + 4"

Max Roach Quartet/Hank Mobley
> Debut OJCCD-202-2 (CD), OJC-202 (LP): "The Max
> Roach Quartet, Featuring Hank Mobley"

Rochester Pops Orchestra/Erich Kunzel
> Pro-Arte CCD-385 (CD), PCD-385 (CS): "Gotta
> Dance - A Tribute to Fred Astaire"

Just One Of Those Things (cont.)

George Shearing/Mel Torme
Concord Jazz CCD-4248 (CD), CJ-248-C (CS): "An Evening At Charlie's"
Bobby Short
Atlantic SD 2-606 (LP): "Bobby Short Loves Cole Porter" 1971
Bobby Short
Atlantic 82062-2 (CD), 82062-4 (CS): "Bobby, Noel & Cole (Bobby Short Loves Cole Porter/Bobby Short Is Mad About Noel Coward)"
Ginny Simms
Motion Picture Tracks MPT 6 (LP): soundtrack from the film *Night and Day* 1945
Ginny Simms
Royale VLP 6055 (LP): "Ginny Simms"
Frank Sinatra
Capitol C2-48470 (CD), C4-48470 (CS): "Songs For Young Lovers & Swing Easy"
Frank Sinatra
K-Tel International 662-2 (CD), 662-4 (CS): "Radio Years"
Frank Sinatra
Capitol C2-91344 (CD): "Frank Sinatra Gift Set"
Frank Sinatra
Intercon OXO-001 (CD): "Original Sessions"
Frank Sinatra
Capitol C2-96611 (CD), C4-96611 (CS): "Frank Sinatra Sings the Select Cole Porter"
Frank Sinatra
Capitol BBX2-99956 (CD), BBX4-99956 (CS): "Concepts"
Frank Sinatra
Capitol C2-99374 (CD), C4-99374 (CS): "At The Movies"
Frank Sinatra
Pair PDK-2-1028 (CS): "Timeless"

Just One Of Those Things (cont.)

Jack Six/Francis Thorne
Composers Recordings 585 (CD): "Porter On My Mind"
Willie The Lion Smith
Milan 35623-2 (CD), 35623-4 (CS): "Echoes of Spring"
Peter Sprague
Concord Jazz CJ-237-C (CS): "Musica Del Mar"
Jo Stafford
Capitol F808 (45) 1950
Ted Straeter, His Piano and His Orchestra
Columbia 35430 (78) 1940
Maxine Sullivan/Scott Hamilton Quintet
Concord Jazz CCD-4351 (CD): "Swingin' Sweet"
Maxine Sullivan/Scott Hamilton Quintet
Concord Jazz CCD-4288 (CD), CJ-288-C (CS): "Uptown"
Art Tatum
Pablo PACD-2405-429-2 (CD): "The Tatum Group Masterpieces, Vol. 6"
Art Tatum
Blue Note C2-92867 (CD): "The Complete Art Tatum, Vol. 2"
Art Tatum
Blue Note B2-98931 (CD): "Capitol Jazz 50th Anniversary Collection"
Jesper Thilo Quartet
Storyville SC-44065 (CS), 4065 (LP): "Swingin' Friends"
Mel Torme
Telarc CD-83328 (CD), CS-33328 (CS): "The Great American Songbook: Live At Michael's Pub"
Sarah Vaughan
Mercury 826333-2 (CD): "Complete Sarah Vaughan on Mercury, Vol. 3: Great Show On Stage (1954-1956)"

Just One Of Those Things (cont.)

Sarah Vaughan
   Verve 314-511-070-2 (CD): "The Cole Porter
   Songbook, Vol. 2"
Sarah Vaughan
   Verve 314-512904-2 (CD), 314-512904-4 (CS): "The
   Essential Sarah Vaughan: The Great Songs"
Sarah Vaughan & Her Trio
   Emarcy 832791-2 (CD), 832791-4 (CS): "Sarah
   Vaughan & Her Trio at Mister Kelly's"
Cedar Walton
   Concord Jazz CCD-4546 (CD): "Live at Maybeck
   Recital Hall, Vol. 25 (Cedar Walton at Maybeck)"
Dionne Warwick
   Arista ARCD-8573 (CD), AC-8573 (CS), AL-8573
   (LP): "Dionne Warwick Sings Cole Porter"
Randy Weston
   Riverside 2508 (LP): "Randy Weston Plays Cole
   Porter in a Modern Mood" 1954
Paul Whiteman and His Orchestra
   Victor 36175 (78) 1935
Mary Lou Williams
   G.N.P. Crescendo GNPS-9029 (LP): "In London"
Garland Wilson
   Brunswick 03115 (78) 1936
Teddy Wilson
   Black Lion BLCD-760166 (CD): "Cole Porter
   Classics"
Teddy Wilson/Marian McPartland
   Halcyon 106 (LP): "Elegant Piano"

Works From 1936

Rolling Home
introduced by the ensemble in the film *Born to Dance*

> **James Stewart/Buddy Ebsen/Sid Silvers**
> Classic International Filmusicals CIF 3001 & Sandy
> Hook SH 2088 (LP): soundtrack from the film *Born
> To Dance* 1936

Rap-Tap On Wood
introduced by Eleanor Powell in the film *Born to Dance*

> **Frances Langford/Jimmy Dorsey and His Orchestra**
> Decca 939 (78) 1936
> **Eleanor Powell**
> Classic International Filmusicals CIF 3001 & Sandy
> Hook SH 2088 (LP): soundtrack from the film *Born
> To Dance* 1936
> **Bobby Short**
> Atlantic SD 2-606 (LP): "Bobby Short Loves Cole
> Porter" 1971
> **Bobby Short**
> Atlantic 82062-2 (CD), 82062-4 (CS): "Bobby, Noel
> & Cole (Bobby Short Loves Cole Porter/Bobby Short
> Is Mad About Noel Coward)"
> **Bobby Short**
> Atlantic 81715-2 (CD), 81715-4 (CS): "50 By Bobby
> Short"

Hey, Babe, Hey
introduced by the ensemble in the film *Born to Dance*

> **Joe Shilkret and His Orchestra**
> American Record Corporation 7-02-14 (78) 1936

Hey, Babe, Hey (cont.)

James Stewart/Eleanor Powell/Una Merkel/Frances Langford/Sid Silvers/Buddy Ebsen
>Classic International Filmusicals CIF 3001 & Sandy Hook SH 2088 (LP): soundtrack from the film *Born To Dance* 1936

Ted Weems and His Orchestra
>Decca 969 (78) 1936

Love Me, Love My Pekinese
introduced by Virginia Bruce in the film *Born to Dance*

Virginia Bruce/Raymond Walburn
>Classic International Filmusicals CIF 3001 & Sandy Hook SH 2088 (LP): soundtrack from the film *Born To Dance* 1936

Easy To Love
introduced by James Stewart in the film *Born to Dance*

Cannonball Adderly Sextet
>Riverside OJCCD-435-2 (CD), OJC-5435 (CS), OJC-435 (LP): "Nippon Soul"

Ray Alexander Sextet
>Nerus NERUS4478 (CD & CS): "Rain in June"

Ambrose Orchestra
>G.N.P. Crescendo GNP-9004 (LP): "Ambrose Tribute to Cole Porter"

Gene Ammons
>Prestige OJCCD-701-2 (CD), P-7192 (LP): "Jug"

Mildred Bailey
>Columbia 35921 (78) 1940

Tony Bennett/Torrie Zito Orchestra
>DRG CDMRS-801 (CD), MRSC-801 (CS): "The Special Magic of Tony Bennett"

Easy To Love (cont.)

William Bolcom/Joan Morris
Omega Record Classics OCD-3002 (CD): "Night &
Day"
Boston Pops Orchestra/Arthur Fiedler
Pair PDC2-1022 (CD): "Popular Favorites by Arthur
Fiedler/Boston Pops"
Al Bowlly
Victor 25422
Virginia Bruce
Brunswick 7765 & Vocalion 523 (78)
Laverne Butler
Chesky JD-91 (CD), JC-91 (CS): "No Looking Back"
Don Byas
Emarcy 833405-2 (CD): "On Blue Star"
Charlie Byrd
Concord Jazz CCD-42014 (CD): "The Washington
Guitar Quintet"
John Campbell
Concord Jazz CCD-4581 (CD): "Live At Maybeck
Recital Hall, Vol. 29 (John Campbell At Maybeck)"
Frankie Carle
RCA EPB-1064 (45)
Paul Chambers
blue Note B2-84437 (CD): "Chambers' Music"
Richie Cole
Palo Alto 8036 (LP): "Alto Annie's Theme"
Ray Conniff
Columbia CK-8117 (CD): "Hollywood in Rhythm"
Vic Damone
Ranwood RCD-8204 (CD), RC-8204 (CS), RLP-8204
(LP): "The Best of Vic Damone Live"
Vic Damone
Vianda VC-1110 (CS), VLP-1110 (LP): "I Just Called
to Say I Love You"
Putney Dandridge and His Orchestra
Vocalion 3351 (78) 1936

Easy To Love (cont.)

Billy Daniels
G.N.P. Crescendo GNPS-16 (LP): "Billy Daniels at the Crescendo"
Sammy Davis, Jr.
Decca ED-2214 (45)
Doris Day/Frank De Vol Orchestra
Columbia CK-8066 (CD) and Sony XPT-5 (CS) and AC2-5 (LP): "Hooray For Hollywood, Vol. I"
Matt Dennis
Glendale 6006 (LP): "Original Mat Dennis"
Jimmy Dorsey and His Orchestra
Decca 940 (78) 1936
Ray Elis and Johnny Douglas conducting the Ray Elis Strings
RCA CAS-2522 (LP): "The Great Hits of Cole Porter"
Skinnay Ennis
Hindsight HSC-164 (CS), HSR-164 (LP): "The Uncollected Skinnay Ennis & His Orchestra (1947-1948)"
Bill Evans
Riverside 12RCD-018-2 (CD), R-018 (LP): "The Complete Riverside Recordings"
Bill Evans
Milestone M-47063 (LP): "Conception"
Bill Evans
Milestone MCD-9170-2 (CD), 5M-9170 (CS), M-9170 (LP): "The Solo Sessions, Vol. 1"
Don Fagerquist Octet
V.S.O.P. 4 (LP): "Eight By Eight"
Percy Faith
Columbia B-1610 (45)
Eileen Farrell
Reference RR-42CD (CD), RR-42CS (CS): "This Time It's Love"
George Feyer
Vanguard VSD-93/94 (LP): "Essential Cole Porter"

Easy To Love (cont.)

George Feyer
Vanguard OVC-6014 (CD): "George Feyer Plays Cole Porter"
Shep Fields and His Rippling Rhythm
Bluebird B-6592 (78) 1936
Ella Fitzgerald
Verve 821989-2/821990-2 (CD), 823278-4 (CS), 823278-1 (LP): "Cole Porter Songbook" 1956
Ella Fitzgerald
Pablo OJCCD-442-2 (CD), OJC-5442 (CS), OJC-442 (LP): "Ella A Nice"
Maureen Forrester
Pro-Arte CDD-374 (CD), PCD-374 (CS): "From Kern to Sondheim"
Judy Garland
DRG SBL-12586 (LP): "Cut! Out Takes From Hollywood's Greatest Musicals, Vol. 1"
Erroll Garner
Emarcy 832994-2 (CD), 832994-4 (CS): "Easy To Love - Erroll Garner Collection, Vol. 1"
Benny Goodman
Musicmasters 65093-2 (CD): "Yale Recordings, Vol. 8: Never Before Released Recordings From Benny Goodman's Private Collection"
Stephane Grappelli
Accord 139004 (CD): "Stephane Grappelli Plays George Gershwin & Cole Porter"
Simon Green
Teldec 75277-2 (CD): "Centennial Gala Concert"
Scott Hamilton/Jake Hanna/Dave McKenna
Concord Jazz CCD-4097 (CD), CJ-97-C (CS): "No Bass Hit"
Barry Harris
Milestone M-40750 (LP): "Stay Right With It"
Billie Holiday
Verve 823064-4 (CS), 823064-1 (LP): "First Verve Sessions"

Easy To Love (cont.)

Billie Holiday
Verve 823233-4 (CS), 8232333-1 (LP): "History of the Real Billie Holiday"
Billie Holiday
Columbia CK-40790 (CD), CJT-40790 (CS): "Quintessential Billie Holiday, Vol. 2, 1936"
Billie Holiday
Verve 847202-2 (CD), 847202-4 (CS): "Night & Day: The Cole Porter Songbook"
Billie Holiday
Columbia C3K-47724 (CD), C3T-47724 (CS): "Billie Holiday: The Legacy Box 1933-1958"
Billie Holiday
Verve 314-519810-2 (CD): "Solitude"
Dick Hyman
Musicmasters 5060-2-C (CD), 5060-4-C (CS): "Cole Porter: All Through the Night"
The Jazz Passengers
New World NW-398-2 (CD), 398-4 (CS): "Implement Yourself"
Irving Joseph
Bainbridge BTC-1014 (CS), 1014 (LP): "Heritage of Broadway - Music of Cole Porter"
Dick Jurgens and His Orchestra
American Record Company 6-12-04 (78) 1936
Hal Kemp and His Orchestra
Brunswick 7745 (78) 1936
Stan Kenton
Capitol SXA-1674 (45)
Stan Kenton
Creative World ST-1018 (LP): "Sophisticated Approach"
Henry King and His Orchestra
Decca 937 (78) 1936
Ernie Krivda Quartet
Inner City 1083 (LP): "Glory Strut"

Easy To Love (cont.)

Steve Lacy
Prestige OJCCD-130-2 (CD), OJC-130 (LP): "Soprano Sax"
Frances Langford
Classic International Filmusicals CIF 3001 & Sandy Hook SH 2088 (LP): soundtrack from the film *Born To Dance* 1936
Frances Langford
Decca 940 (78) 1936
Frances Langford
Take Two TT 214 (LP)
Lester Lanin & His Orchestra
Hindsight HSC-210 (CS), HSR-210 (LP): "The Uncollected Lester Lanin & His Orchestra (1960-1962)"
Julie London
EMI E2-93455 (CD), E4-93455 (CS): "Julie London Sings Cole Porter"
Patti LuPone
RCA 7769-2-RC (CD), 7769-4-RC (CS): "Anything Goes"
Jimmy Lyon
Atlantic 81817-2 (CD), 81817-4 (CS): "The Erteguns' New York, New York Cabaret Music"
Rob McConnell & The Boss Brass
MCA/Impulse MCAD-42123 (CD): "Atras Da Porta"
Kate McGarry
Vital VTL-015 (CD): "Easy to Love"
Donna McKenzie
NSD 109 (7" single)
Adam Makowicz
Concord Jazz CCD-4541 (CD): "Live At Maybeck Recital Hall, Vol. 24 (Adam Makowicz At Maybeck)"
Freddie Martin and His Orchestra
Bluebird B-10678 (78) 1940
Hank Mobley
Blue Note B2-95591 (CD), B4-95591 (CS): "Blue Porter"

Easy To Love (cont.)

Vaughn Monroe
RCA 47-4172 (45), 1951
Ray Noble and His Orchestra
Victor 25422 (78) 1936
Anita O'Day/Billy May
Verve 849266-2 (CD), 849266-4 (CS): "Anita O'Day
Swings Cole Porter"
101 Strings Orchestra
Alshire International ALCD-30 (CD), ALSC-5007
(CS): "Cole Porter"
101 Strings Orchestra
Alshire ALSC-5321 (CS): "Entertainment From the
Movies"
101 Strings Orchestra
Alshire International ALCD-50 (CD), ADBL-406
(CS): "The Best of the Great American Composers,
Vol. VI"
One O'Clock Lab Band
Amazing AMCD-1027 (CD), AMC-1027 (CS): "The
Best Of One O'Clock"
Will Osborne & His Orchestra
Hindsight HSC-197 (CS), HSR-197 (LP): "The
Uncollected Will Osborne & His Orchestra (1936)"
Charlie Parker
Verve 831553-4 (CS): "Charlie Parker With Strings"
Charlie Parker
Verve 821684-4 (CS): "Verve Years (1950-1951)"
Charlie Parker
Verve 823250-2 (CD), 823250-4 (CS): "The Cole
Porter Songbook"
Joe Pass
Pablo OJCCD-602-2 (CD), OJC-5602 (CS), OJC-602
(LP): "I Remember Charlie Parker"
P.J. Perry
The Jazz Alliance TJA-10007 (CD): "Worth Waiting
For"

Easy To Love (cont.)

Oscar Peterson
  Verve 821987-2 (CD), 821987-4 (CS): "Oscar Peterson Plays the Cole Porter Songbook"
Casper Reardon
  Schirmer 511 (78) 1940
Joe Reichman
  Camden CAE-146 (45)
Melora Hardin
  Hollywood 61117-2 (CD), 61117-4 (CS): soundtrack from the film *The Rocketeer* 1991
Hal Schaefer
  Discovery 74002-2 (CD): "Solo, Duo, Trio"
Diane Schuur
  GRP GRD-9540 (CD), GRC-1030 (CS), GR-1030 (LP): "Timeless"
Diane Schuur
  GRP GRD-9521 (CD), GRC-9521 (CS), GR-9521 (LP): "Collection"
Artie Shaw
  RCA PK-5119 (CS): "This is Artie Shaw, Vol. 2"
Artie Shaw
  RCA AXK2-5579 (CS): "Complete Artie Shaw, Vol. 6"
George Shearing
  Concord Jazz CCD-4281 (CD), CJ-281-C (CS): "Grand Piano"
George Shearing/Barry Tuckwell
  Concord Jazz CCD-42010 (CD), CC-2010-C (CS): "George Shearing & Barry Tuckwell Play the Music of Cole Porter"
Dinah Shore
  RCA 66023-2 (CD), 66023-4 (CS): "Love & Kisses, Dinah"
Bobby Short
  Telarc CD83311 (CD), CS-33311 (CS): "Late Night at the Cafe Carlyle"

Easy To Love (cont.)

Frank Sinatra
Reprise 26340-2 (CD), 26340-4 (CS): "The Reprise Collection"

Frank Sinatra/Johnny Mandel
Reprise 27017-2 (CD), 27017-4 (CS): "Ring-A-Ding Ding!"

Jack Six/Francis Thorne
Composers Recordings 585 (CD): "Porter On My Mind"

James Stewart/Eleanor Powell
Classic International Filmusicals CIF 3001 & Sandy Hook SH 2088 (LP): soundtrack from the film *Born To Dance* 1936

James Stewart/Eleanor Powell
Sony AK-47838 (CD), AT-47838 (CS): "Cole Porter in Hollywood - The MGM Years"

Sonny Stitt/Sadik Hakim
Progressive C-7034 (CS), 7034 (LP): "Sonny Stitt Meets Sadik Hakim"

Maxine Sullivan
Vocalion/Okeh 3848 (78) 1937

Ben Webster
Black Lion BLCD-760151 (CD): "There Is No Greater Love"

Gerald Wiggins
Concord Jazz CCD-4450 (CD), CJ-450-C (CS): "Live at Maybeck Recital Hall, Vol. 8"

Lee Wiley
Liberty Music Shop L-295 (78) 1940

Lee Wiley
Audiophile ACD-1 (CD), Monmouth-Evergreen MES-7034 (LP) "Lee Wiley Sings George Gershwin and Cole Porter"

Julie Wilson
DRG CDSL-5208 (CD), SLC-5208 (CS): "Cole Porter Songbook"

Teddy Wilson
Brunswick 7762 (78) 1936

Easy To Love (cont.)

Teddy Wilson
Black Lion BLCD-760166 (CD): "Cole Porter
Classics"

I've Got You Under My Skin
introduced by Virginia Bruce in the film *Born to Dance*

Larry Adler
Audiofidelity Enterprises 6193 (LP): "Larry Adler
Again"
Ambrose Orchestra
G.N.P. Crescendo GNP-9004 (LP): "Ambrose Tribute
to Cole Porter"
Sil Austin
SSS International 14 (LP): "Sil & The Silver Screen"
Tony Bennett/Torrie Zito Orchestra
DRG CDMRS-801 (CD), MRSC-801 (CS): "The
Special Magic of Tony Bennett"
William Bolcom/Joan Morris
Omega Record Classics OCD-3002 (CD): "Night &
Day"
Al Bowlly
Cameo CDN-5131
Clifford Brown/Dinah Washington
Verve 842933-2 (CD): "Compact Jazz - Clifford
Brown"
Les Brown
USA Music Group USACD-685 (CD), USACA-685
(CS): "Anything Goes"
Virginia Bruce
Classic International Filmusicals CIF 3001 & Sandy
Hook SH 2088 (LP): soundtrack from the film *Born
To Dance* 1936
Virginia Bruce
Brunswick 7765 & Vocalion 523 (78)

I've Got You Under My Skin (cont.)

Virginia Bruce
Sony AK-47838 (CD), AT-47838 (CS): "Cole Porter
in Hollywood - The MGM Years"

Carmen Cavallaro
Hindsight HCD-312 (CD), HSC-312 (CS), HSR-312
(LP): "The Best of the Sweet Bands"

Neneh Cherry
Chrysalis F2-21799 (CD), F4-21799 (CS): "Red Hot
& Blue (A Tribute to Cole Porter to Benefit Aids
Research & Relief)"

Rosemary Clooney
Concord Jazz CJ-185 (LP), CCD-4185 (CD), CJ-185-
C (CS): "Rosemary Clooney Sings the Music of Cole
Porter" 1982

Ray Conniff & His Orchestra & Chorus
Columbia CK-8282 (CD): "Say It With Music"

Chris Connor
Progressive 7028 (CS), 7028 (LP): "Sweet &
Swinging"

Vic Damone
Mercury 563X45 (45)

Meyer Davis
Monmouth-Evergreen MES-6813 (LP): "Meyer Davis
Plays Cole Porter"

Paul Desmond
Bluebird 5778-2-RB (CD), 5778-4-RB (CS): "Late
Lament"

Jimmy Dorsey and His Orchestra
Decca 939 (78) 1936

Bill Evans
Verve 831366-2 (CD), 831366-4 (CS): "Compact Jazz
- Bill Evans"

Bill Evans
Verve 813184-4 (CS), 813184-1 (LP): "Bill Evans -
Trio-Duo"

Bill Evans/Jim Hall
Verve 833771-2 (CD), 833771-4 (CS):
"Intermodulation"

I've Got You Under My Skin (cont.)

Frederick Fennell/Eastman-Rochester Pops Orchestra
Mercury 43427-2 (CD): "Fennell Conducts Porter & Gershwin"
George Feyer
Vanguard VSD-93/94 (LP): "Essential Cole Porter"
George Feyer
Vanguard OVC-6014 (CD): "George Feyer Plays Cole Porter"
Shep Fields and His Rippling Rhythm
Bluebird B-6592 (78) 1936
Eddie Fisher
RCA 547-0010 (45) and RCA EPB-3058 (45)
Ella Fitzgerald (accompanied by Nelson
Riddle and His Orchestra)
Atlantic SD-1631 (LP): "Ella Loves Cole"
Ella Fitzgerald
Verve 821989-2/821990-2 (CD), 823278-4 (CS), 823278-1 (LP): "Cole Porter Songbook" 1956
Ella Fitzgerald
Pablo PACD-2310-814-2 (CD), 52310-814 (CS), 2310814 (LP): "Dream Dancing"
Flamingo Orkestra
Voss D2-72944 (CD), D41G-72944 (CS), D11G-72944 (LP): "Flamingo Orkestra Featuring Cynthia Manley"
Stan Freberg
Capitol F1711 (45) 1951
Stan Freberg
Capitol C2-91627 (CD): "Capitol Collectors Series"
Stan Freberg
Capitol/Curb D2-77615 (CD), D4-77615 (CS): "Greatest Hits"
Erroll Garner
Emarcy EP-1-6073 (45)
Erroll Garner
Mercury EP-13168 (45)

I've Got You Under My Skin (cont.)

Stan Getz
>Prestige 42-250 (45) 1962

Stan Getz
>Prestige P-7337 (LP): "Stan Getz Greatest Hits"

Stan Getz
>Prestige OJCCD-121-2 (CD), OJC-5121 (CS), OJC-121 (LP): "Stan Getz Quartets"

Jackie Gleason
>Pair PCD-2-1176 (CD), PDK-2-1176 (CS): "Shangri-La"

Jackie Gleason
>Pair PCD-2-1069 (CD), PDK-2-1069 (CS): "Lush Moods"

Benny Goodman
>Musicmasters 65095-2 (CD): "Yale Recordings, Vols. 1-5, Swing, Swing, Rare Recordings From yale University Music Library"

Joe Henderson
>Milestone M-9017 (LP): "Tetragon"

Woody Herman
>GRP GRD-2-629 (CD), GRC-2-629 (CS): "An Anthology of Big Band Swing (1930-1955)"

John Holmquist/Dan Estrem
>Projazz CDJ-606 (CD), PCJ-606 (CS): "Still of the Night"

Julio Iglesias
>Columbia CD-40180 (CD), DJC-50336 (CS): "Libra"

Irving Joseph
>Bainbridge BTC-1014 (CS), 1014 (LP): "Heritage of Broadway - Music of Cole Porter"

Dick Jurgens and His Orchestra
>American Record Company 6-12-04 (78) 1936

Greta Keller
>Decca F-6263 (78) 1937

Hal Kemp and His Orchestra
>Brunswick 7745 (78) 1936

I've Got You Under My Skin (cont.)

Hal Kemp
Columbia CK-45346 (CD), CT-45346 (CS): "Best of the Big Bands"

Stan Kenton
Capitol EBF-462 (45)

Stan Kenton
Creative World ST-1003 (LP): "Contemporary Concepts"

Stan Kenton
Creative World ST-1042 (LP): "Portraits on Standards"

Stan Kenton
Blue Note B2-97350 (CD): "Retrospective - The Capitol Years, Vol. 1"

Henry King and His Orchestra
Decca 937 (78) 1936

Frances Langford
Decca 939 (78) 1936

Francis Langford
Take Two TT 214 (LP)

Peggy Lee
MCA MCAC-20251 (CS): "Black Coffee"

Dave Liebman Trio
Red 123236-2 (CD): "Dave Liebman Trio Plays Cole Porter"

Julie London
EMI E2-93455 (CD), E4-93455 (CS): "Julie London Sings Cole Porter"

Jimmy Lyon
Atlantic 81817-2 (CD), 81817-4 (CS): "The Erteguns' New York, New York Cabaret Music"

Charles Mingus
Debut 12DCD-4402-2 (CD): "The Complete Debut Recordings"

Ray Noble and His Orchestra
Victor 25422 (78) 1936

I've Got You Under My Skin (cont.)

Red Norvo Trio
> Savoy SJL-2212 (LP): "Red Norvo Trio with Tal
> Farlow & Charles Mingus - The Savoy Sessions"

Red Norvo
> Savoy Jazz SV-0168 (CD): "Move!"

Anita O'Day/Billy May
> Verve 849266-2 (CD), 849266-4 (CS): "Anita O'Day
> Swings Cole Porter"

101 Strings Orchestra
> Alshire International ALCD-30 (CD), ALSC-5007
> (CS): "Cole Porter"

101 Strings Orchestra
> Alshire International ALCD-48 (CD), ADBL-404
> (CS): "The Best of the Great American Composers,
> Vol. IV"

Will Osborne & His Orchestra
> Hindsight HSC-197 (CS), HSR-197 (LP): "The
> Uncollected Will Osborne & His Orchestra (1936)"

Charlie Parker
> Verve 827154-4 (CS), 827154-1 (LP): "Verve Years
> (1952-1954)"

Charlie Parker
> Verve 823250-2 (CD), 823250-4 (CS): "The Cole
> Porter Songbook"

Charlie Parker/Bud Powell/Max Roach
> Prestige 5P-24024 (CS): "The Greatest Jazz Concert
> Ever"

Tony Pastor and His Orchestra
> Bluebird B-10915 (78) 1940

Oscar Peterson
> Verve 821987-2 (CD), 821987-4 (CS): "Oscar
> Peterson Plays the Cole Porter Songbook"

Bud Powell Trio
> Debut OJCCD-111-2 (CD), OJC-5111 (CS), OJC-111
> (LP): "Jazz at Massey Hall, Vol. 2"

Louis Prima
> Gallery 104 (45)

I've Got You Under My Skin (cont.)

Louis Prima
Rhino R2-70225 (CD), R4-70225 (CS): "Zooma Zooma, The Best of Louis Prima"

Louis Prima/Keely Smith
Capitol F4140 (45) 1959

Louis Prima/Keely Smith
Capitol C2-91208 (CD), 4M-1531 (CS), SM-1531 (LP): "Hits of Louis & Keely"

Louis Prima/Keely Smith
Capitol C2-94072 (CD), C4-94072 (CS): "Capitol Collectors Series"

Louis Prima/Keely Smith
Capitol C2-96361 (CD), C4-96361 (CS): "Anything Goes - Capitol Sings Cole Porter"

Sonny Rollins
Blue Note B2-46517 (CD): "A Night at the Village Vanguard, Vol. I"

Renee Rosnes
Blue Note B2-98168 (CD), B4-98168 (CS): "Without Words"

Frank Rosolino/Hal McKusick/Stan Levy/Terry Gibbs/Barry Harris/That Jones/Billy Mitchell
Savoy Jazz SV-0188 (CD): "Swing Not Spring"

George Shearing/Barry Tuckwell
Concord Jazz CCD-42010 (CD), CC-2010-C (CS): "George Shearing & Barry Tuckwell Play the Music of Cole Porter"

Cesare Siepi
London 5705 (LP): "Bravo Siepi! The Broadway Songs of Cole Porter" 1962

Ginny Simms
Royale VLP 6055 (LP): "Ginny Simms"

Frank Sinatra
Capitol 6193 (45) 1956

Frank Sinatra
Capitol EAP-4-653 (45) 1956

Frank Sinatra
Capitol DV-653 (45) 1956

I've Got You Under My Skin (cont.)

Frank Sinatra
> Capitol 4XBB-11357 (CS), SABB-11357 (LP): "Round No. 1"

Frank Sinatra
> Reprise 1016-2 (CD), J5-1016 (CS): "Sinatra - A Man & His Music"

Frank Sinatra
> Reprise 2207-2 (CD), L5F-2207 (CS): "Frank Sinatra - The Main Event ('Live' From Madison Square Garden)"

Frank Sinatra
> Reprise 1019-2 (CD), J5-1019 (CS): "Sinatra At The Sands (In Concert)"

Frank Sinatra
> Reprise FS2-1010 (CD), M5-1010 (CS): "Sinatra's Sinatra"

Frank Sinatra/Nelson Riddle Orchestra
> Capitol C2-46570 (CD): "Songs For Swingin' Lovers"

Frank Sinatra
> Capitol C2-91344 (CD): "Frank Sinatra Gift Set"

Frank Sinatra
> Reprise 26340-2 (CD), 26340-4 (CS): "The Reprise Collection"

Frank Sinatra
> Reprise 26501-2 (CD), 26501-4 (CS): "Sinatra Reprise - The Very Good Years"

Frank Sinatra
> Capitol C2-96611 (CD), C4-96611 (CS): "Frank Sinatra Sings the Select Cole Porter"

Frank Sinatra
> Capitol C2-94777 (CD), C4-94777 (CS), C1-94777 (LP): "The Capitol Years"

Frank Sinatra
> Mobile Fidelity Sound Lab UDCD-538 (CD): "Songs For Swingin' Lovers"

I've Got You Under My Skin (cont.)

Frank Sinatra
Capitol C2-99225 (CD), C4-99225 (CS), C5-99225
(DCC), C8-99225 (MD): "The Best of the Capitol
Years" - Selections from 'The Capitol Years' Box Set
Frank Sinatra
Capitol BBX2-99956 (CD), BBX4-99956 (CS):
"Concepts"
Frank Sinatra
Pair PDK-2-1028 (CS): "Timeless"
Frank Sinatra/Bono
Capitol CDP-27596 (CD - Gold Disc), CDP-89611
(CD), C4-89611 (CS): "Duets"
Paul Smith
Outstanding 023 (LP): "Jazz Spotlight on Cole Porter
& George Gershwin"
Southern Methodist University Band
Fidelity 1234 (LP): "Mustang Jazz"
Stuff Smith
Savoy SJL-2246 (LP): "Black Swing Tradition"
Stuff Smith
Varsity 8242 (78) 1940
Cal Tjader/Terry Gibbs
Savoy ZDS-1207 (CD), SJK-1207 (CS), SJL-1207
(LP): "Good Vibes"
Mel Torme
Columbia PCT-9118 (CS) and Sony BT-13090 (CS)
and P-13090 (LP): "That's All"
Mel Torme
Columbia CK-53779 (CD), CT-53779 (CS): "16 Most
Requested Songs"
Frankie Valli and The Four Seasons
Philips 40393 (45) 1966, Rhino R2-72998 (CD), R4-
72998 (CS), R1-72998 (LP): "25th Anniversary
Collection"
Frankie Valli and The Four Seasons
Collectables 0012: (7" single)

I've Got You Under My Skin (cont.)

Frankie Valli and the Four Seasons
Rhino R2-71490 (CD), R4-71490 (CS), R1-71490
(LP): "Anthology"
Frankie Valli and the Four Seasons
Rhino R2-75095 (CD), R4-75095 (CS): "Greatest
Hits, Vol. 2"
Dionne Warwick
Arista ARCD-8573 (CD), AC-8573 (CS), AL-8573
(LP): "Dionne Warwick Sings Cole Porter"
Dinah Washington
Emarcy 814639-2 (CD), 814639-4 (CS): "Dinah Jams"
Dinah Washington
Verve 847202-2 (CD), 847202-4 (CS): "Night & Day:
The Cole Porter Songbook"
Dinah Washington
Verve 314-512905-2 (CD), 314-512905-4 (CS): "The
Essential Dinah Washington: The Great Songs"
Randy Weston
Riverside 2508 (LP): "Randy Weston Plays Cole
Porter in a Modern Mood" 1954
Lee Wiley
Decca 15034 (78) 1937
Julie Wilson
DRG CDSL-5208 (CD), SLC-5208 (CS): "Cole Porter
Songbook"
Teddy Wilson
Black Lion BLCD-760166 (CD): "Cole Porter
Classics"
Vincent Youmans
Biograph BLP-1007Q (LP): "Forty-Second Street
(Rare Piano Roll Versions From the Musical
Comedies of the 20's & 30's)"

Swingin' The Jinx Away
introduced by Frances Langford and the Foursome Quartet
in the film *Born to Dance*

> **Nat Gonella and His Georgians**
> Parlophone F-645 (78) 1937
> **Francis Langford/Jimmy Dorsey and His Orchestra**
> Decca 940 (78) 1936
> **Francis Langford**
> Classic International Filmusicals CIF 3001 & Sandy
> Hook SH 2088 (LP): soundtrack from the film *Born
> To Dance* 1936
> **Francis Langford**
> Take Two TT 214 (LP)
> **Tempo King and His Kings of Tempo**
> Bluebird B-6643 (78) 1936

Ours
introduced by Dorothy Vernon and Thurston Crane in
Red, Hot and Blue

> **Blossom Dearie/Arthur Siegel**
> Painted Smiles PS-1371 (LP): "Cole Porter Revisited,
> Volume IV"
> **Lena Horne**
> Three Cherries TC-64411 (CD), TC-54411 (CS), TC-
> 44411 (LP): "Men in My Life"
> **Lena Horne**
> DRG CDMRS-510 (CD), MRSC-510 (CS), MRS-510
> (LP): "Lena Goes Latin & Sings Your Requests"
> **Mabel Mercer**
> Atlantic 1213 (LP): "Mabel Mercer Sings Cole Porter"
> 1954
> **Mabel Mercer**
> Atlantic 81817-2 (CD), 81817-4 (CS): "The Erteguns'
> New York, New York Cabaret Music"
> **Mabel Mercer**
> Atlantic 81264-4 (CS): "Mabel Mercer Sings Cole
> Porter (With Cy Walter & Stan Freeman)"

Ours (cont.)

>**Jack Sheldon Quartet**
>>Concord Jazz CJ-229 (LP): "Stand By For..."
>**George Wallington**
>>Prestige 7587 (LP): "George Wallington Trios"

Down In The Depths
introduced by Ethel Merman in *Red, Hot and Blue*

>**Kaye Ballard**
>>Columbia COS-2810 and CBS Special Products AOS-2810 (LP) "The Decline and Fall of the Entire World as Seen Through the Eyes of Cole Porter" 1965
>**William Bolcom/Joan Morris**
>>Omega Record Classics OCD-3002 (CD): "Night & Day"
>**Dial & Oatts**
>>Digital Music Products CD-495 (CD): "Dial & Oatts Play Cole Porter"
>**Peter Duchin**
>>Fiction 2994 (CD), 299 (CS), 299 (LP): "Dance With Peter Duchin"
>**Ella Fitzgerald (accompanied by Nelson Riddle and His Orchestra)**
>>Atlantic SD-1631 (LP): "Ella Loves Cole"
>**Ella Fitzgerald**
>>Pablo PACD-2310-814-2 (CD), 52310-814 (CS), 2310814 (LP): "Dream Dancing"
>**Morgana King**
>>Muse MCD-5326 (CD), MC-5326 (CS), MR-5326 (LP): "Simply Eloquent"
>**Mabel Mercer**
>>Atlantic SD2-605 (LP)
>**Ethel Merman**
>>Liberty Music Shop L-206 (78) 1936
>**Ethel Merman**
>>Decca DX-153 (LP)

Down In The Depths (cont.)

> **Ethel Merman**
> > JJC M-3004 (LP)
>
> **Ethel Merman**
> > Columbia EK-57682 (CD), ET-57682 (CS): "More
> > Songs For Sleepless Nights"
>
> **Portia Nelson**
> > Dolphin 4 and Stanyan SR-10060 (LP)
>
> **Ruby Newman and His Orchestra**
> > Victor 25470 (78) 1936
>
> **Wayne Shorter**
> > G.N.P. Crescendo 2-2075 (LP), GNPD-2-2075 (CD),
> > GNPS-2-2075 (CS): "Wayne Shorter"
>
> **Wayne Shorter**
> > Vee-Jay SRC-3006 (CS), SR-3006 (LP): "Introducing
> > Wayne Shorter"
>
> **Jack Six/Francis Thorne**
> > Composers Recordings 585 (CD): "Porter On My
> > Mind"
>
> **Lisa Stansfield**
> > Chrysalis F2-21799 (CD), F4-21799 (CS): "Red Hot
> > & Blue (A Tribute to Cole Porter to Benefit Aids
> > Research & Relief)"
>
> **Sylvia Syms**
> > Atlantic 81817-2 (CD), 81817-4 (CS): "The Erteguns'
> > New York, New York Cabaret Music"
>
> **Julie Wilson**
> > DRG CDSL-5208 (CD), SLC-5208 (CS): "Cole Porter
> > Songbook"

You've Got Something
introduced by Bob Hope and Ethel Merman in *Red, Hot and Blue*

> **Eddy Duchin/Jerry Cooper**
> > Victor 25432 (78) 1936
>
> **Leo Reisman and His Orchestra**
> > Brunswick 7753 (78) 1936

It's De-Lovely
introduced by Bob Hope and Ethel Merman in *Red, Hot and Blue*

Ray Anthony
 Aero Space RACD-995 (CD), RACS-995 (CS): "Dancing In The Dark"

Carlos Barbosa-Lima
 Concord Jazz CCD-42008 (CD), CC-42008 (CS), CC-42008 (LP): "Barbosa-Lima Plays The Music of Bonfa & Porter"

Buddy Brock
 Bellaire CD-1138 (CD): "Buddy Brock Collection, Vol's 1 & 2"

Kitty Brown
 Thesaurus 325 (78) 1936

Les Brown and His Duke (University) Blue Devils
 Thesaurus 325 (78) 1936

Carmen Cavallaro
 Hindsight HCD-312 (CD), HSC-312 (CS), HSR-312 (LP): "The Best of the Sweet Bands"

Rosemary Clooney
 Concord Jazz CJ-185 (LP), CCD-4185 (CD), CJ-185-C (CS): "Rosemary Clooney Sings the Music of Cole Porter" 1982

J. Lawrence Cook
 Biograph BLP-1023Q (LP) from a piano roll

Francis Day
 HMV B-8790 (78) 1938

Francis Day
 World Records SHB-26 (LP)

Tommy Dorsey
 RCA PK-5121 (CS): "This is Tommy Dorsey, Vol. 2"

Eddy Duchin
 Victor 25432 (78) 1936

Peter Duchin
 Fiction 2994 (CD), 299 (CS), 299 (LP): "Dance With Peter Duchin"

Frederick Fennell/Eastman-Rochester Pops Orchestra
 Mercury 43427-2 (CD): "Fennell Conducts Porter & Gershwin"

It's De-Lovely (cont.)

George Feyer
Vanguard VSD-93/94 (LP): "Essential Cole Porter"
George Feyer
Vanguard OVC-6014 (CD): "George Feyer Plays Cole Porter"
Shep Fields and His Rippling Rhythm
Bluebird B-6639 (78) 1936
Ella Fitzgerald
Verve 821989-2/821990-2 (CD), 823278-4 (CS), 823278-1 (LP): "Cole Porter Songbook" 1956
Freddy Gardner
Rex 9396 (78) 1938
Mitzi Gaynor/Donald O'Connor
Decca DL 8318 (LP): soundtrack from the film *Anything Goes* 1956
Vince Guaraldi Trio
Fantasy OJCCD-149-2 (CD), OJC-5149 (CS), OJC-149 (LP): "Vince Guaraldi Trio"
Goldie Hawkins
Atlantic 81817-2 (CD), 81817-4 (CS): "The Erteguns' New York, New York Cabaret Music"
Irving Joseph
Bainbridge BTC-1014 (CS), 1014 (LP): "Heritage of Broadway - Music of Cole Porter"
Hal Linden/Eileen Rodgers/Barbara Lang
Epic EK-15100 (CD), JST-15100 (CS): "Anything Goes"
Vincent Lopez and His Orchestra
American Record Company 7-02-06 (78)1936
Patti LuPone
RCA 7769-2-RC (CD), 7769-4-RC (CS): "Anything Goes"
Mabel Mercer
Atlantic 1213 (LP): "Mabel Mercer Sings Cole Porter" 1954

It's De-Lovely (cont.)

Mabel Mercer
> Atlantic 81264-4 (CS): "Mabel Mercer Sings Cole Porter (With Cy Walter & Stan Freeman)"

Ethel Merman
> Liberty Music Shop L-206 (78) 1936

Ethel Merman
> Decca 24454 (78)

Ethel Merman
> JJC M-3004 (LP)

Ethel Merman and Bob Hope
> JJA 19745 (LP)

Hugo Montenegro & Orchestra
> Bainbridge BTC-1003 (CS), BT-1003 (LP): "Overture: American Musical Theatre, Vol. Two 1935-1945"

Anita O'Day/Billy May
> Verve 849266-2 (CD), 849266-4 (CS): "Anita O'Day Swings Cole Porter"

Original Cast
> DRG CDSBL-12585 (CD), SBLC-12585 (CS), SBL-12585 (LP): "Forbidden Broadway"

Will Osborne and His Orchestra
> Decca 1058 (78) 1936

Will Osborne & His Orchestra
> Hindsight HSC-197 (CS), HSR-197 (LP): "The Uncollected Will Osborne & His Orchestra (1936)"

Leo Reisman and His Orchestra
> Brunswick 7753 (78) 1936

Burt Reynolds/Cybill Shepherd
> RCA ABL2-0967 (LP)

Dinah Shore
> Columbia CK-45315 (CD), CT-45315 (CS): "16 Most Requested Songs"

Sarah Vaughan
> Verve 847202-2 (CD), 847202-4 (CS): "Night & Day: The Cole Porter Songbook"

A Little Skipper From Heaven Above
introduced by Jimmy Durante in *Red, Hot and Blue*

Ronny Graham
Painted Smiles PS-1340 (LP): "Cole Porter Revisited"

Ridin' High
introduced by Ethel Merman in *Red, Hot and Blue*

Les Brown
Hindsight HCD-408 (CD), HSC-408 (CS): "Les Brown & His Orchestra Play 22 Original Big Band Recordings (1957)"
Louise Carlyle
Walden 301 (LP)
John Colianni Trio/Lew Tabackin
Concord Jazz CCD-4367 (CD), CJ-367-C (CS): "Blues-O-Matic"
Jan De Gaerani
Columbia M-34533 (LP)
Dial & Oatts
Digital Music Products CD-495 (CD): "Dial & Oatts Play Cole Porter"
Frederick Fennell and the Eastman Rochester Pops Orchestra
Mercury 75110 (LP) "Music of Cole Porter"
Frederick Fennell/Eastman-Rochester Pops Orchestra
Mercury 43427-2 (CD): "Fennell Conducts Porter & Gershwin"
George Feyer
Vanguard VSD-93/94 (LP): "Essential Cole Porter"
George Feyer
Vanguard OVC-6014 (CD): "George Feyer Plays Cole Porter"
Ella Fitzgerald
Verve 821989-2/821990-2 (CD), 823278-4 (CS), 823278-1 (LP): "Cole Porter Songbook" 1956

Ridin' High (cont.)

Benny Goodman and His Orchestra
>Columbia 48319 (78) 1937

Benny Goodman
>Columbia CK-40588 (CD), CJT-40588 (CS): "Roll
>'Em"

Benny Goodman
>Columbia C2K-48836 (CD), C2T-48836 (CS): "Benny
>Goodman on the Air (1937-1938)"

Mal Hallett and His Orchestra
>Decca 1163 (78) 1937

Cleo Laine
>RCA 60960-2 (CD), 60960-4 (CS): "Cleo Laine Live
>at Carnegie Hall"

Cleo Laine/John Dankworth Quartet
>DRG MR2SC-608 (CS), MR2S-608 (LP): "Evening
>With Cleo Laine & The John Dankworth Quartet"

Lester Lanin
>Epic EK-53134 (CD), ET-53134 (CS): "This Is
>Society Dance Music"

Peggy Lee
>Hindsight HCD-220 (CD), HSC-220 (CS), HSR-220
>(LP): "The Uncollected Peggy Lee with the David
>Barbour & Billy May Bands (1948)"

Dave Liebman Trio
>Red 123236-2 (CD): "Dave Liebman Trio Plays Cole
>Porter"

Guy Lombardo and His Royal Canadians
>Victor 25440 (78) 1936

Guy Lombardo
>Pair PDC2-1046 (CD): "Musical Yesteryears"

Ethel Merman
>Liberty Music Shop L-207 (78) 1936

Ethel Merman
>JJC M-3004 (LP)

Ethel Merman
>Larynx 567 (LP) from the television version of
>*Panama Hattie*

Ridin' High (cont.)

Sid Phillips
Decca F-7723 (78) 1941
Sue Raney/Bob Florence Group
Discovery DSCD-913 (CD), DS-913MC (CS), DS-913
(LP): "Ridin' High"
Kate Smith
Capitol/Curb D2-77475 (CD), D4-77475 (CS): "The
Best of Kate Smith"
Mel Torme
Telarc CD-83328 (CD), CS-33328 (CS): "The Great
American Songbook: Live At Michael's Pub"

You're A Bad Influence On Me
introduced by Ethel Merman in *Red, Hot and Blue*

David Allen
Painted Smiles PS-1340 (LP): "Cole Porter Revisited"
Sheila M. Sanders
Philips PHM 200-169 (LP)

The Ozarks Are Calling Me Home
introduced by Ethel Merman in *Red, Hot and Blue*

Ramona Davies
Liberty Music Shop L-210 (LP)

Red, Hot and Blue
introduced by Ethel Merman in *Red, Hot and Blue*

Ethel Merman
Liberty Music Shop L-207 (78) 1936
Ethel Merman
JJC M-3004 (LP)
Bobby Short/Kaye Ballard/Bibi Osterwald
Painted Smiles PS-1340 (LP): "Cole Porter Revisited"

Bertie and Gertie
written for but unused in *Red, Hot and Blue*

Alice Playten/Edward Earle
Painted Smiles PS-1358 (LP): "Unpublished Cole Porter" (second pressing only)

Goodbye, Little Dream, Goodbye
introduced by Yvonne Printemps in the English show
O Mistress Mine

William Bolcom/Joan Morris
Omega Record Classics OCD-3002 (CD): "Night & Day"
Jan De Gaerani
Columbia M-34533 (LP)
Dial & Oatts
Digital Music Products CD-495 (CD): "Dial & Oatts Play Cole Porter"
Patti LuPone
RCA 7769-2-RC (CD), 7769-4-RC (CS): "Anything Goes"
Yvonne Printemps and Pierre Fresnay
HMV DA-1539 (78)
Yvonne Printemps and Pierre Fresnay
World SHB-26 (LP)
Jack Six/Francis Thorne
Composers Recordings 585 (CD): "Porter On My Mind"

Close
introduced by Nelson Eddy in the film *Rosalie*

Leo Reisman and His Orchestra
Victor 25698 (78) 1937

In The Still Of The Night
introduced by Nelson Eddy in the film *Rosalie*

Carlos Barbosa-Lima
Concord Jazz CCD-42008 (CD), CC-42008 (CS), CC-42008 (LP): "Barbosa-Lima Plays The Music of Bonfa & Porter"
William Bolcom/Joan Morris
Omega Record Classics OCD-3002 (CD): "Night & Day"
Al Bowlly
HMV BD-502, Decca F-6605 (78) 1938
Kenny Burrell
Muse MR-5216 (LP): "Live at the Village Vanguard"
Betty Carter
Verve 314-513870-2 (CD), 314-513870-4 (CS): "It's Not About the Melody"
Frank Chacksfield and His Orchestra
London SP-44185 (LP): "The Music of Cole Porter"
Cynthia Clarey
Teldec 75277-2 (CD): "Centennial Gala Concert"
Clebanoff
Mercury SR-613 (45)
Rosemary Clooney
Concord Jazz CJ-185 (LP), CCD-4185 (CD), CJ-185-C (CS): "Rosemary Clooney Sings the Music of Cole Porter" 1982
Ray Conniff & His Orchestra
Columbia CK-8037 (CD): "'S Marvelous"

In The Still Of The Night (cont.)

Michael Crawford
> Columbia CK-44321 (CD), OCT-44321 (CS), OC-44321 (LP): "Songs From the Stage & Screen"

Michael Crawford
> Atlantic 82427-2 (CD), 82427-4 (CS): "Songs From the Stage & Screen"

Vic Damone
> Ranwood RCD-8204 (CD), RC-8204 (CS), RLP-8204 (LP): "The Best of Vic Damone Live"

Vic Damone
> Pair PCD-2-1303 (CD), PDK-2-1303 (CS): "Let's Face the Music & Sing"

Meyer Davis
> Monmouth-Evergreen MES-6813 (LP): "Meyer Davis Plays Cole Porter"

Doris Day/Frank De Vol Orchestra
> Columbia CK-8066 (CD) and Sony XPT-5 (CS) and AC2-5 (LP): "Hooray For Hollywood, Vol. I"

Dion
> Collectables COL-5027 (CS, LP): "Runaround Sue"

Dion
> Pair PDK-2-1142 (CS): "The Best of Dion"

Dion & the Belmonts
> Laurie 3059 (45) 1960

Dion & the Belmonts
> Collectables COL-5026 (CS): "Wish Upon a Star With Dion & the Belmonts"

Dion & the Belmonts
> Laurie LCD-4092 (CD), LE5-4092 (CS): "20 Great Love Songs of the 50's & 60's, Vol. 2"

Dion & the Belmonts
> Laurie 3CD-102 (CD): "Their Best"

Dion & the Belmonts
> Laurie 3CD-105 (CD): "The Wanderer"

Tommy Dorsey and His Orchestra
> Victor 25663 (78) 1937

In The Still Of The Night (cont.)

Tommy Dorsey
>RCA AXK2-5573 (CS): "Complete Tommy Dorsey, Vol. 5 (1937)"

Tommy Dorsey/Jack Leonard
>Pair PDC-2-1312 (CD), PDK-2-1312 (CS): "Great Singers - Great Bands"

Billy Eckstine
>Savoy ZDS-4401 (CD), SJK-2214 (CS), SJL-2214 (LP): "Mister B. & The Band"

Billy Eckstine
>Verve 847202-2 (CD), 847202-4 (CS): "Night & Day: The Cole Porter Songbook"

Billy Eckstine/Quincy Jones
>Mercury 832592-2 (CD), 832592-4 (CS): "At Basin Street East"

Nelson Eddy
>Sony AK-47838 (CD), AT-47838 (CS): "Cole Porter in Hollywood - The MGM Years"

Ray Elis and Johnny Douglas conducting the Ray Elis Strings
>RCA CAS-2522 (LP): "The Great Hits of Cole Porter"

Frederick Fennell/Eastman-Rochester Pops Orchestra
>Mercury 43427-2 (CD): "Fennell Conducts Porter & Gershwin"

George Feyer
>Vanguard VSD-93/94 (LP): "Essential Cole Porter"

George Feyer
>Vanguard OVC-6014 (CD): "George Feyer Plays Cole Porter"

Shep Fields and His Rippling Rhythm
>Bluebird B-7185 (78) 1937

Ella Fitzgerald
>Verve 821989-2/821990-2 (CD), 823278-4 (CS), 823278-1 (LP): "Cole Porter Songbook" 1956

In The Still Of The Night (cont.)

Bruce Forman
> Kamei KR7000CD (CD), KR-7000C (CS): "Still of
> the Night"

Erroll Garner
> MGM SE-4361 (45)

Stephane Grappelli
> Accord 139004 (CD): "Stephane Grappelli Plays
> George Gershwin & Cole Porter"

Dick Hyman
> Concord Jazz CCD-4415 (CD), CJ-415-C (CS): "Live
> at Maybeck Recital Hall, Vol. 3 (Dick Hyman at
> Maybeck - Music of 1937)"

Dick Hyman
> Concord Jazz CCD-7001 (CD): "The Maybeck Recital
> Hall Collection"

Irving Joseph
> Bainbridge BTC-1014 (CS), 1014 (LP): "Heritage of
> Broadway - Music of Cole Porter"

Dave Liebman Trio
> Red 123236-2 (CD): "Dave Liebman Trio Plays Cole
> Porter"

Julie London
> EMI E2-93455 (CD), E4-93455 (CS): "Julie London
> Sings Cole Porter"

Julie London
> Rhino R2-70737 (CD), R4-70737 (CS): "Time For
> Love/The Best of Julie London"

Dorothy Malone/Cary Grant
> Motion Picture Tracks MPT 6 (LP): soundtrack from
> the film *Night and Day* 1945

Jack Marshard and His Orchestra
> Brunswick 8417 (78) 1939

Johnny Mathis
> Columbia CGT-2 (CS): "Warm/Open Fire, Two
> Guitars"

Johnny Mathis
> Columbia CK-8056 (CD): "Open Fire, Two Guitars"

In The Still Of The Night (cont.)

Neville Brothers
Chrysalis F2-21799 (CD), F4-21799 (CS): "Red Hot & Blue (A Tribute to Cole Porter to Benefit Aids Research & Relief)"

Ozzie Nelson & His Orchestra
Hindsight HSC-208 (CS), HSR-208 (LP): "The Uncollected Ozzie Nelson & His Orchestra, Vol. 3 (1938)"

Michael Nesmith
Pacific Arts Audio PAAD-5000 (CD), PAAC-5000 (CS): "Tropical Campfire's"

Jessye Norman
Philips Classics 412 625 (LP) "Jessye Norman--With a Song in My Heart" 1984

Jessye Norman/Boston Pops Orchestra
Philips 412625-2 (CD), 412625-4 (CS): "With a Song in My Heart"

Jessye Norman/Boston Pops Orchestra
Philips 422893-2 (CD), 422893-4 (CS): "The Jessye Norman Collection"

Helen O'Connell
Capitol C2-96361 (CD), C4-96361 (CS): "Anything Goes - Capitol Sings Cole Porter"

101 Strings Orchestra
Alshire International ALCD-30 (CD), ALSC-5007 (CS): "Cole Porter"

101 Strings Orchestra
Alshire International ALCD-48 (CD), ADBL-404 (CS): "The Best of the Great American Composers, Vol. IV"

Will Osborne and His Orchestra
Decca 1467 (78) 1937

Charlie Parker
Verve 827154-4 (CS), 827154-1 (LP): "Verve Years (1952-1954)"

Charlie Parker
Verve 823250-2 (CD), 823250-4 (CS): "The Cole Porter Songbook"

In The Still Of The Night (cont.)

Charlie Parker
Verve 833288-2 (CD), 833288-4 (CS): "Compact - Charlie Parker"
Oscar Peterson
Verve 821987-2 (CD), 821987-4 (CS): "Oscar Peterson Plays the Cole Porter Songbook"
Della Reese
Jubilee 45-6002 (45)
Della Reese
Virgo 6002 (45)
Leo Reisman and His Orchestra
Brunswick 7985 (78) 1937
Django Reinhardt
Inner City TIC-1104 (CS), 1104 (LP): "Django, Vol. 1"
Django Reinhardt
Disques Swing CDSW-8421/23 (CD), SWC-8421/23 (CS): "Djangologie/USA, Vol. 1"
Artie Shaw
MCA MCAC2-4081 (CS): "The Best of Artie Shaw"
George Shearing/Barry Tuckwell
Concord Jazz CCD-42010 (CD), CC-2010-C (CS): "George Shearing & Barry Tuckwell Play the Music of Cole Porter"
Scott Shirley
Prestige P-7312 (LP): "Soul Shouting"
Frank Sinatra/Johnny Mandel
Reprise 27017-2 (CD), 27017-4 (CS): "Ring-A-Ding Ding!"
Candi Staton
Sugar Hill 265 (LP): "Nightlites"
Louis Van Dijk/Elly Ameling
Philips 7337284 (CS), 6514284 (LP): "After Hours"
Fred Waring & the Pennsylvanians
Capitol EAP-2-845 (45)
Randy Weston
Riverside 2508 (LP): "Randy Weston Plays Cole Porter in a Modern Mood" 1954

I've A Strange New Rhythm In My Heart
introduced by Eleanor Powell in the film *Rosalie*

Bob Crosby and His Orchestra
Decca 1555 (78) 1937
Artie Shaw
Brunswick 7971 (78) 1937

Rosalie
introduced by Nelson Eddy in the film *Rosalie*

Al Bowlly
HMV BD-502, Decca F-6605
Ray Brown/Jimmy Rowles
Concord Jazz CJ-66-C (CS): "As Good As It Gets"
Chorus
Motion Picture Tracks MPT 6 (LP): soundtrack from
the film *Night and Day* 1945
Buddy Clark
Columbia CK-48976 (CD), CT-48976 (CS): "16 Most
Requested Songs"
George Feyer
Vanguard VSD-93/94 (LP): "Essential Cole Porter"
George Feyer
Vanguard OVC-6014 (CD): "George Feyer Plays Cole
Porter"
Jan Garber
Brunswick 7969 (78) 1937
Erroll Garner/Slam Stewart
Savoy ZDS-4422 (CD), SJK-1118 (CS), SJL-1118
(LP): "Yesterdays"
Erroll Garner
Mercury 834910-2 (CD), 834910-4 (CS): "The
Original Misty"
Horace Heidt
Brunswick 8028 (78) 1937
Art Kassel and His "Kassels-In-The-Air"
Bluebird B-7255 (78) 1937

Rosalie (cont.)

Swing and Sway With Sammy Kaye
Vocalion 3700 (78) 1937
Vincent Lopez and His Orchestra
American Record Company 7-12-09 (78) 1937
Will Osborne and His Orchestra
Decca 1467 (78) 1937
Tony Pastor
Roulette EPR-1-1308 (45)
Louis Prima and His New Orleans Gang
Decca 1618 (78) 1938
Leo Reisman and His Orchestra
Victor 25698 (78) 1937
Roy Ross and His Orchestra
Decca 24083 (78) 1942
Jimmy Rowles/Ray Brown
Concord Jazz CCD-4066 (CD): "As Good As It Gets"
Artie Shaw and His New Music
Thesaurus 455 (78) 1937
Artie Shaw and His Orchestra
Bluebird B-10126 (78) 1939
Artie Shaw
RCA AXK2-5517 (CS) "Complete Artie Shaw, Vol. 1 (1938-1939)"
Artie Shaw/Tony Pastor
Bluebird 61099-2 (CD), 61099-4 (CS): "Personal Best"

Who Knows?
introduced by an unidentified female vocalist
in the film *Rosalie*

Tommy Dorsey and His Orchestra
Victor 25663 (78) 1937
Shep Fields and His Rippling Rhythm
Bluebird B-7185 (78) 1937
Vincent Lopez and His Orchestra
American Record Company 7-12-01 (78) 1937

Who Knows? (cont.)

Leo Reisman and His Orchestra
Brunswick 7985 (78) 1937

Why Should I Care?
introduced by Frank Morgan in the film *Rosalie*

Bob Crosby and His Orchestra
Decca 1555 (78) 1937
Swing and Sway with Sammy Kaye
Vocalion 3700 (78) 1937
Dave Liebman Trio
Red 123236-2 (CD): "Dave Liebman Trio Plays Cole Porter"

I Know It's Not Meant For Me
written for but unused in the film *Rosalie*

Charles Rydell/Karen Morrow
Painted Smiles PS-1358 (LP): "Unpublished Cole Porter"

Works From 1938

You Never Know
introduced by Libby Holman in *You Never Know*

Larry Clinton and His Orchestra
Victor 26014 (78) 1938
Lena Horne
RCA LPM LSP 1879 (LP): "Give the Lady What She Wants" 1958
Kay Kyser and His Orchestra
Brunswick 8210 (78) 1938
Casa Loma Orchestra
Decca 2010 (78) 1938

For No Rhyme Or Reason
introduced by Toby Wing, Charles Kemper and the Debonairs in *You Never Know*

Al Donahue and His Orchestra
Vocalion 4349 (78) 1938
Kay Kyser and His Orchestra
Brunswick 8209 (78) 1938
Joseph Rines and His Hotel St. Regis Orchestra
Victor 26022 (78) 1938
Bobby Short
Atlantic 1285 (LP)

From Alpha To Omega
introduced by Clifton Webb and Lupe Velez in *You Never Know*

Duilio Del Prete/Madeline Kahn
RCA ABL2-0967 (LP)
Kay Kyser and His Orchestra
Brunswick 8210 (78) 1938

From Alpha To Omega (cont.)

> **Joseph Rines and His Hotel St. Regis Orchestra**
> Victor 26022 (78) 1938

What Shall I Do?
introduced by Lupe Velez in *You Never Know*

> **Carmen Alvarez, Harold Lang, William Hickey**
> Columbia COS-2810 and CBS Special Products AOS-2810 (LP): "The Decline and Fall of the Entire World as Seen Through the Eyes of Cole Porter") 1965

At Long Last Love
introduced by Clifton Webb in *You Never Know*

> **William Bolcom/Joan Morris**
> Omega Record Classics OCD-3002 (CD): "Night & Day"
> **Casa Loma Orchestra**
> Decca 2010 (78) 1938
> **Larry Clinton and His Orchestra**
> Victor 26014 (78) 1938
> **Duilio Del Prete/Madeline Kahn/Burt Reynolds/Cybill Shepherd**
> RCA ABL2-0967 (LP)
> **Jan De Gaetani**
> Columbia M-34533 (LP)
> **Dial & Oatts**
> Digital Music Products CD-495 (CD): "Dial & Oatts Play Cole Porter"
> **Al Donahue and His Orchestra**
> Vocalion 4349 (78) 1938
> **Ella Fitzgerald (accompanied by Nelson Riddle and His Orchestra)**
> Atlantic SD-1631 (LP): "Ella Loves Cole"

At Long Last Love (cont.)

Ella Fitzgerald
Pablo PACD-2310-814-2 (CD), 52310-814 (CS), 2310814 (LP): "Dream Dancing"

Buddy Greco
Columbia CK-53775 (CD), CT-53775 (CS): "16 Most Requested Songs"

Grant Green
Blue Note B2-95591 (CD), B4-95591 (CS): "Blue Porter"

Bill Henderson
Verve 847202-2 (CD), 847202-4 (CS): "Night & Day: The Cole Porter Songbook"

Bill Henderson/Oscar Peterson Trio
Verve 837937-2 (CD), 837937-4 (CS): "Bill Henderson with the Oscar Peterson Trio"

Lena Horne
Pickwick Entertainment PMTD-16006 (CD), PMTT-16006 (CS): "Stormy Lady"

Lena Horne
RCA 66021-2 (CD), 66021-4 (CS): "At Long Last Lena"

Sammy Kaye
Ranwood RC-8220 (CS): "Swing & Sway with Sammy Kaye"

Kay Kyser and His Orchestra
Brunswick 8209 (78) 1938

Frances Langford
Decca 2197 (78) 1938

Julie London
EMI E2-93455 (CD), E4-93455 (CS): "Julie London Sings Cole Porter"

Susannah McCorkle
Pausa PC-7208 (CS), 7208 (LP): "Dream"

Carmen McRae
Atlantic 81817-2 (CD), 81817-4 (CS): "The Erteguns' New York, New York Cabaret Music"

Carmen McRae
Atlantic SD-904-2 (CD): "Great American Songbook"

At Long Last Love (cont.)

Ozzie Nelson and His Orchestra
Bluebird B-7825 (78) 1938
Ellyn Rucker
Capri 74010-2 (CD), 74010-4 (CS): "This Heart of
Mine"
Bobby Short
Atlantic SD 2-606 (LP): "Bobby Short Loves Cole
Porter" 1971
Bobby Short
Atlantic 1262 (LP)
Bobby Short
Atlantic 82062-2 (CD), 82062-4 (CS): "Bobby, Noel
& Cole (Bobby Short Loves Cole Porter/Bobby Short
Is Mad About Noel Coward)"
Frank Sinatra
Capitol EAP-2-803 (45) 1956
Frank Sinatra
Reprise 27021-2 (CD), 27021-4 (CS), FS-1005 (LP):
"Sinatra & Swingin' Brass"
Frank Sinatra
Capitol C2-94518 (CD), C4-94518 (CS): "A Swingin'
Affair!"
Frank Sinatra
Capitol C2-96611 (CD), C4-96611 (CS): "Frank
Sinatra Sings the Select Cole Porter"
Frank Sinatra
Capitol BBX2-99956 (CD), BBX4-99956 (CS):
"Concepts"
Jack Six/Francis Thorne
Composers Recordings 585 (CD): "Porter On My
Mind"
Frank Stallone
USA Music Group USACD-695 (CD), USACA-695
(CS): "Day In and Day Out"
Weslia Whitfield
Cabaret CACD-5007-2 (CD), CACS-5007-4 (CS):
"Beautiful Love"

I'm Yours
written for but unused in *You Never Know*

Patrice Munsel
Painted Smiles PS-1371 (LP): "Cole Porter Revisited, Volume IV"

By Candlelight
written for but unused in *You Never Know*

Bobby Short
Atlantic SD 2-606 (LP: "Bobby Short Loves Cole Porter") 1971
Bobby Short
Atlantic 82062-2 (CD), 82062-4 (CS): "Bobby, Noel & Cole (Bobby Short Loves Cole Porter/Bobby Short Is Mad About Noel Coward)"

Get Out Of Town
introduced by Tamara in *Leave It To Me*

David Allyn
Discovery DS-803 (LP): "I Only Have Eyes For You"
Tony Bennett/Torrie Zito Orchestra
DRG CDMRS-801 (CD), MRSC-801 (CS): "The Special Magic of Tony Bennett"
Les Brown
Bluebird B-10009 (78) 1938
Eddie Cano
RCA International 3459-2-RL (CD): "Cole Porter, Duke Ellington & Me"
Louise Carlyle
Waldon 301 (LP)
Rosemary Clooney
Concord Jazz CJ-185 (LP), CCD-4185 (CD), CJ-185-C (CS): "Rosemary Clooney Sings the Music of Cole Porter" 1982

Get Out Of Town (cont.)

Sammy Davis, Jr.
Decca ED-2285 (45)

Sammy Davis, Jr.
MCA MCAC2-4109 (CS & LP): "Hey there (It's Sammy Davis, Jr. At His Dynamite Greatest)"

Eddy Duchin
Brunswick 8252 (78) 1938

Eddy Duchin
Columbia CK-46150 (CD), CT-46150 (CS): "Best of the Big Bands"

Eileen Farrell
Reference RR-34CD (CD), RR-34CS (CS): "Eileen Farrell Sings Torch Songs"

George Feyer
Vanguard VSD-93/94 (LP): "Essential Cole Porter"

George Feyer
Vanguard OVC-6014 (CD): "George Feyer Plays Cole Porter"

Ella Fitzgerald
Verve 821989-2/821990-2 (CD), 823278-4 (CS), 823278-1 (LP): "Cole Porter Songbook" 1956

Ella Fitzgerald
Pablo OJCCD-442-2 (CD), OJC-5442 (CS), OJC-442 (LP): "Ella A Nice"

John Holmquist/Dan Estrem
Projazz CDJ-606 (CD), PCJ-606 (CS): "Still of the Night"

Shirley Horn
Verve CD 314-511-070-2 (CD): "The Cole Porter Songbook, Vol. II"

Shirley Horn
Verve 837933-2 (CD), 837933-4 (CS), 837933-1 (LP): "Close Enough For Love"

Lena Horne
RCA EPA-4329 (45)

Get Out Of Town (cont.)

Lena Horne
RCA 66021-2 (CD), 66021-4 (CS): "At Long Last Lena"
Dick Johnson
Concord Jazz CCD-4107 (CD): "Dick Johnson Plays Alto Sax & Flute & Soprano Sax & Clarinet"
Irving Joseph
Bainbridge BTC-1014 (CS), 1014 (LP): "Heritage of Broadway - Music of Cole Porter"
Thad Jones
Debut OJCCD-625-2 (CD), OJC-5625 (CS), OJC-625 (LP): "Fabulous Thad Jones"
Swing and Sway with Sammy Kaye
Victor 26080 (78) 1938
Barney Kessel
Concord Jazz CCD-6033 (CD): "Soaring"
Rahsaan Roland Kirk
Mercury 826988-2 (CD): "Domino"
Frances Langford
Decca 2229 (78) 1938
Peggy Lee/George Shearing
Blue Note B2-98454 (CD): "Beauty & The Beat!"
Dave Liebman Trio
Red 123236-2 (CD): "Dave Liebman Trio Plays Cole Porter"
Julie London
Liberty LRP-3434 (LP)
Julie London
EMI E2-93455 (CD), E4-93455 (CS): "Julie London Sings Cole Porter"
Doug MacDonald Quartet
Cexton CR-5678-D (CD): "Doug MacDonald Quartet"
Susannah McCorckle
Concord Jazz CCD-4491 (CD), CJ-491-C (CS): "I'll Take Romance"
Adam Makowicz
Concord Jazz CCD-4541 (CD): "Live At Maybeck Recital Hall, Vol. 24 (Adam Makowicz At Maybeck)"

Get Out Of Town (cont.)

Charles Mingus
 Debut 12DCD-4402-2 (CD): "The Complete Debut
 Recordings"
Ruby Newman and His Orchestra
 Decca 2192 (78) 1938
Anita O'Day/Billy May
 Verve 849266-2 (CD), 849266-4 (CS): "Anita O'Day
 Swings Cole Porter"
Ellyn Rucker
 Capri 74010-2 (CD), 74010-4 (CS): "This Heart of
 Mine"
Hal Schaefer
 Discovery 74002-2 (CD): "Solo, Duo, Trio"
Hal Schaefer
 Discovery 75005-2 (CD), 75005-4 (CS): "Malibu
 Sunset"
Jack Sheldon Quartet
 Concord Jazz CJ-229 (LP): "Stand By For..."
Jeri Southern
 Capitol T-1173 (LP)
Jeri Southern/Billy May
 Capitol C2-96361 (CD), C4-96361 (CS): "Anything
 Goes - Capitol Sings Cole Porter"
The Champagne Music of Lawrence Welk
 Vocalion 4512 (78) 1938
Randy Weston
 Riverside 2508 (LP): "Randy Weston Plays Cole
 Porter in a Modern Mood" 1954
Teddy Wilson
 Black Lion BLCD-760166 (CD): "Cole Porter
 Classics"
Steve Wolfe/Nancy King
 Inner City 1049 (LP): "First Date"

Most Gentlemen Don't Like Love
introduced by Sophie Tucker in *Leave It To Me*

Eileen Brennan/Madeline Kahn/Cybill Shepherd
RCA ABL2-0967 (LP)

Kaye Ballard, Carmen Alvarez and Elmarie Wendel
Columbia COS-2810 and CBS Special Products AOS-2810 (LP) "The Decline and Fall of the Entire World as Seen Through the Eyes of Cole Porter" 1965

Betty Carter
Roulette 5005 (LP): "Now It's My Turn"

Larry Clinton and His Orchestra
Victor 26100 (78) 1938

Pat Kirkwood/Jack Hylton and His Orchestra
HMV BD-785 (78)

Pat Kirkwood/Jack Hylton and His Orchestra
World Records SHB-26 (LP)

Julia McKenzie/Elizabeth Power/Angela Richards
RCA LRL2-5054 (LP): "Cole"

Mary Martin with Eddy Duchin's Orchestra
Brunswick 8282 (78) 1938

Mary Martin with Eddy Duchin's Orchestra
Columbia KS-31456 (LP)

Mary Martin with Eddy Duchin's Orchestra
Columbia CK-46150 (CD), CT-46150 (CS): "Best of the Big Bands"

Sheila M. Sanders
Philips PHM 200-169 (LP)

Julie Wilson, with the Marshall Grant Trio
Victor LX-1118 (LP): "Julie Wilson at the St. Regis" 1957

Julie Wilson
DRG CDSL-5208 (CD), SLC-5208 (CS): "Cole Porter Songbook"

From Now On
introduced by William Gaxton and Tamara in *Leave It To Me*

> **Les Brown and His Orchestra**
> > Bluebird B-10009 (78) 1938
> **Eddy Duchin**
> > Brunswick 8252 (78) 1938
> **Swing and Sway with Sammy Kaye**
> > Victor 26080 (78) 1938
> **Frances Langford**
> > Decca 2229 (78) 1938
> **Peggy Lee**
> > Capitol C2-96361 (CD), C4-96361 (CS): "Anything Goes - Capitol Sings Cole Porter"
> **Ruby Newman and His Orchestra**
> > Decca 2192 (78) 1938
> **The Champagne Music of Lawrence Welk**
> > Vocalion 4512 (78) 1938
> **Bobby Short**
> > Atlantic 1285 (LP)
> **Bobby Short**
> > Atlantic 81715-2 (CD), 81715-4 (CS): "50 By Bobby Short"

I Want To Go Home
introduced by Victor Moore in *Leave It To Me*

> **Ethel Levey**
> > HMV B-4401 (78) 1933

My Heart Belongs To Daddy
introduced by Mary Martin in *Leave It To Me*

> **Ambrose Orchestra/Evelyn Dall**
> > G.N.P. Crescendo GNP-9004 (LP): "Ambrose Tribute to Cole Porter"
> **Chet Baker/Gerry Mulligan**
> > Pacific Jazz B2-46857 (CD): "Reunion"

My Heart Belongs To Daddy (cont.)

William Bolcom/Joan Morris
Omega Record Classics OCD-3004 (CD): "Let's Do it
- Bolcom & Morris at Aspen"

William Bolcom/Joan Morris
Omega Record Classics OCD-3002 (CD): "Night &
Day"

Frank Chacksfield and His Orchestra
London SP-44185 (LP): "The Music of Cole Porter"

Terry Clark Quintet
Riverside OJCCD-764-2 (CD): "Top & Bottom Brass"

Larry Clinton and His Orchestra
Victor 26100 (78) 1938

Count Basie
Decca 2249 (78) 1939

Rosemary Clooney
Concord Jazz CJ-185 (LP), CCD-4185 (CD), CJ-185-
C (CS): "Rosemary Clooney Sings the Music of Cole
Porter" 1982

Eddie DeLange and His Orchestra
Bluebird B-10080 (78) 1938

Les Elgart
Columbia CK-48909 (CD), CT-48909 (CS): "Best of
the Big Bands, Vol. 2"

Les & Larry Elgart
Columbia 4-43081(45) 1964

Les & Larry Elgart
Columbia PCT-38341 (CS): "Swingtime"

Les & Larry Elgart
Columbia CK-45337 (CD), CT-45337 (CS): "Best of
the Big Bands"

Frederick Fennell/Eastman-Rochester Pops Orchestra
Mercury 43427-2 (CD): "Fennell Conducts Porter &
Gershwin"

George Feyer
Vanguard VSD-93/94 (LP): "Essential Cole Porter"

George Feyer
Vanguard OVC-6014 (CD): "George Feyer Plays Cole
Porter"

My Heart Belongs To Daddy (cont.)

Ella Fitzgerald
GRP GRD-2-623 (CD), GRC-2-623 (CS): "The Early Years, Part 2"
Ella Fitzgerald (accompanied by Nelson Riddle and His Orchestra)
Atlantic SD-1631 (LP): "Ella Loves Cole"
Ella Fitzgerald
Pablo PACD-2310-814-2 (CD), 52310-814 (CS), 2310814 (LP): "Dream Dancing"
Ella Fitzgerald
EPM Musique 157762 (CD): "Ladies Sing Jazz, Vol. 2"
Dizzy Gillespie
Verve 314-515392-2 (CD), 314-515392-4 (CS): "Jazz 'Round Midnight - The George Gershwin & Cole Porter Songbook"
Billie Holiday/Ella Fitzgerald
MCA MCAC2-4099 (CS), MCA2-4099 (LP): "Billie Holiday & Ella Fitzgerald"
Kitty Kallen
Everest 367 (LP): "Big Bands of the Swinging Years, Vol. II"
Kitty Kallen/Artie Shaw
Collectables COL-5097 (CD, CS): "Big Bands of the Swinging Years, Vol. II"
Pat Kirkwood/Jack Hylton and His Orchestra
HMV BD-785
Pat Kirkwood/Jack Hylton and His Orchestra
World Records SHB-26 (LP)
Eartha Kitt
MCA MCAC-1554 (CS): "The Best of Eartha Kitt"
Eartha Kitt
RCA 66022-2 (CD), 66022-4 (CS): "'Miss Kitt', To You"
Peggy Lee
MCA MCAC2-4049 (CS): "The Best of Peggy Lee"
Peggy Lee
MCA MCAC-20251 (CS): "Black Coffee"

My Heart Belongs To Daddy (cont.)

Julie London
EMI E2-93455 (CD), E4-93455 (CS): "Julie London
Sings Cole Porter"
Julie London
Rhino R2-70737 (CD), R4-70737 (CS): "Time For
Love/The Best of Julie London"
Julie London
Liberty LRP-3434 (LP)
Mary Martin with Eddie Duchin's Orchestra
Brunswick 8282 (78) 1938
Mary Martin with Eddie Duchin's Orchestra
Columbia KS-31456 (LP)
Mary Martin with Eddie Duchin's Orchestra
Columbia CK-46150 (CD), CT-46150 (CS): "Best of
the Big Bands"
Mary Martin
Warner Bros 3XX2736 and Motion Picture Tracks
MPT 6 (LP): soundtrack from the film *Night and Day*
1945
Mary Martin
Decca 9-245 (45) 1951
Mary Martin
Columbia CK-53777 (CD), CT-53777 (CS): "16 Most
Requested Songs"
Mary Martin/Noel Coward
DRG CDXP-1103 (CD), DARC-2-1103 (LP):
"Together With Music"
Mary Martin/Ethel Merman
Decca DL-7027 (LP)
Marilyn Monroe
Sony BT-8327 (CS), ACS-8327 (LP): soundtrack from
the film *Let's Make Love* 1960
Marilyn Monroe
Accord 339372 (CD): "Goodbye Primadonna"
Marilyn Monroe
DRG CDXP-15005 (CD), DARC2C-15005 (CS):
"Never Before Never Again"

My Heart Belongs To Daddy (cont.)

Paul Motian
>Verve 834430-2 (CD), 834430-1 (LP): "Paul Motian on Broadway, Vol. 1"

Anita O'Day
>Verve 314-511-070-2 (CD): "The Cole Porter Songbook, Vol. II"

Anita O'Day
>Emily 32383 (LP): "Night Has A Thousand Eyes"

Anita O'Day
>Verve 314-515392-2 (CD), 314-515392-4 (CS): "Jazz 'Round Midnight - The George Gershwin & Cole Porter Songbook"

Anita O'Day/Billy May
>Verve 849266-2 (CD), 849266-4 (CS): "Anita O'Day Swings Cole Porter"

Charlie Parker
>Verve 827154-4 (CS), 827154-1 (LP): "Verve Years (1952-1954)"

Charlie Parker
>Verve 823250-2 (CD), 823250-4 (CS): "The Cole Porter Songbook"

Cybill Shepherd
>MCA MCAC-25173 (CS), MCA-25173 (LP): "Cybill Does It...To Cole Porter"

Cybill Shepherd
>Paramount PAS-1018 (LP)

Zoot Sims/Harry Sweets Edison
>Pablo OJCCD-499-2 (CD), OJC-5499 (CS), OJC-499 (LP): "Just Friends"

Valaida
>Sonora 3557 (78) 1939

Bennie Wallace
>Enja 4046 (LP): "Big Jim's Tango"

Chick Webb
>Decca 2309 (78) 1939

Julie Wilson
>DRG CDSL-5208 (CD), SLC-5208 (CS): "Cole Porter Songbook"

Tomorrow
introduced by Sophie Tucker in *Leave It To Me*

> **Kaye Ballard/Harold Lang/Carmen Alvarez/William Hickey/Elmarie Wendel**
> > Columbia COS-2810 and CBS Special Products AOS-2810 (LP): "The Decline and Fall of the Entire World as Seen Through the Eyes of Cole Porter" 1965
>
> **Chorus**
> > RCA LRL2-5054 (LP): "Cole"

Far Away
introduced by William Gaxton and Tamara in *Leave It To Me*

> **David Allen/Kaye Ballard**
> > Painted Smiles PS-1340 (LP): "Cole Porter Revisited"

River God
introduced by Todd Duncan in the English show
The Sun Never Sets

> **Todd Duncan**
> > English Columbia DB-1778 (78) 1938

Works From 1939

Please Don't Monkey With Broadway
introduced by Fred Astaire and George Murphy in the film
Broadway Melody of 1940

Fred Astaire and George Murphy
MGM 25987 and Classic International Filmusicals CIF
3002 (LP): soundtrack from the film *Broadway
Melody of 1940* 1939
Ray Cornell/Rod McLennan/Kenneth Nelson
RCA LRL2-5054 (LP): "Cole"
Jack Six/Francis Thorne
Composers Recordings 585 (CD): "Porter On My
Mind"

Between You and Me
introduced by George Murphy in the film *Broadway Melody of 1940*

Mitchell Ayres and His Fashions in Music
Bluebird BB-10585 (78) 1940
Mary Healy
Columbia DB-1927 (78) 1940
Dick Jurgens and His Orchestra
Vocalion 5442 (78) 1940
George Murphy
Classic International Filmusicals CIF 3002 (LP):
soundtrack from the film *Broadway Melody of 1940*
1939

I've Got My Eyes On You
introduced by Fred Astaire and Eleanor Powell in the film
Broadway Melody of 1940

Fred Astaire
> Classic International Filmusicals CIF 3002 (LP):
> soundtrack from the film *Broadway Melody of 1940*
> 1939

Fred Astaire
> Sony AK-47838 (CD), AT-47838 (CS): "Cole Porter
> in Hollywood - The MGM Years"

Ambrose Orchestra
> G.N.P. Crescendo GNP-9004 (LP): "Ambrose Tribute
> to Cole Porter"

Les Brown
> Bluebird B-10551 (78) 1939

Chick Bullock
> Vocalion 5342 (78) 1940

Bob Crosby
> Decca 2991 (78) 1940

Tommy Dorsey
> Victor 26470 (78) 1939

Jan Garber
> Vocalion 5253 (78) 1939

Mary Healy
> Columbia DB-1927 (78) 1940

Gene Krupa
> Columbia 36361 (78) 1940

Barbara Lea
> Prestige OJCCD-1742-2 (CD): "Lea in Love"

Frankie Masters and His Orchestra
> Vocalion 5352 (78) 1939

Artie Shaw
> Victor LPT-6000 (78) 1939

Dinah Shore
> Bluebird B-10592 (78) 1939

I Concentrate On You
introduced by Douglas McPhail in the film
Broadway Melody of 1940

Cannonball Adderly
> Capitol/Curb D2-77399 (Cd), D4-77399 (CS): "Best of Cannonball Adderly"

Fred Astaire
> Verve 847202-2 (CD), 847202-4 (CS): "Night & Day: The Cole Porter Songbook"

Tony Bennett
> Columbia CK-57424 (CD), CT-57424 (CS): "Steppin' Out"

Les Brown and His Orchestra
> Bluebird B-10551 (78) 1939

Mike Campbell/Tom Garvin
> ITI 4XT-72959 (CS), ST-72959 (LP): "Blackberry Winter"

Casa Loma Orchestra
> Decca 3008, (78) 1940

The Clayton Brothers
> Capri 74037-2 (CD), 74037-4 (CS): "The Music"

Rosemary Clooney
> Concord Jazz CJ-185 (LP), CCD-4185 (CD), CJ-185-C (CS): "Rosemary Clooney Sings the Music of Cole Porter" 1982

Perry Como
> RCA 547-0078 (45)

Perry Como
> RCA 66098-2 (CD), 66098-4 (CS): "Yesterday & Today - A Celebration in Song"

Ray Conniff
> Columbia CK-8678 (CD): "Rhapsody in Rhythm"

Sammy Davis, Jr.
> MCA MCAC2-4109 (CS & LP): "Hey there (It's Sammy Davis, Jr. At His Dynamite Greatest)"

Tommy Dorsey
> Victor 26470 (78) 1939

Eddy Duchin
> Columbia 35369 (78) 1940

I Concentrate On You (cont.)

> **Peter Duchin**
>> Decca 7-34158 (45)
> **Nelson Eddy**
>> Everest 354 (LP): "Love Songs"
> **Herb Ellis**
>> Concord Jazz CCD-4077 (CD): "Soft & Mellow"
> **Michael Feinstein**
>> Elektra 60743-2 (CD), 60743-4 (CS): "Live at the Algonquin"
> **Michael Feinstein**
>> Teldec 75277-2 (CD): "Centennial Gala Concert"
> **George Feyer**
>> Vanguard VSD-93/94 (LP): "Essential Cole Porter"
> **George Feyer**
>> Vanguard OVC-6014 (CD): "George Feyer Plays Cole Porter"
> **Ella Fitzgerald (accompanied by Nelson Riddle and His Orchestra)**
>> Atlantic SD-1631 (LP): "Ella Loves Cole"
> **Ella Fitzgerald**
>> Verve 821989-2/821990-2 (CD), 823278-4 (CS), 823278-1 (LP): "Cole Porter Songbook" 1956
> **Ella Fitzgerald**
>> Pablo PACD-2310-814-2 (CD), 52310-814 (CS), 2310814 (LP): "Dream Dancing"
> **Bruce Forman**
>> Kamei KR-7004CD (CD), KR-7004C (CS): "Forman on the Job"
> **Gary Foster**
>> Concord Jazz CCD-4459 (CD), CJ-459-C: "Make Your Own Fun"
> **Judy Garland**
>> Pair PCD-2-1030 (CD), PDK-2-1030 (CS): "Golden Memories of Judy Garland"
> **Scott Hamilton**
>> Concord Jazz CCD-4538 (CD), CJ-538-C (CS): "Scott Hamilton With Strings"

I Concentrate On You (cont.)

Mary Cleere Haran
Columbia CK-52403 (CD), CT-52403 (CS): "There's
A Small Hotel (Live at the Algonquin)"
Mary Healy
Columbia DB-1927 (78) 1940
Steve Houben/Michel Benita
Ricercar RIC-121106 (CD): "Embraceable You
(American Songs)"
J.J. Johnson & Kai Winding
Impulse AS-1 (45)
J.J. Johnson & Kai Winding
MCA/Impulse MCAD-42012 (CD), MCAC-39109
(CS): "The Great Kai & J.J."
Sheila Jordan
Muse MCD-5390 (CD), MC-5390 (CS), MR-5390
(LP): "Lost & Found"
Dick Jurgens and His Orchestra
Vocalion 5442 (78) 1940
Richie Kamuca
Concord Jazz CJ-41 (LP): "Richie"
Stan Kenton
Creative World ST-1032 (LP): "Stan Kenton - At the
Tropicana"
Teddi King
Storyville SLP 302 (LP): "'Round Midnight" 1953
Douglas MacPhail
Sony AK-47838 (CD), AT-47838 (CS): "Cole Porter
in Hollywood - The MGM Years"
Susannah McCorckle
Concord Jazz CCD-4491 (CD), CJ-491-C (CS): "I'll
Take Romance"
Dave McKenna/Dick Johnson Reed Section
Concord Jazz CJ-146-C (CS): "Piano Mover"
Douglas McPhail
Classic International Filmusicals CIF 3002 (LP):
soundtrack from the film *Broadway Melody of 1940*
1939

I Concentrate On You (cont.)

Carmen McRae
GRP GRD-631 (CD), GRC-631 (CS): "Carmen
McRae Sings Great American Songwriters"
Adam Makowicz
Concord Jazz CCD-4541 (CD): "Live At Maybeck
Recital Hall, Vol. 24 (Adam Makowicz At Maybeck)"
Johnny Mathis
Columbia CGT-2 (CS): "Warm/Open Fire, Two
Guitars"
Johnny Mathis
Columbia CK-8056 (CD): "Open Fire, Two Guitars"
Paul Motian
Verve 834430-2 (CD), 834430-1 (LP): "Paul Motian
on Broadway, Vol. 1"
Joe Pass
Pablo PACD-2310-931-2 (CD), 52310-931 (CS),
2310-931 (LP): "Blues For Fred"
Houston Person
Muse MR-5136 (LP): "The Big Horn"
Oscar Peterson
Pablo 52625-711 (CS), 2625-711 (LP): "Oscar
Peterson in Russia"
Hal Schaefer
Discovery 74002-2 (CD): "Solo, Duo, Trio"
Artie Shaw
Columbia PCT-32031 (CS): "Best of the Big Bands"
George Shearing/Barry Tuckwell
Concord Jazz CCD-42010 (CD), CC-2010-C (CS):
"George Shearing & Barry Tuckwell Play the Music
of Cole Porter"
Frank Sinatra
Columbia CGK-40897 (CD), CGT-40897 (CS): "Hello
Young Lovers"
Frank Sinatra
Capitol C2-46573 (CD), C4-46573 (CS): "Sinatra's
Swingin' Session!!!! (& More)"

I Concentrate On You (cont.)

Frank Sinatra
Reprise 1021-2 (CD), M5-1021 (CS): "Francis Albert Sinatra/Antonio Carlos Jobin"
Frank Sinatra
Sony A2-20709 (CD), XPT-6 (CS), CC2-6 (LP): "Frank Sinatra Story in Music"
Frank Sinatra
Capitol C2-91344 (CD): "Frank Sinatra Gift Set"
Frank Sinatra
Reprise 26340-2 (CD), 26340-4 (CS): "The Reprise Collection"
Frank Sinatra
Capitol C2-96611 (CD), C4-96611 (CS): "Frank Sinatra Sings the Select Cole Porter"
Frank Sinatra
Capitol BBX2-99956 (CD), BBX4-99956 (CS): "Concepts"
Frank Sinatra
Pair PDK-2-1028 (CS): "Timeless"
Frank Sinatra
Columbia CXK-48673 (CD): "The Columbia Years (1943-1952) The Complete Recordings"
Jim Snidero
Red 123241-2 (CD): "While Your Here"
Cal Tjader
Fantasy OJC-5274 (CS), OJC-274 (LP): "Tjader Plays Mambo"
Mel Torme
Telarc CD-83328 (CD), CS-33328 (CS): "The Great American Songbook: Live At Michael's Pub"
Dionne Warwick
Arista ARCD-8573 (CD), AC-8573 (CS), AL-8573 (LP): "Dionne Warwick Sings Cole Porter"
Dinah Washington
Mercury 70694X45 (45) 1955
Sadao Watanabe
Inner City 6015 (LP): "I'm Old Fashioned"

I Concentrate On You (cont.)

> **Chuck Wayne**
> > Statiras C-7008 (CS), 7008 (LP): "Traveling"

I Happen To Be In Love
written for but unused in the film *Broadway Melody of 1940*

> **Eddy Duchin**
> > Columbia 35369 (78) 1940
> **Mary Healy**
> > Columbia DB-1927 (78) 1940

It Ain't Etiquette
introduced by Bert Lahr and Jean Moorhead in
Du Barry Was a Lady

> **Ronny Graham**
> > Painted Smiles PS-1340 (LP): "Cole Porter Revisited"

When Love Beckoned
introduced by Ethel Merman in *Du Barry Was a Lady*

> **Del Courtney and His Orchestra**
> > Vocalion 5291 (78) 1939
> **Gertrude Niesen/Leo Reisman and His Orchestra**
> > Victor 26434 (78) 1939
> **Artie Shaw and His Orchestra**
> > Bluebird B-10509 (78) 1939
> **Elaine Stritch**
> > Painted Smiles PS-1370 (LP): "Cole Porter Revisited,
> > Volume III"

Come On In
introduced by Ethel Merman in *Du Barry Was a Lady*

Ronny Graham/Kaye Ballard/Bibi Osterwald
Painted Smiles PS-1340 (LP): "Cole Porter Revisited"

But In The Morning, No
introduced by Bert Lahr and Ethel Merman in *Du Barry Was a Lady*

Eileen Brennan/John Hillerman/Burt Reynolds/Cybill Shepherd
RCA ABL2-0967 (LP)
Frances Day/Bud Flanagan
Decca F-7951 (78)
Ronny Graham/Kaye Ballard
Painted Smiles PS-1340 (LP): "Cole Porter Revisited"
George Shearing/Barry Tuckwell
Concord Jazz CCD-42010 (CD), CC-2010-C (CS): "George Shearing & Barry Tuckwell Play the Music of Cole Porter"
Cybill Shepherd
MCA MCAC-25173 (CS), MCA-25173 (LP): "Cybill Does It...To Cole Porter"
Julie Wilson/William Roy
DRG CDSL-5208 (CD), SLC-5208 (CS): "Cole Porter Songbook"

Do I Love You?
introduced by Ronald Graham and Ethel Merman in
Du Barry Was a Lady

Aztec Camera
Chrysalis F2-21799 (CD), F4-21799 (CS): "Red Hot & Blue (A Tribute to Cole Porter to Benefit Aids Research & Relief)"
Chick Bullock
Vocalion 5278 (78) 1939

Do I Love You? (cont.)

Frances Day
> Decca F-7867 (78)

Bill Evans
> Riverside 12RCD-018-2 (CD), R-018 (LP): "The
> Complete Riverside Recordings"

Ella Fitzgerald
> Verve 821989-2/821990-2 (CD), 823278-4 (CS),
> 823278-1 (LP): "Cole Porter Songbook" 1956

Judy Garland
> Pair PCD-2-1030 (CD), PDK-2-1030 (CS): "Golden
> Memories of Judy Garland"

Scott Hamilton
> Concord Jazz CJ-165-C (CS): "Apples & Oranges"

Woody Herman
> Decca 2971 (78) 1940

Don Ho
> Reprise GRE-705 (7" single)

Dick Jurgens and His Orchestra
> Vocalion 5288 (78) 1939

Gene Kelly
> Sony AK-47838 (CD), AT-47838 (CS): "Cole Porter
> in Hollywood - The MGM Years"

Kay Kyser and His Orchestra
> Columbia 35337 (78) 1939

Peggy Lee
> Hindsight HCD-220 (CD), HSC-220 (CS), HSR-220
> (LP): "The Uncollected Peggy Lee with the David
> Barbour & Billy May Bands (1948)"

Peggy Lee
> Chesky JD-84 (CD), JC-84 (CS): "Moments Like
> This"

Peggy Lee/George Shearing
> Blue Note B2-98454 (CD): "Beauty & The Beat!"

Ethel Merman
> Decca DX-153 (LP)

Tom Postilio
> Elba 4002-2 (CD), 4002-4 (CS): "What Matters Most"

Do I Love You? (cont.)

Leo Reisman and His Orchestra
Victor 26421 (78) 1939
The Ronettes
Collectables 3207 (7" single)
Artie Shaw
Bluebird B-10509 (78) 1939
Artie Shaw
RCA AXK2-5566 (CS): "Complete Artie Shaw, Vol. 3 (1939-1940)"
George Shearing/Barry Tuckwell
Concord Jazz CCD-42010 (CD), CC-2010-C (CS): "George Shearing & Barry Tuckwell Play the Music of Cole Porter"
Bobby Short
Atlantic SD 2-606 (LP): "Bobby Short Loves Cole Porter" 1971
Bobby Short
Atlantic 82062-2 (CD), 82062-4 (CS): "Bobby, Noel & Cole (Bobby Short Loves Cole Porter/Bobby Short Is Mad About Noel Coward)"
Ginny Simms
Motion Picture Tracks MPT 6 (LP): soundtrack from the film *Night and Day* 1945
Julie Wilson
DRG CDSL-5208 (CD), SLC-5208 (CS): "Cole Porter Songbook"

Give Him The Oo-La-La
introduced by Ethel Merman in *Du Barry Was a Lady*

Cybill Shepherd
MCAMCAC-25173 (CS), MCA-25173 (LP): "Cybill Does It...To Cole Porter"
Elmarie Wendel
Columbia COS-2810 and CBS Special Products AOS-2810 (LP) "The Decline and Fall of the Entire World as Seen Through the Eyes of Cole Porter" 1965

Well, Did You Evah!
introduced by Betty Grable and Charles Walters in
Du Barry Was a Lady

Bing Crosby/Frank Sinatra
Capitol F3507 (45) 1956
Bing Crosby/Frank Sinatra
Capitol SW 750 and SW-12235 (LP): soundtrack from
the film *High Society* 1956
Debbie Harry/Iggy Pop
Chrysalis F2-21799 (CD), F4-21799 (CS): "Red Hot
& Blue (A Tribute to Cole Porter to Benefit Aids
Research & Relief)"
Cole Porter and Bing Crosby
RCA A-22702 (CD from a telecast) 1956
Burt Reynolds/Madeline Kahn/Cybill Shepherd/Mildred Natwick
RCA ABL2-0967 (LP)

It Was Written In The Stars
introduced by Ronald Graham in *Du Barry Was a Lady*

Del Courtney and His Orchestra
Vocalion 5291 (78) 1939
Chick Bullock
Vocalion 5278 (78) 1939
Glenn Miller & His Orchestra
Bluebird BB-10498 (78)
Glenn Miller & His Orchestra
Bluebird 61015-2 (CD): "Complete Glenn Miller &
His Orchestra"
Leo Reisman and His Orchestra
Victor 26434 (78) 1939

Katie Went To Haiti
introduced by Ethel Merman in *Du Barry Was a Lady*

Tommy Dorsey/Jo Stafford/Dick Haymes
Sony AK-47838 (CD), AT-47838 (CS): "Cole Porter
in Hollywood - The MGM Years"
Dick Jurgens and His Orchestra
Vocalion 5288 (78) 1939
Mary Martin
Decca 23150 (78) 1940
Gertrude Niesen
Victor 26434 (78) 1939
Ray Noble and His Orchestra
Columbia 35335 (78) 1939
Leo Reisman and His Orchestra
Victor 26421 (78) 1939
Bobby Short
Atlantic SD 2-606 (LP): "Bobby Short Loves Cole
Porter" 1971
Bobby Short
Atlantic 82062-2 (CD), 82062-4 (CS): "Bobby, Noel
& Cole (Bobby Short Loves Cole Porter/Bobby Short
Is Mad About Noel Coward)"

Friendship
introduced by Bert Lahr and Ethel Merman in *Du Barry Was a Lady*

Lucille Ball/Red Skelton/Gene Kelly/Virginia O'Brian
Sony AK-47838 (CD), AT-47838 (CS): "Cole Porter
in Hollywood - The MGM Years"
Frank Chacksfield and His Orchestra
London SP-44185 (LP): "The Music of Cole Porter"
Ray Charles/Ricky Skaggs
Columbia CK-39415 (CD), PCT-39415 (CS):
"Friendship"
Tommy Dorsey
Bluebird B-10804 (78) 1940

Friendship (cont.)

Ralph Emery/Shotgun Red
RCA 9719-2-R (CD), 9719-4-R (CS): "Songs For Children"

Judy Garland and Johnny Mercer
MCA 907 (LP): "Judy Garland from the Decca Vaults" 1940

Judy Garland and Johnny Mercer
Decca MCAD-31345 (CD), MCAC-31345 (CS): "The Best of the Decca Years, Vol. 1 - Hits!"

Judy Garland
Pro-Arte CDD-547 (CD), PCD-547 (CS): "Over the Rainbow"

Dick Jurgens and His Orchestra
Vocalion 5383 (78) 1940

Madeline Kahn/Cybill Shepherd/Burt Reynolds/Duilio De Prete
RCA ABL2-0967 (LP)

Kay Kyser and His Orchestra
Columbia 35368 (78) 1940

Ernie Kucera
Czech SC8-28 (CS), 0086 (LP): "Still More Polkas & Waltzes"

Hal Linden/Eileen Rodgers/Barbara Land
Epic EK-15100 (CD), JST-15100 (CS): "Anything Goes"

Hal Linden/Eileen Rodgers/Mickey Deems
Epic FLM-13100 and FLS-15100 (LP)

Patti LuPone
RCA 7769-2-RC (CD), 7769-4-RC (CS): "Anything Goes"

Ethel Merman and Bert Lahr
JJA 19745 (LP)

Ethel Merman
Decca DX-153 (LP)

Bert Lahr
JJA 19765 (LP)

Visit Panama
introduced by Ethel Merman in *Panama Hattie*

> **Xavier Cugat and his Waldorf-Astoria Orchestra**
> Victor 27259 (78) 1940

My Mother Would Love You
introduced by Ethel Merman and James Dunn in *Panama Hattie*

> **Dick Jurgens and His Orchestra**
> Okeh 5871 (78) 1940
> **Freddie Martin and His Orchestra**
> Bluebird B-10921 (78) 1940
> **Ethel Merman**
> Decca 23200 (78) 1940
> **Ethel Merman**
> JJA 19732 (LP): "Cole Porter--1924-1944"
> **Ethel Merman**
> MCA MCAD-10521 (CD), MCAC-10521 (CS): "12
> Songs from 'Call Me Madam' (With Selections from
> 'Panama Hattie')"
> **Ruby Newman and His Orchestra**
> Decca 3489 (78) 1940
> **Leo Reisman and His Orchestra**
> Victor 27200 (78) 1940

I've Still Got My Health
introduced by Ethel Merman in *Panama Hattie*

> **Kaye Ballard**
> Painted Smiles PS-1340 (LP): "Cole Porter Revisited"
> **Ethel Merman**
> Decca 23200 (78) 1940

I've Still Got My Health (cont.)

> **Ethel Merman**
> JJA 19732 (LP): "Cole Porter--1924-1944"
> **Ethel Merman**
> MCA MCAD-10521 (CD), MCAC-10521 (CS): "12
> Songs from 'Call Me Madam' (With Selections from
> 'Panama Hattie')"
> **Bette Midler**
> Atlantic 81933-2 (CD), 81933-4 (CS), 81933-1 (LP):
> "Beaches"
> **Ann Sothern**
> Sony AK-47838 (CD), AT-47838 (CS): "Cole Porter
> in Hollywood - The MGM Years"

Fresh As A Daisy
introduced by Betty Hutton, Pat Harrington and Frank Hyers
in *Panama Hattie*

> **Kay Kyser and His Orchestra**
> Columbia 35790 (78) 1940
> **Glenn Miller & His Orchestra**
> Victor AXM2-5565 (LP): "Complete Glenn Miller,
> Vol. 5"
> **Glenn Miller & His Orchestra**
> Bluebird 61015-2 (CD): "Complete Glenn Miller &
> His Orchestra"
> **Leo Reisman and His Orchestra**
> Victor 26797 (78) 1940

Let's Be Buddies
introduced by Ethel Merman and Joan Carroll in *Panama Hattie*

> **Connie Boswell**
> Decca 3478
> **Les Brown**
> Okeh 5937 (78) 1940

Let's Be Buddies (cont.)

Al Cohn
Concord Jazz 194 (LP): "Overtones"
Doris Day/Les Brown
Columbia CK-46224 (CD), CT-46224 (CS): "Best of
the Big Bands"
Eddy Duchin
Columbia 35780 (78) 1940
Shep Fields and His Rippling Rhythm
Bluebird B-10923 (78) 1940
Ethel Merman
Decca 23199 (78) 1940
Ethel Merman
Decca 9-245 (45) 1951
Ethel Merman
MCA MCAD-10521 (CD), MCAC-10521 (CS): "12
Songs from 'Call Me Madam' (With Selections from
'Panama Hattie')"
Ethel Merman and Joan Carroll
Decca 23199 (78)
Ethel Merman and Joan Carroll
Decca 18187 (78)
Ethel Merman and Joan Carroll
JJA 19732 (LP): "Cole Porter--1944-1924"
Ruby Newman and His Orchestra
Decca 3489 (78) 1940
Leo Reisman and His Orchestra
Victor 26797 (78) 1940

Who Would Have Dreamed?
introduced by Janis Carter and Lipman Duckat (Larry Douglas)
in *Panama Hattie*

Dolores Gray
Painted Smiles PS-1370 (LP): "Cole Porter Revisited,
Volume III"

I'm Throwing a Ball Tonight
introduced by Ethel Merman in *Panama Hattie*

> **Mabel Mercer/Bobby Short**
> > Atlantic 2-604 (LP): "Town Hall"
>
> **Ethel Merman**
> > JJA 19745 (LP)
>
> **Bobby Short**
> > Atlantic SD2-604 (LP)
>
> **Bobby Short**
> > Painted Smiles PS-1340 (LP): "Cole Porter Revisited"

Make It Another Old-Fashioned, Please
introduced by Ethel Merman in *Panama Hattie*

> **Carmen Alvarez**
> > Columbia COS-2810 and CBS Special Products AOS-2810 (LP) "The Decline and Fall of the Entire World as Seen Through the Eyes of Cole Porter" 1965
>
> **Mitchell Ayres and His Fashions in Music**
> > Bluebird B-10940 (78) 1940
>
> **Xavier Cugat and his Waldorf-Astoria Orchestra**
> > Columbia 35789 (78) 1940
>
> **Julie London**
> > EMI E2-93455 (CD), E4-93455 (CS): "Julie London Sings Cole Porter"
>
> **Ethel Merman**
> > Decca 23199 (78) 1940
>
> **Ethel Merman**
> > Decca 18187 (78)
>
> **Ethel Merman**
> > JJA 19732 (LP): "Cole Porter--1924- 1944"
>
> **Ethel Merman**
> > JJA-19745 (LP) from a live performance
>
> **Ethel Merman**
> > MCA MCAD-10521 (CD), MCAC-10521 (CS): "12 Songs from 'Call Me Madam' (With Selections from 'Panama Hattie')"

Make It Another Old-Fashioned, Please (cont.)

> **Leo Reisman and His Orchestra**
>> Victor 27200 (78) 1940
> **Angela Richards**
>> RCA LRL2-5054 (LP): "Cole"
> **Sheila M. Sanders**
>> Philips PHM 222-169 and PHS 600-169 (LP)
> **Jack Six/Francis Thorne**
>> Composers Recordings 585 (CD): "Porter On My Mind"
> **Marti Stevens**
>> Teldec 75277-2 (CD): "Centennial Gala Concert"

Works From 1941

Boogie Barcarolle
danced by Fred Astaire and Rita Hayworth in the film
You'll Never Get Rich

> **The Orchestra**
>> Hollywood Soundstage 5001 (LP): soundtrack from
>> the film *You'll Never Get Rich* 1941

Dream Dancing
danced by Fred Astaire and Rita Hayworth in the film
You'll Never Get Rich

> **Fred Astaire**
>> Decca 18188 (78) 1941
>
> **Tony Bennett/Torrie Zito Orchestra**
>> DRG CDMRS-801 (CD), MRSC-801 (CS): "The
>> Special Magic of Tony Bennett"
>
> **Ruby Braff Trio**
>> Concord Jazz CCD-4381 (CD), CJ-381-C (CS): "Me,
>> Myself & I"
>
> **Barbara Carroll**
>> Discovery DS-847 (LP): "Barbara Carroll At The
>> Piano"
>
> **Ella Fitzgerald**
>> Pablo PACD-2310-814-2 (CD), 52310-814 (CS),
>> 2310814 (LP): "Dream Dancing"
>
> **Anita Gravine**
>> Progressive 7074 (LP): "Dream Dancing"
>
> **Dick Hyman**
>> Musicmasters 5060-2-C (CD), 5060-4-C (CS): "Cole
>> Porter: All Through the Night"
>
> **Dick Jurgens and His Orchestra**
>> Okeh 6389 (78) 1941

Dream Dancing (cont.)

Dave Liebman Trio
Red 123236-2 (CD): "Dave Liebman Trio Plays Cole
Porter"

Dave McKenna
Concord Jazz CCD-4410 (CD), CJ-410-C (CS): "Live
at Maybeck Recital Hall, Vol. 2 (Dave McKenna at
Maybeck"

Dave McKenna
Concord Jazz CCD-7001 (CD): "The Maybeck Recital
Hall Collection"

Andrea Marcovicci
Cabaret CACD-6001-2 (CD), CACS-6001-4 (CS):
"I'll Be Seeing You (Love Songs of World War II)"

The Orchestra
Hollywood Soundstage 5001 (LP): soundtrack from
the film *You'll Never Get Rich* 1941

Tony Pastor and His Orchestra
Bluebird B-11267 (78) 1941

Spike Robinson
Capri 74029-2 (CD): "Reminiscin"

Kenny Rogers
RCA PCD1-5335 (CD), AJK1-5335 (CS): "What
About Me"

Bud Shank Quartet
Contemporary 5C-14019 (CS), C-14019 (LP): "That
Old Feeling"

Bobby Short
Atlantic 81715-2 (CD), 81715-4 (CS): "50 By Bobby
Short"

Zoot Simms/Jimmy Rowles
Pablo PACD02310-831-2 (CD), 52310-831 (CS),
2310831 (LP): "Warm Tenor"

Jack Six/Francis Thorne
Composers Recordings 585 (CD): "Porter On My
Mind"

Billy Stritch
DRG CDSL-5215 (CD), SLC-5215 (CS): "Billy
Stritch"

Dream Dancing (cont.)

Mel Torme/George Shearing
Concord Jazz CJ-278-C (CS): "The Concord Sound, Vol. I"
Cedar Walton Trio/Jay Thomas
Discovery DSCD-956 (CD): "Easy Does It"
Julie Wilson
DRG CDSL-5208 (CD), SLC-5208 (CS): "Cole Porter Songbook"

Shootin' The Works For Uncle Sam
introduced by Fred Astaire in the film *You'll Never Get Rich*

Fred Astaire
Hollywood Soundstage 5001 (LP): soundtrack from the film *You'll Never Get Rich* 1941

Since I Kissed My Baby Goodbye
introduced by the Delta Rhythm Boys and danced by Fred Astaire in the film *You'll Never Get Rich*

David Allen
Painted Smiles PS-1340 (LP): "Cole Porter Revisited"
Fred Astaire with the Delta Rhythm Boys
Decca 18187 (78)
Fred Astaire with the Delta Rhythm Boys
JJA 19732 (LP): "Cole Porter--1924-1944"
The Delta Rhythm Boys
Hollywood Soundstage 5001 (LP): soundtrack from the film *You'll Never Get Rich* 1941

So Near And Yet So Far
introduced by Fred Astaire in the film *You'll Never Get Rich*

Fred Astaire
Hollywood Soundstage 5001 (LP): soundtrack from the film *You'll Never Get Rich* 1941
Fred Astaire
Decca 18187 (78) 1941
Ella Fitzgerald (accompanied by Nelson Riddle and His Orchestra)
Atlantic SD-1631 (LP): "Ella Loves Cole"
Ella Fitzgerald
Pablo PACD-2310-814-2 (CD), 52310-814 (CS), 2310814 (LP): "Dream Dancing"
Tony Pastor and His Orchestra
Bluebird B-11267 (78) 1941
Bobby Short
Atlantic SD 2-606 (LP): "Bobby Short Loves Cole Porter" 1971
Bobby Short
Atlantic 82062-2 (CD), 82062-4 (CS): "Bobby, Noel & Cole (Bobby Short Loves Cole Porter/Bobby Short Is Mad About Noel Coward)"
Bobby Short
Atlantic 81715-2 (CD), 81715-4 (CS): "50 By Bobby Short"

The Wedding Cake-Walk
introduced by Martha Tilton in the film *You'll Never Get Rich*

Fred Astaire and the Delta Rhythm Boys
Decca 18188 (78) 1941
Martha Tilton
Hollywood Soundstage 5001 (LP): soundtrack from the film *You'll Never Get Rich* 1941
Martha Tilton
Decca 4029
Martha Tilton
JJA 19732 (LP): "Cole Porter--1924-1944"

A-Stairable Rag (instrumental)
written for but unused in the film *You'll Never Get Rich*

Jazz Group
Hollywood Soundstage 5001 (LP): soundtrack from
the film *You'll Never Get Rich* 1941

A Lady Needs A Rest
introduced by Eve Arden, Vivian Vance and Edith Meiser in
Let's Face It

Lynn Redgrave
Painted Smiles PS-1371 (LP): "Cole Porter Revisited,
Volume IV"

Let's Face It
introduced by Tommy Gleason and the Royal Guards in *Let's Face It*

Chorus
JJA-119767 (LP)

Farming
introduced by Danny Kaye, Benny Baker, Jack Williams,
Sunnie O'Dea and Nanette Fabray in *Let's Face It*

Kaye Ballard, Harold Lang, Carmen Alvarez, William Hickey and Elmarie Wendel
Columbia COS-2810 and CBS Special Products AOS-
2810 (LP) "The Decline and Fall of the Entire World
as Seen Through the Eyes of Cole Porter" 1965
Hildegarde
Decca 23244 (78) 1941
Danny Kaye
Columbia 36583 (78)
Danny Kaye
Columbia KS-31456 (LP)

Farming (cont.)

Mary Jane Walsh
Liberty Music Shop L-343 (78) 1941
William Scotti and His Cotillion Room Orchestra
Liberty Music Shop L-345 (78)
Mary Jane Walsh
JJA 19732 (LP): "Cole Porter--1924-1944"

Ev'rything I Love
introduced by Danny Kaye and Mary Jane Walsh in *Let's Face It*

Warren Bernhardt Trio
Digital Music Products CD-478 (CD), CS-478 (CS):
"Ain't Life Grand"
Alan Broadbent Trio
Discovery DSCD-929 (CD), DS-929 (LP):
"Everything I Love"
Bob Brookmeyer Small Band
Gryphon 2-785 (LP): "Bob Brookmeyer Small Band
(Recorded 'Live' at Sandy's Jazz Revival, July 28-29,
1978)"
Ray Brown Trio/Ralph Moore
Concord Jazz CCD-4477 (CD), CJ-477-C (CS):
"Moore Makes 4"
Concord Jazz All Stars
Concord Jazz CJ-182 (LP): "Concord Jazz All Stars at
the Northsea Jazz Festival, Vol. 1"
Paul Desmond
CBS Associated ZK-40806 (CD), FZT-40806 (CS):
"Pure Desmond"
Dial & Oatts
Digital Music Products CD-495 (CD): "Dial & Oatts
Play Cole Porter"
Jimmy Dorsey and His Orchestra
Decca 4123 (78) 1941
Peter Erskine/John Taylor/Palle Danielsson
ECM 51753-2 (CD): "You Never Know"

Ev'rything I Love (cont.)

Bill Evans
>   Riverside 12RCD-018-2 (CD), R-018 (LP): "The
>   Complete Riverside Recordings"

Bill Evans Trio
>   Riverside OJCCD-369-2 (CD), OJC-5369 (CS), OJC-
>   369 (LP): "How My Heart Sings!"

Tommy Flanagan
>   Progressive 7059 (LP): "The Magnificent Tommy
>   Flanagan"

Benny Goodman
>   Okeh 6516 (78) 1941

Benny Goodman/Peggy Lee
>   Columbia CK-53422 (CD), CT-53422 (CS): "Best of
>   the Big Bands, Vol. 2"

Benny Goodman/Peggy Lee
>   Columbia CK-53422 (CD), CT-53422 (CS): "Benny
>   Goodman Featuring Peggy Lee"

Tom Harrell
>   Contemporary CCD-14063-2 (CD): "Visions"

John Hart
>   Somethin' Else B2-95206 (CD): "Trust"

Hildegarde
>   Decca 23242 (78) 1941

Dick Hyman
>   Musicmasters 5060-2-C (CD), 5060-4-C (CS): "Cole
>   Porter: All Through the Night"

Ina Ray Hutton and Her Melodears
>   Elite 5008 (78) 1941

Dick Johnson
>   Concord Jazz CCD-4107 (CD): "Dick Johnson Plays
>   Alto Sax & Flute & Soprano Sax & Clarinet"

Vic Juris
>   Muse MR-5265 (LP): "Bleecker Street"

Swing and Sway with Sammy Kaye
>   Victor 27711 (78) 1941

Dave McMurdo
>   The Jazz Alliance TJA-10001 (CD): "The Dave
>   McMurdo Jazz Orchestra"

Ev'rything I Love (cont.)

Glenn Miller
RCA AXK2-5570 (CS): "Complete Glenn Miller, Vol.
7"

Glenn Miller/Ray Eberle
Bluebird 0693-2-RB (CD), CPK2-0693 (CS): "A
Legendary Performer"

Glenn Miller & His Orchestra
Bluebird 61015-2 (CD): "Complete Glenn Miller &
His Orchestra"

Red Norvo
Musicmasters 65090-2 (CD), 65090-4 (CS): "Red
Norvo Orchestra Live From the Blue Gardens"

Ken Peplowski Quintet
Concord Jazz CCD-4376 (CD), CJ-376-C (CS):
"Sonny Side"

Renee Rosnes
Blue Note B2-93561 (CD): "Renee Rosnes" 1990

William Scotti and His Cotillion Room Orchestra
Liberty Music Shop L-345 (78)

George Shearing/Barry Tuckwell
Concord Jazz CCD-42010 (CD), CC-2010-C (CS):
"George Shearing & Barry Tuckwell Play the Music
of Cole Porter"

Claude Thornhill and His Orchestra
Columbia 36456 (78) 1941

Mary Jane Walsh
Liberty Music Shop L-344 (78) 1941

Mary Jane Walsh
JJA 19732 (LP): "Cole Porter--1924-1944"

Weslia Whitfield
Cabaret CACD-5007-2 (CD), CACS-5007-4 (CS):
"Beautiful Love"

James Williams
Concord Jazz CJ-104 (LP): "Everything I Love"

Phil Woods Quartet
Clean Cuts CCD-702 (CD), CS-702 (CS), 702 (LP):
"Phil Woods Quartet, Live - Vol. 1"

Ace In The Hole
introduced by Mary Jane Walsh, Sunnie O'Dea and
Nanette Fabray in *Let's Face It*

Dukes of Dixieland
> MCA MCAC-268 (CS): "Dixieland's Greatest Hits"

George Feyer
> Vanguard VSD-93/94 (LP): "Essential Cole Porter"

George Feyer
> Vanguard OVC-6014 (CD): "George Feyer Plays Cole
> Porter"

Ella Fitzgerald
> Verve 821989-2/821990-2 (CD), 823278-4 (CS),
> 823278-1 (LP): "Cole Porter Songbook" 1956

Hildegarde
> Decca 23242 (78) 1941

Mabel Mercer
> Atlantic 81264-4 and Rhino R4-81264 (CS): "Mabel
> Mercer Sings Cole Porter (with Cy Walter & Stan
> Freeman)"

Mom & Dads
> G.N.P. Crescendo GNP5-2117 (CS), GNPS-2117
> (LP): "Gratefully Yours"

Jimmy Roselli
> M&R 1007 (LP & CS): "Saloon Songs, Vol. I"

William Scotti and His Cotillion Room Orchestra
> Liberty Music Shop L-345 (78)

Roberta Sherwood
> MCA 60105 (LP)

Bobby Short
> Atlantic 1285 (LP)

George Strait
> MCA 42266 (CD & CS & LP): "Beyond the Blue
> Neon"

Dave Von Ronk
> Prestige 7800 (LP): "In The Tradition"

Ace In The Hole (cont.)

> **Jimmy Roselli**
> > M&R CA-1007 (CS), 1007 (LP): "Saloon Songs, Vol. 1"
> **Mary Jane Walsh**
> > Liberty Music Shop L-344 (78) 1941
> **Mary Jane Walsh**
> > JJA 19732 (LP): "Cole Porter--1924-1944"

You Irritate Me So
introduced by Nanette Fabray and Jack Williams in
Let's Face It

> **Louise Carlyle/Bob Shaver**
> > Walden 301 (LP)
> **Hildegarde**
> > Decca 23243 (78) 1941
> **William Scotti and His Cotillion Room Orchestra**
> > Liberty Music Shop L-345 (78)

I've Got Some Unfinished Business With You
Mary Jane Walsh, Nanette Fabray, Sunnie O'Dea,
Helen Devlin, Betty Moran, Joseph Macaulay and
Fred Irving Lewis in *Let's Face It*

> **Sheila M. Saunders**
> > Philips PHM 200-169 and PHS 600-169 (LP)

Let's Talk About Love
introduced by Danny Kaye and Eve Arden in *Let's Face It*

> **Dolores Gray**
> > Painted Smiles PS-1371 (LP): "Cole Porter Revisited, Volume IV"

Let's Not Talk About Love
introduced by Danny Kaye and Eve Arden in *Let's Face It*

> **Betty Hutton**
> > JJA-19767 (LP)
> **Danny Kaye**
> > Columbia 36583 (78)
> **Danny Kaye**
> > Columbia KS-31456 (LP)
> **Andrea Marcovicci**
> > DRG 91405 (CD & CS): "Marcovicci Sings Movies"

A Little Rumba Numba
introduced by Tommy Gleason, Marguerite Benton, Mary Parker and Billy Daniel in *Let's Face It*

> **Hildegarde**
> > Decca 23243 (78) 1941

I Hate You, Darling
introduced by Vivian Vance, James Todd, Mary Jane Walsh and Danny Kaye in *Let's Face It*

> **Hildegarde**
> > Decca 23244 (78) 1941
> **William Scotti and His Cotillion Room Orchestra**
> > Liberty Music Shop L-345 (78)
> **Bobby Short**
> > Atlantic SD 2-606 (LP): "Bobby Short Loves Cole Porter" 1971
> **Bobby Short**
> > Atlantic 82062-2 (CD), 82062-4 (CS): "Bobby, Noel & Cole (Bobby Short Loves Cole Porter/Bobby Short Is Mad About Noel Coward)"
> **Claude Thornhill and His Orchestra**
> > Columbia 36456 (78) 1941
> **Mary Jane Walsh**
> > Liberty Music Shop L-343 (78) 1941

I Hate You, Darling (cont.)

Mary Jane Walsh
JJA 19732 (LP): "Cole Porter--1924-1944"

What Are Little Husbands Made Of?
written for but unused in *Let's Face It*

Lynn Redgrave
Painted Smiles PS-1371 (LP): "Cole Porter Revisited, Volume IV"

Make A Date With A Great Psychoanalyst
written for but unused in *Let's Face It*

Helen Gallagher
Painted Smiles PS-1371 (LP): "Cole Porter Revisited, Volume IV"

Pets
written for but unused in *Let's Face It*

Alice Playten
Painted Smiles PS-1358 (LP): "Unpublished Cole Porter"

Get Yourself a Girl
introduced by Tommy Gleason and The Royal Guards in *Let's Face It*

Edward Earle
Painted Smiles PS-1358 (LP): "Unpublished Cole Porter"

You'd Be So Nice To Come Home To
introduced by Janet Blair and Don Ameche in the film
Something to Shout About

Cannonball Adderly
> Verve 842930-2 (CD), 842930-4 (CS): "Compact Jazz - Cannonball Adderly"

Ambrose Orchestra
> G.N.P. Crescendo GNP-9004 (LP): "Ambrose Tribute to Cole Porter"

Gene Ammons
> Prestige PCD-24079-2 (CD), P-24079 (LP): "The Gene Ammons Story: Gentle Jug"

Dorothy Ashby
> Prestige P-7639 (LP): "Dorothy Ashby (Plays For Beautiful People)"

Dorothy Ashby
> Prestige PCD-24120-2 (CD): "In A Minor Groove"

Chet Baker
> Riverside OJCCD-087-2 (CD), OJC-5087 (CS), OJC-087 (LP): "Chet"

Tony Bennett/Torrie Zito Orchestra
> DRG CDMRS-801 (CD), MRSC-801 (CS): "The Special Magic of Tony Bennett"

William Bolcom/Joan Morris
> Omega Record Classics OCD-3002 (CD): "Night & Day"

Bob Brookmeyer Small Band
> Gryphon 2-785 (LP): "Bob Brookmeyer Small Band (Recorded 'Live' at Sandy's Jazz Revival, July 28-29, 1978)"

Tony Campise
> Heart Music 004-CD (CD), 004-CT (CS): "Once in a Blue Moon"

Frank Chacksfield and His Orchestra
> London SP-44185 (LP): "The Music of Cole Porter"

You'd Be So Nice To Come Home To (cont.)

Paul Chambers
> Blue Note B2-46533 (CD): "Bass On Top"

Paul Chambers
> Blue Note B2-95591 (CD), B4-95591 (CS): "Blue Porter"

Rosemary Clooney
> Concord Jazz CCD-4444 (CD), CJ-444-C (CS): "For the Duration"

Al Cohn/Zoot Sims
> Verve 840031-2 (CD), 840031-4 (CS): "Jazz-Club Tenor Sax"

Al Cohn/Zoot Sims
> Verve 314-515392-2 (CD), 314-515392-4 (CS): "Jazz 'Round Midnight - The George Gershwin & Cole Porter Songbook"

Perry Como
> Pilz America 449344-2 (CD): "Take Me In Your Arms"

Connie Crothers
> New Artists NA-1002CD (CD), NA-1002 (LP): "Concert at Cooper Union"

Ray Conniff Singers
> Columbia CK-8442 (CD): "Somebody Loves Me"

Bobby Darin
> Bainbridge BTC-6220 (CS), 6220 (LP): "Darin at the Copa"

Paul Desmond
> CBS ZK-45484 (CD), ZT-45484 (CS): "The Best of Paul Desmond"

Ray Elis and Johnny Douglas conducting the Ray Elis Strings
> RCA CAS-2522 (LP): "The Great Hits of Cole Porter"

Tal Farlow
> Concord Jazz CJ-204 (LP): "Cookin' on All Burners"

Frederick Fennell/Eastman-Rochester Pops Orchestra
> Mercury 43427-2 (CD): "Fennell Conducts Porter & Gershwin"

You'd Be So Nice To Come Home To (cont.)

Ella Fitzgerald
Verve 833294-2 (CD), 8332994-4 (CS): "Compact Jazz - Ella Fitzgerald Live"
Liz Gorrill/Charley Krachy
New Artists NA-1007CD (CD): "A Jazz Duet"
Liz Gorrill
New Artists NA-1010CD (CD): "Dreamflight"
Gigi Gryce/Duke Jordan/Hall Overton
Savoy SJL-2231 (LP): "Signals"
Jim Hall
CBS Associated ZK-40807 (CD), FZT-40807 (CS): "Concierto"
Scott Hamilton Quartet
Progressive 7026 (LP): "Grand Appearance"
Coleman Hawkins
Verve 823120-2 (CD): "Coleman Hawkins Encounters Ben Webster"
Coleman Hawkins/Ben Webster
Verve 833296-2 (CD), 833296-4 (CS): "Compact Jazz - Coleman Hawkins & Ben Webster"
Robert Hicks
Velocity VCD-82863 (CD): "New Standards"
Dick Hyman
Musicmasters 5060-2-C (CD), 5060-4-C (CS): "Cole Porter: All Through the Night"
Milt Jackson
Riverside OJCCD-366-2 (CD), OJC-5366 (CS), OJC-366 (LP): "Big Bags"
Sheila Jordan/Harold Danko/Cameron Brown/Lou Grassi
Jazz JR-3 (LP): "Lennie Tristano Memorial Concert"
Irving Joseph
Bainbridge BTC-1014 (CS), 1014 (LP): "Heritage of Broadway - Music of Cole Porter"
Dick Jurgens & His Orchestra
Columbia C2K-48516 (CD), C2T-48516 (CS): "Words & Music of World War II"
Wayne King
Decca ED-2662 (45)

You'd Be So Nice To Come Home To (cont.)

Lee Konitz
Prestige P-7827 (LP): "Ezzz-thetic"
Barbara Lea
Prestige OJCCD-1742-2 (CD): "Lea in Love"
Julie London
EMI E2-93455 (CD), E4-93455 (CS): "Julie London
Sings Cole Porter"
Julie London
Rhino R2-70737 (CD), R4-70737 (CS): "Time For
Love/The Best of Julie London"
Fraser MacPherson
Concord Jazz CJ-269 (LP): "Jazz Prose"
Adam Makowicz
Concord Jazz CCD-4541 (CD): "Live At Maybeck
Recital Hall, Vol. 24 (Adam Makowicz At Maybeck)"
Helen Merrill
Mercury 826340-2 (CD): "Complete Helen Merrill on
Mercury (1954-1958)"
Helen Merrill
Verve 314-515392-2 (CD), 314-515392-4 (CS): "Jazz
'Round Midnight - The George Gershwin & Cole
Porter Songbook"
Helen Merrill/Clifford Brown
Emarcy 814643-2 (CD): "Helen Merrill With Clifford
Brown"
Helen Merrill
Verve 847202-2 (CD), 847202-4 (CS): "Night & Day:
The Cole Porter Songbook"
Anita O'Day
Emily 13081 (LP): "Angel Eyes"
Anita O'Day
Emily 9578 (LP): "Anita O'Day Live in Tokyo, 1975"
Anita O'Day
Disques Swing 8435 (CD & CS): "Anita O'Day at
Vine St. Live"
Anita O'Day/Billy May
Verve 849266-2 (CD), 849266-4 (CS): "Anita O'Day
Swings Cole Porter"

You'd Be So Nice To Come Home To (cont.)

Hall Overton/Duke Jordan
Savoy Jazz SV-0130 (CD): "Do It Yourself Jazz, Vol. 1 & 2"
Art Pepper
Contemporary OJCCD-338-2 (CD), OJC-5338 (CS), OJC-338 (LP): "Art Pepper Meets the Rhythm Section"
Bud Powell
Roulette B2-93902 (CD): "Bud Powell Trio Plays"
Andre Previn's Jazz Trio
Contemporary OJCCD-691-2 (CD): "King Size!"
Judy Roberts Band
Pausa PC-7147 (CS), 7147 (LP): "Trio"
Jimmy Roselli
M & R CA-1027 (CS), 1027 (LP): "More I See You"
George Shearing/Mel Torme
Concord Jazz CCD-4190 (CD), CJ-190-C (CS): "An Evening with George Shearing & Mel Torme"
Dinah Shore
Victor 20-1519 (78) 1942
Frank Sinatra
Capitol EAP-1-803 (45) 1956
Frank Sinatra
Capitol C2-94518 (CD), C4-94518 (CS): "A Swingin' Affair!"
Frank Sinatra
Capitol C2-96611 (CD), C4-96611 (CS): "Frank Sinatra Sings the Select Cole Porter"
Frank Sinatra
Capitol BBX2-99956 (CD), BBX4-99956 (CS): "Concepts"
Frank Sinatra
Pair PDK-2-1028 (CS): "Timeless"
Jo Stafford
Corinthian 108-CD (CD), COR-108 (LP): "Jo Plus Jazz"
Cecil Taylor
Blue Note B2-84462 (CD): "Jazz Advance"

You'd Be So Nice To Come Home To (cont.)

McCoy Tyner
GRP GRD-106 (CD): "Today & Tomorrow"
Sarah Vaughan
Mercury 826333-2 (CD): "Complete Sarah Vaughan
on Mercury, Vol. 3: Great Show On Stage (1954-
1956)"
Warren Vache
Concord Jazz CCD-4323 (CD), CJ-323-C (CS): "Easy
Going"
Dionne Warwick
Arista ARCD-8573 (CD), AC-8573 (CS), AL-8573
(LP): "Dionne Warwick Sings Cole Porter"
Ben Webster/Coleman Hawkins
Verve 833549-4 (CS), 833549-1 (LP): "Tenor Giants"
Carla White
Milestone 5M-9147 (CS), M-9147 (LP): "Orient
Express"
James Williams Trio
Concord Jazz CJ-192 (LP): "Arioso Touch"
Julie Wilson
DRG CDSL-5208 (CD), SLC-5208 (CS): "Cole Porter
Songbook"
Nancy Wilson
Capitol C2-96361 (CD), C4-96361 (CS): "Anything
Goes - Capitol Sings Cole Porter"
**Phil Woods/Hall Overton Quartet/George Wallington
Quintet**
Savoy ZDS-1179 (CD), SJK-1179 (CS), SJL-1179
(LP): "Bird Calls, Vol. 1"

It Might Have Been
written for but unused in the film *Something to Shout About*

Hal McIntyre and His Orchestra
Victor 20-1599 (78) 1942

Works From 1943

See That You're Born In Texas
introduced by the ensemble in the film *Something For The Boys*

Chorus
Soundstage 2305 (LP)

Something For The Boys
introduced by Ethel Merman in the film *Something For The Boys*

Chorus
JJA 19732 (LP): "Cole Porter--1924-1944"
Evelyn Dall
Decca F-8429 (78)
Betty Garrett
Decca 23363 (78)
Paula Lawrence
Decca 23363 (78)
Paula Lawrence
JJA 19732 (LP): "Cole Porter--1924-1944"
Ethel Merman and Bill Johnson
JJA 19732 (LP): "Cole Porter--1924-1944"
Ethel Merman
A&M SP-4775 (LP)
Ethel Merman
JJA 19732 (LP): "Cole Porter--1924-1944"

Could It Be You?
introduced by Bill Johnson in the film *Something For The Boys*

Bill Johnson
JJA 19732 (LP): "Cole Porter--1924-1944"
Ethel Merman and Bill Johnson
JJA 19732 (LP): "Cole Porter--1924-1944"

Could It Be You? (cont.)

Orchestra
Soundstage 2305 (LP)
Jack Saunders Orchestra
Everest LPBR-5011 and SD-1011 (LP)

Hey, Good Lookin'
introduced by Ethel Merman and Bill Johnson in the film
Something For The Boys

Evelyn Dall
Decca F-8429
Ethel Merman and Betty Garrett
JJA 19732 (LP): "Cole Porter--1924-1944"
Ethel Merman/Bill Johnson
JJA 19732 (LP): "Cole Porter--1924-1944"

He's A Right Guy
introduced by Ethel Merman in the film *Something For The Boys*

Ethel Merman
Decca DX-153 (LP)
Ethel Merman
JJA 19732 (LP): "Cole Porter--1924-1944"
Ethel Merman and Bill Johnson
JJA 19732 (LP): "Cole Porter--1924-1944"

The Leader Of A Big-Time Band
introduced by Ethel Merman in the film *Something For The Boys*

Kaye Ballard, Carmen Alvarez and Elmarie Wendel
Columbia COS-2810 and CBS Special Products AOS-2810 (LP) "The Decline and Fall of the Entire World as Seen Through the Eyes of Cole Porter" 1965

The Leader Of A Big-Time Band (cont.)

Julia McKenzie/Elizabeth Power/Angela Richards/Rod McLennan/Kenneth Nelson
RCA LRL2-5054 (LP): "Cole"

I'm In Love With A Soldier Boy
introduced by Betty Garret in the film *Something For The Boys*

Betty Garrett
Take Home Tunes THT-777 (LP)

By The Mississinewah
introduced by Ethel Merman and Paula Laurence in the film
Something For The Boys

Kaye Ballard/Bibi Osterwald
Painted Smiles PS-1340 (LP): "Cole Porter Revisited"
Paula Lawrence and Betty Garrett
Decca 23363 (78)
Paula Lawrence and Betty Garrett
JJA 19732 (LP): "Cole Porter--1924-1944"

My Broth of a Boy
written for but unused in the unproduced film
Mississippi Belle

Mimi Bessette
Music For Little People MLP-244 (CS): "Lullabies of Broadway"

Sing To Me Guitar
introduced by Corinna Mura in *Mexican Hayride*

> **Corinna Mura**
>> Decca DL-5232 (LP): original cast of the Broadway
>> show *Mexican Hayride* 1944
>
> **Corinna Mura**
>> Decca 23336 (78)
>
> **Corinna Mura**
>> JJA 19745 (LP): "Cole Porter (Music and Lyrics)"

I Love You
introduced by Wilbur Evans in *Mexican Hayride*

> **Joe Albany/Warne Marsh**
>> Riverside OJCCD-1749-2 (CD), OJC-1749 (LP):
>> "Right Combination"
>
> **Chet Baker**
>> Sony JCL-549 (LP): "Chet Baker & Strings"
>
> **Chet Baker**
>> Columbia CK-46174 (CD), CT-46174 (CS): "Chet
>> Baker: With Strings"
>
> **Robert Russell Bennett Orchestra**
>> AE1-2106 (LP)
>
> **Art Blakey & The Jazz Messengers**
>> Concord Jazz CCD-4307 (CD), CJ-307-C (CS): "Live
>> at Kimball's"
>
> **The Brass Connection**
>> The Jazz Alliance TJA-10014 (CD): "Standards"
>
> **Ray Brown/Milt Jackson**
>> Pablo 52310-867 (CS), 2310-867 (LP): "Big Mouth"
>
> **Ray Brown/Monty Alexander/Herb Ellis**
>> Concord Jazz CCD-4394 (CD), CJ-394-C (CS):
>> "Triple Treat III"

I Love You (cont.)

Tony Campise
> Heart Music 021-CD (CD), 021-CT (CS): "First Takes"

Eddie Cano
> RCA International 3459-2-RL (CD): "Cole Porter, Duke Ellington & Me"

Louise Carlyle
> Walden 301 (LP)

Al Cohn
> Concord Jazz CJ-194 (LP): "Overtones"

John Coltrane
> Prestige OJCCD-131-2 (CD), OJC-5131 (CS), OJC-131 (LP): "Lush Life"

John Coltrane
> Prestige 5P-24014 (CS), P-24014 (LP): "More Lasting Than Bronze"

John Coltrane
> Prestige P-7426 (LP): "Plays For Lovers"

John Coltrane
> Prestige 16PCD-4405-2 (CD): "John Coltrane - The Prestige Recordings"

Ray Conniff & His Orchestra
> Columbia CK-8037 (CD): "'S Marvelous"

Bing Crosby
> MCA MCAD4-10887 (CD), MCAC4-10887 (CS): "Bing! His Legendary Years, 1931 to 1957"

Dial & Oatts
> Digital Music Products CD-495 (CD): "Dial & Oatts Play Cole Porter"

Kenny Dorham Quintet
> Debut OJCCD-113-2 (CD), OJC-113 (LP): "Kenny Dorham Quintet"

Don Ellis
> Candid CCD-79032 (CD): "Out of Nowhere"

Herb Ellis
> Concord Jazz CJ-116-C (CS): "Herb Ellis at Montreux"

I Love You (cont.)

Bill Evans
Milestone M-47063 (LP): "Conception"
Bill Evans
Fantasy OJCCD-644-2 (CD), OJC-5644 (CS), OJC-644 (LP): "Montreux III"
Bill Evans
Riverside OJCCD-025-2 (CD), OJC-5025 (CS), OJC-025 (LP): "New Jazz Conceptions"
Wilbur Evans
Decca DL-5232 (LP): original cast of the Broadway show *Mexican Hayride* 1944
Wilbur Evans
Decca 23337 (78)
Wilbur Evans
JJA 19745 (LP): "Cole Porter (Music and Lyrics)"
Art Farmer
Blue Note B2-84459 (CD): "Modern Art" 1991
George Feyer
Vanguard VSD-93/94 (LP): "Essential Cole Porter"
George Feyer
Vanguard OVC-6014 (CD): "George Feyer Plays Cole Porter"
Clare Fischer/Gary Foster
Starbright DS-885MC (CS), DS-885 (LP): "Starbright"
Stan Getz
Emarcy 838770-2 (CD), 838770-4 (CS): "Serenity"
Coleman Hawkins
Bluebird 5717-2-RB (CD), 5658-4-RB (CS): "Body & Soul"
Elmo Hope
Inner City 1037 (LP): "Last Sessions"
Elmo Hope
Specialty OJCCD-1765-2 (CD): "Final Sessions, Vol. 1"
J.J. Johnson
Concord Jazz CCD-4523 (CD): "Vivian"

I Love You (cont.)

Barney Kessel
Concord Jazz CCD-6033 (CD): "Soaring"
Barney Kessel
Contemporary OJCCD-746-2 (CD): "Music to Listen to Barney Kessel By"
L.A. 4
Concord Jazz CJ-100-C (CS): "The L.A. 4 Live at Montreux - Summer 1979"
Dave Liebman Trio
Red 123236-2 (CD): "Dave Liebman Trio Plays Cole Porter"
Guy Lombardo
Decca ED-1071 (45)
Guy Lombardo/Kenny Gardner
Hindsight HCD-187 (CD), HSC-187 (CS), HSR-187 (LP): "The Uncollected Guy Lombardo & His Royal Canadians (1950)"
Julie London
Liberty 2-3006 (45)
Julie London
EMI E2-93455 (CD), E4-93455 (CS): "Julie London Sings Cole Porter"
Julie London
EMI Records Group North America E2-99804 (CD), E4-99804 (CS): "Julie Is Her Name, Vol. 1 & 2"
Rob McConnell & The Boss Brass
Sea Breeze CD-SB-106 (CD), D-SB-9106 (Digital Audio Tape) "Live in Digital"
Jackie McLean
Blue Note B2-95591 (CD), B4-95591 (CS): "Blue Porter"
Marian McPartland
Concord Jazz CJ-118 (LP): "At The Festival"
Marian McPartland/Bill Evans
The Jazz Alliance TJA-12004 (CD): "Marian McPartland's Piano Jazz With Guest Bill Evans"
Herbie Mann/Bill Evans Trio
Atlantic 90141-4 (CS): "Nirvana (Jazzlore)"

I Love You (cont.)

Frank Marocco
  Discovery DS-979 (LP): "Jazz Accordion"
Warne Marsh/Eddie Gomez/Peter Scattaretico
  Jazz JR-3 (LP): "Lennie Tristano Memorial Concert"
Tony Mottola
  Project 3 Records PRC-5010 (CS), 5010 (LP): "A
  Latin Love-In"
Jessye Norman/Boston Pops Orchestra
  Philips 412625-2 (CD), 412625-4 (CS): "With a Song
  in My Heart"
Anita O'Day
  Verve 847202-2 (CD), 847202-4 (CS): "Night & Day:
  The Cole Porter Songbook"
Anita O'Day/Billy May
  Verve 849266-2 (CD), 849266-4 (CS): "Anita O'Day
  Swings Cole Porter"
101 Strings Orchestra
  Alshire International ALCD-30 (CD), ALSC-5007
  (CS): "Cole Porter"
101 Strings Orchestra
  Alshire International ALCD-48 (CD), ADBL-404
  (CS): "The Best of the Great American Composers,
  Vol. IV"
Art Pepper
  Contemporary OJCCD-387-2 (CD), OJC-5387 (CS),
  OJC-387 (LP): "Intensity"
Art Pepper
  Galaxy 16GCD-1016-2 (CD): "The Complete Galaxy
  Recordings"
Oscar Peterson
  Verve SLV-8476 (45)
Oscar Peterson
  Verve 833772-4 (CS), 833772-1 (LP): "Something
  Warm"
Ruth Price
  Contemporary OJCCD-1770-2 (CD), OJC-1770 (LP):
  "Ruth Price with Shelly Manne & His Men at the
  Manne-Hole"

I Love You (cont.)

John Raitt
> Capitol C2-97616 (CD), C4-97616 (CS): "Highlights of Broadway/Under Open Skies"

Django Reinhardt
> G.N.P. Crescendo GNP5-9038 (CS), GNPS-9038 (LP): "Immortal Django Reinhardt"

Saint Louis Brass
> Summit DCD-140 (CD), DCC-140 (CS): "Pops"

Jack Saunders Orchestra
> Everest LPBR-5011 and SD-1011 (LP)

Misha Segal
> Musicmasters 65068-2 (CD), 65068-4 (CS): "Zambooka"

Jim Self
> Concord Jazz CCD-4430 (CD), CJ-430-C (CS): "Tricky Lix"

George Shearing
> Pair PCD-2-1226 (CD), PDK-2-1226 (CS): "Mellow Moods"

Jack Sheldon Quartet
> Concord Jazz CJ-229 (LP): "Stand By For..."

Bobby Shew/Chuck Findley
> Delos International 4003 (CD): "Trumpets No End"

Frank Sinatra
> Capitol F2638 (45) 1953

Frank Sinatra
> Reprise 27021-2 (CD), 27021-4 (CS), FS-1005 (LP): "Sinatra & Swingin' Brass"

Jo Stafford
> Capitol C2-91638 (CD): "Capitol Collectors Series"

Jo Stafford
> Pair PCD-2-1225 (CD), PDK-2-1225 (CS): "You Belong To Me"

Turtle Island String Quartet
> Windham Hill 10132-2 (CD), 10132-4 (CS): "On the Town"

I Love You (cont.)

> **Warren Vache/Scott Hamilton**
>> Concord Jazz CJ-70 (LP): "Scott Hamilton & Warren Vache (With Scott's Band in New York)"
>
> **Randy Weston**
>> Riverside 2508 (LP): "Randy Weston Plays Cole Porter in a Modern Mood" 1954
>
> **Buster Williams**
>> Muse MCD-5430 (CD), MC-5430 (CS): "Crystal Reflections"
>
> **Teddy Wilson**
>> Black Lion BLCD-760166 (CD): "Cole Porter Classics"
>
> **Phil Woods Quartet**
>> Portrait RK-44408 (CD), CS RJT-44408 (CS): "Warm Woods"

There Must Be Someone For Me
introduced by June Havoc in *Mexican Hayride*

> **June Havoc**
>> Decca DL-5232 (LP): original cast of the Broadway show *Mexican Hayride* 1944
>
> **June Havoc**
>> Decca 23338 (78)
>
> **June Havoc**
>> JJA 19745 (LP): "Cole Porter (Music and Lyrics)"

Carlotta
introduced by Corinna Mura in *Mexican Hayride*

> **Corinna Mura**
>> Decca DL-5232 (LP): original cast of the Broadway show *Mexican Hayride* 1944
>
> **Corinna Mura**
>> Decca 23336 (78)

Carlotta (cont.)

Corinna Mura
JJA 19745 (LP): "Cole Porter (Music and Lyrics)"

Girls
introduced by Bobby Clark in *Mexican Hayride*

Wilbur Evans
Decca DL-5232 (LP): original cast of the Broadway
show *Mexican Hayride* 1944
Wilbur Evans
Decca 23337 (78)
Wilbur Evans
JJA 19745 (LP): "Cole Porter (Music and Lyrics)"

What a Crazy Way to Spend Sunday
introduced by the ensemble in *Mexican Hayride*

Chorus
Decca DL-5232 (LP): original cast of the Broadway
show *Mexican Hayride* 1944
Chorus
Decca 23339 (78)
Chorus
JJA 19745 (LP): "Cole Porter (Music and Lyrics)"

Abracadabra
introduced by June Havoc in *Mexican Hayride*

June Havoc
Decca DL-5232 (LP): original cast of the Broadway
show *Mexican Hayride* 1944
June Havoc
Decca 23338 (78)

Abracadabra (cont.)

> **June Havoc**
>> JJA 19745 (LP): "Cole Porter (Music and Lyrics)"

Count Your Blessings
introduced by June Havoc, Bobby Clark and George Givot in
Mexican Hayride

> **June Havoc**
>> Decca DL-5232 (LP): original cast of the Broadway
>> show *Mexican Hayride* 1944
> **June Havoc**
>> Decca 23339 (78)
> **June Havoc**
>> JJA 19745 (LP): "Cole Porter (Music and Lyrics)"

A Humble Hollywood Executive
written for but unused in *Mexican Hayride*

> **Carmen Alvarez**
>> Painted Smiles PS-1358 (LP): "Unpublished Cole
>> Porter"

It's Just Yours
written for but unused in *Mexican Hayride*

> **Lynn Redgrave/Arthur Siegel**
>> Painted Smiles PS-1370 (LP): "Cole Porter Revisited,
>> Volume III"

Big Town
introduced by Nan Wynn, Jere McMahon, Paula Bane,
Billie Worth, Bill Tabbert, Dolores Gray, and Mary Roche
in *Seven Lively Arts*

Chorus
Painted Smiles PS-1371 (LP): "Cole Porter Revisited,
Volume IV"

Is It The Girl? (Or Is It The Gown?)
introduced by Dolores Gray in *Seven Lively Arts*

Dolores Gray
Painted Smiles PS-1371 (LP): "Cole Porter Revisited,
Volume IV"
Gene Walsh
Soundstage 2305 (LP)
Thomas L. Thomas
JJA-19745 (LP)

Only Another Boy And Girl
introduced by Mary Roche and Bill Tabbert in *Seven Lively Arts*

Benny Goodman and His Quintet/Jane Harvey
Columbia 36767 (78)
Benny Goodman and His Quintet/Jane Harvey
JJA 19732 (LP): "Cole Porter --1924-1944"
Benny Goodman
Columbia CK-44437 (CD), CJT-44437 (CS): "Small
Groups: 1941-1945"
Dorothy Kirsten
RCA 10-11156 and JJA-19745 (LP)

When I Was A Little Cuckoo
introduced by Beatrice Lillie in *Seven Lively Arts*

Kaye Ballard
Painted Smiles PS-1358 (LP): "Unpublished Cole Porter" - second pressing only.
Charlotte Rae
Vanguard VRS-9004 and Soundstage 2305 (LP)

Frahngee-Pahnee
introduced by Bill Tabbert in *Seven Lively Arts*

Thomas L. Thomas
JJA-19745 (LP)

Ev'ry Time We Say Goodbye
introduced by Nan Wynn in *Seven Lively Arts*

Karen Akers
DRG DRG-5214 (CD), DRGC-5214 (CS): "Unchained Melodies"
Chet Baker
Novus 3054-2-N (CD), 3054-4-N (CS), 3054-1-N (LP): "Let's Get Lost"
Chet Baker
Verve 840632-2 (CD), 840632-4 (CS): "Compact Jazz - Chet Baker"
Warren Bernhardt
Digital Music Products CD-489 (CD): "Reflections"
Ruby Braff & His New England Songhounds
Concord Jazz CCD-4478 (CD), CJ-478-C (CS): "Ruby Braff & His New England Songhounds, Vol. 1"
Charlie Byrd
Fantasy F-9496 (LP): "Top Hat"
Betty Carter
Verve 847202-2 (CD), 847202-4 (CS): "Night & Day: The Cole Porter Songbook"

Ev'ry Time We Say Goodbye (cont.)

Betty Carter
Verve 843274-2 (CD), 843274-4 (CS): "Compact Jazz - Betty Carter"
Betty Carter
Roulette B2-95999 (CD), B4-95999 (CS): "'Round Midnight"
Frank Chacksfield and His Orchestra
London SP-44185 (LP): "The Music of Cole Porter"
Chorus
RCA LRL2-5054 (LP): "Cole"
Rosemary Clooney
Concord Jazz CCD-4444 (CD), CJ-444-C (CS): "For the Duration"
John Coltrane Quartet
Natashi Imports NI-4003 (CD): "Live Australia 1962"
John Coltrane
Pablo PACD-2405-417-2 (CD), 52405-417 (CS), 2405-417 (LP): "The Best of John Coltrane"
John Coltrane
Atlantic SD-1361-2 and Rhino R2-1361 (CD), Atlantic CS-1361 and Rhino R4-1361 (CS): "My Favorite Things"
John Coltrane
Pablo OJCCD-781-2 (CD), PRES-2308-217 (CD): "The Paris Concert"
Michael Crawford
Quality CDL-15105-2 (CD), 4XL-15105-4 (CS): "Phantom Unmasked"
Michael Crawford/London Symphony Orchestra
Atlantic 82430-2 (CD), 82430-4 (CS): "With Love"
Elaine Delmar
Teldec 75277-2 (CD): "Centennial Gala Concert"
Bill Evans
Fantasy OJCCD-718-2 (CD), 5F-9568 (CS): "Crosscurrents"
George Feyer
Vanguard VSD-93/94 (LP): "Essential Cole Porter"

Ev'ry Time We Say Goodbye (cont.)

George Feyer
>Vanguard OVC-6014 (CD): "George Feyer Plays Cole Porter"

Ella Fitzgerald
>Verve 821989-2/821990-2 (CD), 823278-4 (CS), 823278-1 (LP): "Cole Porter Songbook" 1956

Ella Fitzgerald
>Pablo PACD-2310-711-2 (CD): "Ella - In London"

Ella Fitzgerald
>Verve 314-517898-2 (CD): "First Lady of Song"

Ella Fitzgerald
>Verve 314-519804-2 (CD), 314-519804-4 (CS): "The Best of the Song Books"

The Four Freshman
>Pausa PC-9029 (CS), 9040 (LP): "Jazz Origin - Four Freshman & Five Trumpets"

Larry Goldings
>Verve 314-511069-2 (CD), 314-511069-4 (CS): "The Intimacy of the Blues"

Benny Goodman and His Quintet with Peggy Mann
>Columbia 36767 (78)

Benny Goodman and His Quintet with Peggy Mann
>Soundstage 2305 (LP): from the original cast of the Broadway show *Seven Lively Arts* 1944

Benny Goodman
>Columbia CK-44437 (CD), CJT-44437 (CS): "Small Groups: 1941-1945"

Charlie Haden/Quartet West/Jeri Southern
>Verve 314-513078-2 (CD), 314-513078-4 (CS), 314-513078-5 (DCC): "Haunted Heart"

Lance Hayward
>Island 422-842859-2 (CD), 422-842859-4 (CS), 422-842859-1 (LP): "Killing Me Softly"

Lance Hayward
>Antilles 314-510092-2 and 422-842859-2 (CD), 314-510092-4 and 422-842859-4 (CS), 422-842859-1 (LP): "Killing Me Softly"

Ev'ry Time We Say Goodbye (cont.)

Christopher Hollyday
Novus 3118-2-N (CD), 3118-4-N (CS): "The Natural Moment"

Lena Horne
Three Cherries TC-64411 (CD), TC-54411 (CS), TC-44411 (LP): "Men in My Life"

Milt Jackson
Musicmasters 5061-2-C (CD), 5061-4-C (CS): "The Harem"

Stan Kenton
Creative World ST-1044 (LP): "Stage Door Swings"

Stan Kenton/June Christy
Capitol C2-96361 (CD), C4-96361 (CS): "Anything Goes - Capitol Sings Cole Porter"

Morgana King
Muse MCD-5326 (CD), MC-5326 (CS), MR-5326 (LP): "Simply Eloquent"

Dorothy Kirsten
RCA 10-11156 and JJA-19745 (LP)

Karen Knowles
Vital VTL-017 (CD): "Moonglow"

Cleo Laine
Columbia MK-39736 (CD), PMT-39736 (CS): "That Old Feeling"

Peggy Lee
MCA Special Products MCAC-20187 (CS): "Peggy Lee"

Annie Lennox
Chrysalis F2-21799 (CD), F4-21799 (CS): "Red Hot & Blue (A Tribute to Cole Porter to Benefit Aids Research & Relief)"

Annie Lennox
Milan 66076-2 (CD), 66076-4 (CS): "Prelude to a Kiss"

Julie London
EMI E2-93455 (CD), E4-93455 (CS): "Julie London Sings Cole Porter"

Ev'ry Time We Say Goodbye (cont.)

London Symphony Orchestra
    MCA MCAD-25932 (CD), MCAC-25932 (CS),
    MCA-25932 (LP): "Crossing Over the Bridge"
Geoff Love Orchestra
    Moss Music Group 703 (LP): "Very Special Love
    Themes"
Rob McConnell & the Boss Brass
    Sea Breeze CD-SB-106 (CD), D-SB-9106 (DAT):
    "Live in Digital"
Carmen MacRae
    GRP GRD-631 (CD), GRC-631 (CS): "Carmen
    MacRae Sings Great American Songwriters"
Doug MacDonald Trio
    Cexton CR-5680-D (CD): "The Doug MacDonald
    Trio"
Dave MacKay Trio
    Mama Foundation 1APDM3IJ-1 (CD): "Windows"
Mabel Mercer
    Atlantic 81264-4 (CS): "Mabel Mercer Sings Cole
    Porter (With Cy Walter & Stan Freeman)"
Mulgrew Miller
    Landmark LCD-1507-2 (CD), LLP-51507 (CS), LLP-
    1507 (LP): "Keys to the City"
Nana Mouskouri
    Philips 832900-2 (CD), 832900-4 (CS), 832900-1
    (LP): "Nana"
Nana Mouskouri
    Philips 314-510229-2 (CD), 314-510229-4 (CS):
    "Only Love - The Very Best of Nana Mouskouri"
P.J. Perry
    The Jazz Alliance TJA-10007 (CD): "Worth Waiting
    For"
Oscar Peterson
    Verve 314-515392-2 (CD), 314-515392-4 (CS): "Jazz
    'Round Midnight - The George Gershwin & Cole
    Porter Songbook"
Sue Raney
    Discovery 74001-2 (CD): "In Good Company"

Ev'ry Time We Say Goodbye (cont.)

Simply Red
>Elektra 60727-2 (CD), 60727-4 (CS): "Men & Women"

Sonny Rollins
>Spotlite CD-15112 (CD), C-15112 (CS), 7024 (LP): "The Sound of Sony"

Sonny Rollins
>Riverside OJCCD-029-2 (CD), OJC-5029 (CS), OJC-029 (LP): "The Sound of Sonny"

Sonny Rollins
>Riverside FCD-60-020 (CD): "The Essential Sonny Rollins on Riverside"

Annie Ross
>Savoy ZDS-1200 (CD), SJK-1200 (CS), SJL-1200 (LP): "The Badies"

Diane Schuur
>GRP GRD-2006 (CD), GRC-2006 (CS): "In Tribute"

Little Jimmy Scott
>Sire 26955-2 (CD), 26955-4 (CS): "All The Way"

George Shearing/Barry Tuckwell
>Concord Jazz CCD-42010 (CD), CC-2010-C (CS): "George Shearing & Barry Tuckwell Play the Music of Cole Porter"

Bobby Short
>Telarc CD83311 (CD), CS-33311 (CS): "Late Night at the Cafe Carlyle"

Bob Stewart
>Virginia Westchester Corporation VWCD-4101 (CD): "Welcome to the Club"

Bob Thiele Collective
>Red Baron AK-52445 (CD), AT-52445 (CS): "Louis Satchmo"

Mel Torme
>Concord Jazz CCD-4542 (CD), CJ-542-C (CS): "Sing, Sing, Sing - Mel Torme Live at the Fujitsu-Concord Jazz Festival, 1992"

Ev'ry Time We Say Goodbye (cont.)

Mel Torme/Cleo Laine
Concord Jazz CCD-4515 (CD), CJ-515-C (CS):
"Nothing Without You"

Sarah Vaughan
Roulette B2-94983 (CD), B4-94983 (CS): "The
Roulette Years"

Dinah Washington
Verve 314-515392-2 (CD), 314-515392-4 (CS): "Jazz
'Round Midnight - The George Gershwin & Cole
Porter Songbook"

Julie Wilson
DRG CDSL-5208 (CD), SLC-5208 (CS): "Cole Porter
Songbook"

Teddy Wilson and His Quintet/Maxine Sullivan
Musicraft 317 (78)

Teddy Wilson and His Quintet/Maxine Sullivan
JJA 19732 (LP): "Cole Porter--1924-1944"

Teddy Wilson
Musicraft MUSCD-59 (CD): "Everytime We Say
Goodbye"

Dick Wittington Trio
Concord Jazz CCD-4498 (CD), CJ-498-C (CS): "The
Dick Wittington Trio in New York"

Phil Woods/Chris Swansen
Sea Breeze SB-2008 (LP): "Crazy Horse"

Hence It Don't Make Sense
introduced by Nan Wynn, Mary Roche, Dolores Gray,
Billie Worth and Jere McMahon in *Seven Lively Arts*

Tony Pastor and His Orchestra
Victor 20-1640 (78)
Tony Pastor and His Orchestra
JJA-19745 (LP)

Dainty Quainty Me
written for but unused in *Seven Lively Arts*

> **Edward Earle**
>> Painted Smiles PS-1358 (LP): "Unpublished Cole Porter" - second pressing only.

I Wrote A Play
written for but unused in *Seven Lively Arts*

> **Arthur Siegel**
>> Painted Smiles PS-1370 (LP): "Cole Porter Revisited, Volume III"

Pretty Little Missus Bell
written for but unused in *Seven Lively Arts*

> **Georgia Engel**
>> Painted Smiles PS-1370 (LP): "Cole Porter Revisited, Volume III"

Don't Fence Me In
written in 1934 for the unproduced film *Adios Argentina*
introduced by Roy Rogers and the Sons of the Pioneers
(and reprised by the Andrews Sisters) in the film
Hollywood Canteen

> **Lynn Anderson**
>> Laserlight 12128 (CD), 72128 (CS): "Cowboy's Sweetheart"
> **The Andrews Sisters**
>> MCA Special Products MCAD-22012 (CD), MCAC-22012 (CS): "Rarities"
> **The Andrews Sisters/Bing Crosby**
>> Capitol/Curb D2-77400 (CD), D4-77400 (CS): "Greatest Hits"

Don't Fence Me In (cont.)

Louis Armstrong
Laserlight 15773 (CD), 79773 (CS0: "Louis
Armstrong & His All-Stars"
Gene Autry
Columbia CK-37465 (CD), PCT-37465 (CS):
"Columbia Historic Edition"
Hoyt Axton
Jeremiah 5003 (LP): "Pistol Packin' Mama"
Moe Bandy
K-TEL International 3023-2 (CD), 3023-4 (CS): "Moe
Bandy Sings Great American Cowboy Songs"
Boston Pops Orchestra/Arthur Fiedler
RCA 5695-4-RV (CS), AGL1-4946 (LP): "Pops Goes
West"
Boston Pops Orchestra/Arthur Fiedler
RCA 61666-2 (CD), 61666-4 (CS): "Pops Roundup"
David Byrne
Chrysalis F2-21799 (CD), F4-21799 (CS): "Red Hot
& Blue (A Tribute to Cole Porter to Benefit Aids
Research & Relief)"
Rosemary Clooney
Concord Jazz CCD-4444 (CD), CJ-444-C (CS): "For
the Duration"
Ray Conniff Singers
Columbia CK-8442 (CD): "Somebody Loves Me"
Bing Crosby/The Andrews Sisters
Decca 23364 (78) 1944
Bing Crosby/The Andrews Sisters
MCA MCAD-31036 (CD): "Andrews Sisters Rarities"
Bing Crosby/The Andrews Sisters
Capitol/Curb D2-77353 (CD), D4-77353 (CS): "Great
Records of the Decade - 40's Hits - Pop, Vol. 1"
Bing Crosby/The Andrews Sisters
Capitol/Curb D2-77340 (CD), D4-77340 (CS): "The
All Time Best of Bing Crosby"
Bing Crosby/The Andrews Sisters
MCA MCAD-1620 (CD), MCAC-1620 (CS): "Bing
Crosby's Greatest Hits"

Don't Fence Me In (cont.)

Bing Crosby
MCA MCAC2-4045 (CS): "The Best of Bing"
Bing Crosby
MCA MCAD4-10887 (CD), MCAC4-10887 (CS):
"Bing! His Legendary Years, 1931 to 1957"
Tommy Edwards
MGM 12871 (45) 1960
George Feyer
Vanguard VSD-93/94 (LP): "Essential Cole Porter"
George Feyer
Vanguard OVC-6014 (CD): "George Feyer Plays Cole
Porter"
Ella Fitzgerald
Verve 821989-2/821990-2 (CD), 823278-4 (CS),
823278-1 (LP): "Cole Porter Songbook" 1956
Marian McPartland/Rosemary Clooney
The Jazz Alliance TJA-12003 (CD): "Marian
McPartland's Piano Jazz With Guest Rosemary
Clooney"
George Maharis
Epic 5-9569 (45) 1963
Mitch Miller
Columbia CK-8004 (CD), PCT-8004 (CS): "Sing
Along With Mitch"
Mom & Dads
G.N.P. Crescendo GNP5-2-2123 (CS), GNPS-2-2123
(LP): "Golden Country"
Willie Nelson/Leon Russell
Columbia CGK-36064 (CD), CGT-36064 (CS): "One
For the Road"
Jimmy C. Newman
Plantation 530 (CS & LP): "Cajun Cowboy"
Johnny Puleo
Audiofidelity Enterprises 5919 (LP): "Western Songs"
Roy Rogers/Sons of the Pioneers
Varese Sarabande 81212 (LP): "Roy Rogers & The
Sons of the Pioneers"

Don't Fence Me In (cont.)

Roy Rogers/Lorrie Morgan/Oak Ridge Boys
RCA 3024-2-R (CD), 3024-4-R (CS): "Tribute"
Roy Rogers
Motion Picture Tracks MPT 6 (LP): soundtrack from
the film *Night and Day* 1945
Sons of the Pioneers
RCA PK-5116 (CS): "This is the Era of Memorable
Song Hits - Decade of the 40's"
Sons of the Pioneers
Pair PDC-2-1217 (CD), PDK-2-1217 (CS): "Songs of
the Trail"
**Toru Takemitsu/Seiichi Tanaka & The San Francisco
Takio Dojo**
Fox 11003-2 (CD), 11003-4 (CS): "Rising Sun"
Grady Tate
Skye 458 (45
Roger Williams
MCA MCAC2-4177 (CS): "Music of the 1940's"

Works From 1946

Look What I Found
introduced by Julie Warren and Larry Laurence (Enzo Stuarti)
in *Around the World in Eighty Days*

> **Larry Laurence (Enzo Stuarti)**
> Real 1195A-B (78)
> **Larry Laurence (Enzo Stuarti)**
> JJA 19745 (LP): "Cole Porter (Music and Lyrics)"

Should I Tell You I Love You?
introduced by Mary Healy in *Around the World in Eighty Days*

> **Larry Laurence (Enzo Stuarti)**
> Real 1195A-B (78)
> **Larry Laurence (Enzo Stuarti)**
> JJA 19745 (LP): "Cole Porter (Music and Lyrics)"

Pipe Dreaming
introduced by Larry Laurence (enzo Stuarti) in
Around the World in Eighty Days

> **Larry Laurence (Enzo Stuarti)**
> Real 1195C-D (78)
> **Larry Laurence (Enzo Stuarti)**
> JJA 19745 (LP): "Cole Porter (Music and Lyrics)"

If You Smile At Me
introduced by Victoria Cordova (and reprised by
Julie Warren) in *Around the World in Eighty Days*

> **Larry Laurence (Enzo Stuarti)**
> Real 1195C-D (78)

If You Smile At Me (cont.)

Larry Laurence (Enzo Stuarti)
JJA 19745 (LP): "Cole Porter (Music and Lyrics)"

Works From 1948

Be A Clown
introduced by Gene Kelly and Judy Garland in
the film *The Pirate*

> **Boston Pops Orchestra/John Williams**
> Philips 438070-2 (CD), 438070-4 (CS): "Over the
> Rainbow - Songs From the Movies"
> **Judy Garland/Gene Kelly**
> MCA 39080 (CD): soundtrack from the film *The
> Pirate* 1948
> **Judy Garland/Gene Kelly**
> MGM 30097 (78) 1948
> **Judy Garland/Gene Kelly**
> MGM E3234 (LP)
> **Judy Garland/Gene Kelly**
> Sony AK-47838 (CD), AT-47838 (CS): "Cole Porter
> in Hollywood - The MGM Years"
> **Julia McKenzie/Una Stubbs**
> RCA LRL2-5054 (LP): "Cole"

Love Of My Life
introduced by Judy Garland in the film *The Pirate*

> **Judy Garland**
> MCA 39080 (CD): soundtrack from the film *The
> Pirate* 1948
> **Judy Garland**
> MGM 30098 (78) 1948
> **Judy Garland**
> MGM E-3234 (LP)
> **Artie Shaw**
> Victor AXM2-5572 (LP): "Complete Artie Shaw, Vol.
> 4"

Mack The Black
introduced by Judy Garland in the film *The Pirate*

>
> **Judy Garland**
>> MCA 39080 (CD): soundtrack from the film *The Pirate* 1948
>
> **Judy Garland**
>> MGM 30099 (78) 1948
>
> **Judy Garland**
>> MGM E-3234 (LP)

Nina
introduced by Gene Kelly in the film *The Pirate*

>
> **Gene Kelly**
>> MCA 39080 (CD): soundtrack from the film *The Pirate* 1948
>
> **Gene Kelly**
>> MGM 30099 (78) 1948
>
> **Gene Kelly**
>> MGM E-3234 (LP)
>
> **Bobby Short**
>> Atlantic 82062-2 (CD), 82062-4 (CS): "Bobby, Noel & Cole (Bobby Short Loves Cole Porter/Bobby Short Is Mad About Noel Coward)"

You Can Do No Wrong
introduced by Judy Garland in the film *The Pirate*

>
> **Judy Garland**
>> MCA 39080 (CD): soundtrack from the film *The Pirate* 1948
>
> **Judy Garland**
>> MGM 30098 (78) 1948
>
> **Judy Garland**
>> MGM E-3234 (LP)

You Can Do No Wrong (cont.)

Judy Garland
Sony AK-47838 (CD), AT-47838 (CS): "Cole Porter
in Hollywood - The MGM Years"

Voodoo
written for but unused in the film *The Pirate*

Judy Garland
MCA 39080 (CD): soundtrack from the film *The
Pirate* 1948
Judy Garland
DRG SBL-12586 (LP): "Cut! Out Takes From
Hollywood's Greatest Musicals, Vol. 1"

Another Op'nin', Another Show
introduced by Annabelle Hill and ensemble in
Kiss Me Kate

Chorus
RCA LRL2-5054 (LP): "Cole"
**Thomas Hampson/Damon Evans/Kim Criswell/Josephine
Barstow/Karla Burns/George Dvorsky**
Angel C-54033-B (CD), 4D2S-54033 (CS): "Kiss Me
Kate"
Annabelle Hill/Ensemble
Angel ZDM-64760 (CD), Angel EG-64760 (CS),
Columbia OL 4140 (LP): original cast of the
Broadway show *Kiss Me Kate* 1949
Howard Keel/Anne Jeffreys
RCA LPM-1984 (LP): "Kiss Me Kate"
The Starsound Orchestra
Dominion Entertainment 3170-2 (CD): "45 Broadway
Showstoppers"
Earl Wrightson/Mary Mayo
Columbia Harmony HL 7155 (LP): "Cole Porter's
Kiss Me Kate"

Why Can't You Behave?
introduced by Lisa Kirk in *Kiss Me Kate*

Buddy Collette/Dick Marx
V.S.O.P. 37 (LP): "Marx Makes Broadway"

Meyer Davis
Monmouth-Evergreen MES-6813 (LP): "Meyer Davis Plays Cole Porter"

George Feyer
Vanguard VSD-93/94 (LP): "Essential Cole Porter"

George Feyer
Vanguard OVC-6014 (CD): "George Feyer Plays Cole Porter"

Ella Fitzgerald
Verve 821989-2/821990-2 (CD), 823278-4 (CS), 823278-1 (LP): "Cole Porter Songbook" 1956

Gogi Grant
RCA LPM-1984 (LP): "Kiss Me Kate"

Lisa Kirk/Harold Lang
Angel ZDM-64760 (CD), Angel EG-64760 (CS), Columbia OL 4140 (LP): original cast of the Broadway show *Kiss Me Kate* 1949

Lisa Kirk
MGM E-3737 (LP)

Lisa Kirk
Sinclair OSS-2250 (LP)

Four Lads
Columbia CK-46158 (CD), CT-46158 (CS): "16 Most Requested Songs"

Paula Lockheart
Flying Fish FF-213 (LP): "It Ain't the End of the World"

Julia McKenzie/Elizabeth Power/Angela Richards
RCA LRL2-5054 (LP): "Cole"

Mary Mayo
Columbia Harmony HL 7155 (LP): "Cole Porter's Kiss Me Kate"

Why Can't You Behave? (cont.)

Ann Miller
> MGM E-3077 (LP), MCA MCAC-25003 (CS):
> soundtrack from the film *Kiss Me Kate* 1953

Estelle Reiner
> Iti 4XT-72955 (CS), ST-72955 (LP): "Just in Time"

Frank Sinatra
> Columbia CXK-48673 (CD): "The Columbia Years
> (1943-1952) The Complete Recordings"

Wunderbar
introduced by Patricia Morison and Alfred Drake
in *Kiss Me Kate*

Boston Pops Orchestra/Arthur Fiedler
> RCA AGK1-7134 (CS): "Greatest Hits of the 40's,
> Vol. 2"

Frank Chacksfield and His Orchestra
> London SP-44185 (LP): "The Music of Cole Porter"

Meyer Davis
> Monmouth-Evergreen MES-6813 (LP): "Meyer Davis
> Plays Cole Porter"

Tommy Dorsey
> Decca ED-552 (45)

Alfred Drake/Patricia Morison
> Angel ZDM-64760 (CD), Angel EG-64760 (CS),
> Columbia OL 4140 (LP): original cast of the
> Broadway show *Kiss Me Kate* 1949

George Feyer
> Vanguard VSD-93/94 (LP): "Essential Cole Porter"

George Feyer
> Vanguard OVC-6014 (CD): "George Feyer Plays Cole
> Porter"

Myron Floren
> Ranwood RC-8119 (CS), RLP-8119 (LP): "The Best
> of the Wurstfest"

Wunderbar (cont.)

Dick Hyman
> Musicmasters 5060-2-C (CD), 5060-4-C (CS): "Cole Porter: All Through the Night"

Howard Keel/Kathryn Grayson
> MGM E-3077 (LP), MCA MCAC-25003 (CS): soundtrack from the film *Kiss Me Kate* 1953

Howard Keel/Anne Jeffreys
> RCA LPM-1984 (LP): "Kiss Me Kate"

Guy Lombardo
> MCA MCAC2-4082 (CS): "Best of Guy Lombardo, Vol. 2"

Mary Mayo/Earl Wrightson
> Columbia Harmony HL 7155 (LP): "Cole Porter's Kiss Me Kate"

Arthur Murray Orchestra
> RCA 1909-4-R (CS): "Arthur Murray's Music For Dancing"

Arthur Murray Orchestra
> RCA 2153-4-R (CS): "Arthur Murray's Music For Dancing - Waltz"

101 Strings Orchestra
> Alshire ALSC-5079 (CS): "Memories of Germany"

Jo Stafford/Gordon MacRae/Paul Weston
> Capitol F1659 (45) 1951

Jo Stafford/Gordon MacRae/Paul Weston
> Capitol C2-96361 (CD), C4-96361 (CS): "Anything Goes - Capitol Sings Cole Porter"

The Three Suns
> RCA 447-0232 (45)

So In Love
introduced by Patricia Morison (and reprised by Alfred Drake) in *Kiss Me Kate*

Toshiko Akiyoshi
> Concord Jazz CCD-4324 (CD), CJ-324-C (CS): "Interlude"

So In Love (cont.)

Julie Andrews
> USA Music Group, Records Division USACD-539 (CD) USACA-539 (CS), USALP-539 (LP): "Love, Julie"

William Bolcom/Joan Morris
> Omega Record Classics OCD-3002 (CD): "Night & Day"

Frankie Carle
> RCA EPB-1064 (45)

Chick Corea
> GRP GRD-9582 (CD), GRC-9582 (CS), GR-9582 (LP): "Chick Corea Akoustic Band"

The Classics
> Collectables 1274 (7" single)

Meyer Davis
> Monmouth-Evergreen MES-6813 (LP): "Meyer Davis Plays Cole Porter"

Dial & Oatts
> Digital Music Products CD-495 (CD): "Dial & Oatts Play Cole Porter"

Placido Domingo
> Atlantic 82350-2 (CD), 82350-4 (CS): "The Broadway I Love"

Tommy Dorsey/The Sentimentalists
> Laserlight 15755 (CD), 79755 (CS): "Tommy Dorsey, Vol. 1"

Alfred Drake
> Angel ZDM-64760 (CD), Angel EG-64760 (CS), Columbia OL 4140 (LP): original cast of the Broadway show *Kiss Me Kate* 1949

David L. Esleck
> Yes Yes SMS1000C (CS), SMS1000 (LP): "Nocturne"

Frederick Fennell/Eastman-Rochester Pops Orchestra
> Mercury 43427-2 (CD): "Fennell Conducts Porter & Gershwin"

George Feyer
> Vanguard VSD-93/94 (LP): "Essential Cole Porter"

So In Love (cont.)

George Feyer
Vanguard OVC-6014 (CD): "George Feyer Plays Cole Porter"
Ella Fitzgerald
Verve 821989-2/821990-2 (CD), 823278-4 (CS), 823278-1 (LP): "Cole Porter Songbook" 1956
Sergio Franchi
RCA 6875-2-R (CD), 6875-4-R (CS): "This is Sergio Franchi"
Gogi Grant/Howard Keel
RCA LPM-1984 (LP): "Kiss Me Kate"
Kathryn Grayson/Howard Keel
MGM E-3077 (LP), MCA MCAC-25003 (CS): soundtrack from the film *Kiss Me Kate* 1953
Kathryn Grayson/Howard Keel
Sony AK-47838 (CD), AT-47838 (CS): "Cole Porter in Hollywood - The MGM Years"
Robert Hale/Dean Wilder
Word 8527 (LP): "Love Songs"
Hampton Hawes
Dore 1001 (LP): "Hampton Hawes Trio"
Hampton Hawes
Contemporary OJCCD-316-2 (CD), OJC-316 (LP): "The Trio: Vol. 1"
Lance Hayward
Island 422-842859-2 (CD), 422-842859-4 (CS), 422-842859-1 (LP): "Killing Me Softly"
Lance Hayward
Antilles 314-510092-2 and 422-842859-2 (CD), 314-510092-4 and 422-842859-4 (CS), 422-842859-1 (LP): "Killing Me Softly"
Fred Hersch Trio
Chesky JD90 (CD), JC90 (CS): "Dancing In The Dark"
Masbumi Poo Kikuchi/Gary Peacock/Paul Motian
Evidence Music ECD-22071-2 (CD): "Tethered Moon"

So In Love (cont.)

Kiri Te Kanawa/Nelson Riddle Orchestra
> London 414666-2 (CD), 414666-4 (CS), 414666-1
> (LP): "Kiri - Blue Skies"

Kiri Te Kanawa/Nelson Riddle Orchestra
> London 440280-2 (CD), 440280-4 (CS): "Kiri On
> Broadway"

**Stan Kurtis/Mary Rowell/Russell Savakus/William
Schimmel/Michael Sahl**
> Nonesuch 79057-4 (CS): "The Tango Project II"

Harold Land
> Jazzland OJCCD-493-2 (CD), OJC-5493 (CS), OJC-
> 493 (LP): "Eastward Ho!"

KD Lang
> Chrysalis F2-21799 (CD), F4-21799 (CS): "Red Hot
> & Blue (A Tribute to Cole Porter to Benefit Aids
> Research & Relief)"

Julie London
> EMI E2-93455 (CD), E4-93455 (CS): "Julie London
> Sings Cole Porter"

Brian Lynch
> Ken Music KEN-011 (CD): "In Process"

Mabel Mercer
> Atlantic 81264-4 (CS): "Mabel Mercer Sings Cole
> Porter (With Cy Walter & Stan Freeman)"

Julia Migenes-Johnson
> RCA RCD1-7034 (CD), ARL1-7034 (LP): "In Love"

Vaughn Monroe
> RCA 47-4171 (45) 1951

Patricia Morison
> Angel ZDM-64760 (CD), Angel EG-64760 (CS),
> Columbia OL 4140 (LP): original cast of the
> Broadway show *Kiss Me Kate* 1949

Paul Motian
> Verve 834430-2 (CD), 834430-1 (LP): "Paul Motian
> on Broadway, Vol. 1"

Walter Norris
> Concord Jazz CCD-4486 (CD), CJ-486-C (CS):
> "Sunburst"

So In Love (cont.)

Patti Page
Mercury 5230X45 (45) 1949
Roberta Peters & Robert Merrill
RCA 49-3786 (45)
John Raitt
Capitol C2-96361 (CD), C4-96361 (CS): "Anything
Goes - Capitol Sings Cole Porter"
John Raitt
Capitol C2-97616 (CD), C4-97616 (CS): "Highlights
of Broadway/Under Open Skies"
George Shearing/Barry Tuckwell
Concord Jazz CCD-42010 (CD), CC-2010-C (CS):
"George Shearing & Barry Tuckwell Play the Music
of Cole Porter"
Cedar Walton
Delos International D/CD-4008 (CD): "Cedar Walton
Plays"
Dinah Washington
Verve CD 314-511-070-2 (CD): "The Cole Porter
Songbook, Vol. II"
Earl Wrightson
Columbia Harmony HL 7155 (LP): "Cole Porter's
Kiss Me Kate"

We Open in Venice
introduced by Alfred Drake, Patricia Morison, Lisa Kirk
and Harold Lang in *Kiss Me Kate*

Alfred Drake/Patricia Morison/Lisa Kirk/Harold Lang
Angel ZDM-64760 (CD), Angel EG-64760 (CS),
Columbia OL 4140 (LP): original cast of the
Broadway show *Kiss Me Kate* 1949
Gogi Grant/Howard Keel/Anne Jeffreys
RCA LPM-1984 (LP): "Kiss Me Kate"
Kathryn Grayson/Howard Keel/Ann Miller/Tommy Rall
MGM E-3077 (LP), MCA MCAC-25003 (CS):
soundtrack from the film *Kiss Me Kate* 1953

We Open In Venice (cont.)

Mary Mayo/Earl Wrightson
Columbia Harmony HL 7155 (LP): "Cole Porter's
Kiss Me Kate"

Tom, Dick or Harry
introduced by Lisa Kirk, Harold Lang, Edwin Clay
and Charles Wood in *Kiss Me Kate*

Gogi Grant
RCA LPM-1984 (LP): "Kiss Me Kate"
Lisa Kirk/Harold Lang/Edwin Clay/Charles Wood
Angel ZDM-64760 (CD), Angel EG-64760 (CS),
Columbia OL 4140 (LP): original cast of the
Broadway show *Kiss Me Kate* 1949
Ann Miller/Bobby Van/Tommy Randall/Bob Fosse
MGM E-3077 (LP), MCA MCAC-25003 (CS):
soundtrack from the film *Kiss Me Kate* 1953

I've Come To Wive It Wealthily In Padua
introduced by Alfred Drake in *Kiss Me Kate*

Alfred Drake/Ensemble
Angel ZDM-64760 (CD), Angel EG-64760 (CS),
Columbia OL 4140 (LP): original cast of the
Broadway show *Kiss Me Kate* 1949
Howard Keel
MGM E-3077 (LP), MCA MCAC-25003 (CS):
soundtrack from the film *Kiss Me Kate* 1953
Howard Keel
RCA LPM-1984 (LP): "Kiss Me Kate"

I Hate Men
introduced by Patricia Morison in *Kiss Me Kate*

> **Kathryn Grayson**
>> MGM E-3077 (LP), MCA MCAC-25003 (CS): soundtrack from the film *Kiss Me Kate* 1953
>
> **Anne Jeffreys**
>> RCA LPM-1984 (LP): "Kiss Me Kate"
>
> **Patricia Morison**
>> Angel ZDM-64760 (CD), Angel EG-64760 (CS), Columbia OL 4140 (LP): original cast of the Broadway show *Kiss Me Kate* 1949

Were Thine That Special Face
introduced by Alfred Drake in *Kiss Me Kate*

> **Alfred Drake**
>> Angel ZDM-64760 (CD), Angel EG-64760 (CS), Columbia OL 4140 (LP): original cast of the Broadway show *Kiss Me Kate* 1949
>
> **Dick Hyman**
>> Musicmasters 5060-2-C (CD), 5060-4-C (CS): "Cole Porter: All Through the Night"
>
> **Howard Keel**
>> MGM E-3077 (LP), MCA MCAC-25003 (CS): soundtrack from the film *Kiss Me Kate* 1953
>
> **Howard Keel**
>> RCA LPM-1984 (LP): "Kiss Me Kate"
>
> **Earl Wrightson**
>> Columbia Harmony HL 7155 (LP): "Cole Porter's Kiss Me Kate"

Kiss Me Kate
introduced by Alfred Drake and Patricia Morison
in *Kiss Me Kate*

> **Kathryn Grayson/Howard Keel**
>> MGM E-3077 (LP), MCA MCAC-25003 (CS):
>> soundtrack from the film *Kiss Me Kate* 1953
> **Jo Stafford & Gordon MacRae**
>> Capitol CDF-157 (45) 1948

Too Darn Hot
introduced by Lorenzo Fuller, Eddie Sledge and Fred Davis
in *Kiss Me Kate*

> **Erasure**
>> Chrysalis F2-21799 (CD), F4-21799 (CS): "Red Hot
>> & Blue (A Tribute to Cole Porter to Benefit Aids
>> Research & Relief)"
> **Ella Fitzgerald and Count Basie**
>> Pablo 2625701 (LP): "Jazz at the Santa Monica Civic
>> '72" 1972
> **Ella Fitzgerald**
>> Verve 821989-2/821990-2 (CD), 823278-4 (CS),
>> 823278-1 (LP): "Cole Porter Songbook" 1956
> **Ella Fitzgerald**
>> Verve 314-519564-2 and 825670-2 (CD),
>> 825670-4 (CS), 825670-1 and 6-4141 (LP):
>> "Mack the Knife - Ella in Berlin"
> **Lorenzo Fuller/Eddie Sledge/Fred Davis**
>> Angel ZDM-64760 (CD), Angel EG-64760 (CS),
>> Columbia OL 4140 (LP): original cast of the
>> Broadway show *Kiss Me Kate* 1949
> **Gogi Grant/Howard Keel/Anne Jeffreys**
>> RCA LPM-1984 (LP): "Kiss Me Kate"

Too Darn Hot (cont.)

Ann Miller
MGM E-3077 (LP), MCA MCAC-25003 (CS):
soundtrack from the film *Kiss Me Kate* 1953
Ann Miller
Sony AK-47838 (CD), AT-47838 (CS): "Cole Porter
in Hollywood - The MGM Years"
The Ritz
Pausa PC-7190 (CS), 7190 (LP): "Born to Bop"
Mel Torme
Verve 314-511-070-2 (CD): "The Cole Porter
Songbook, Vol. II"
Mel Torme
Verve 821581 (CD), 821581-4 (CS): "Mel Torme
Swings Shubert Alley"
Mel Torme
Concord Jazz CCD-4433 (CD), CJ-433-C (CS):
"Night at the Concord Pavilion"

Where is the Life That Late I Led?
introduced by Alfred Drake in *Kiss Me Kate*

Alfred Drake
Angel ZDM-64760 (CD), Angel EG-64760 (CS),
Columbia OL 4140 (LP): original cast of the
Broadway show *Kiss Me Kate* 1949
Howard Keel
MGM E-3077 (LP), MCA MCAC-25003 (CS):
soundtrack from the film *Kiss Me Kate* 1953
Howard Keel
RCA LPM-1984 (LP): "Kiss Me Kate"

Always True To You In My Fashion
introduced by Lisa Kirk in *Kiss Me Kate*

Pearl Bailey
Roulette 42004 (LP): "Pearl Bailey"

Always True To You In My Fashion (cont.)

Frankie Carle
RCA EPB-1064 (45)
Blossom Dearie
DRG DARC-2-1105 (LP): "Blossoms On Broadway"
Blossom Dearie
Verve 847202-2 (CD), 847202-4 (CS): "Night & Day:
The Cole Porter Songbook"
Ella Fitzgerald
Verve 821989-2/821990-2 (CD), 823278-4 (CS),
823278-1 (LP): "Cole Porter Songbook" 1956
Gogi Grant
RCA LPM-1984 (LP): "Kiss Me Kate"
Lisa Kirk
Angel ZDM-64760 (CD), Angel EG-64760 (CS),
Columbia OL 4140 (LP): original cast of the
Broadway show *Kiss Me Kate* 1949
Peggy Lee
Chesky JD-84 (CD), JC-84 (CS): "Moments Like
This"
Peggy Lee/George Shearing
Capitol C2-96361 (CD), C4-96361 (CS): "Anything
Goes - Capitol Sings Cole Porter"
Peggy Lee/George Shearing
Blue Note B2-98454 (CD): "Beauty & The Beat!"
Julie London
EMI E2-93455 (CD), E4-93455 (CS): "Julie London
Sings Cole Porter"
Mary Mayo
Columbia Harmony HL 7155 (LP): "Cole Porter's
Kiss Me Kate"
Ann Miller/Tommy Rall
MGM E-3077 (LP), MCA MCAC-25003 (CS):
soundtrack from the film *Kiss Me Kate* 1953
George Shearing/Peggy Lee
Blue Note B2-98454 (CD): "Beauty & the Beat!"

Always True To You In My Fashion (cont.)

Cybill Shepherd
MCA MCAC-25173 (CS), MCA-25173 (LP): "Cybill
Does It...To Cole Porter"
Julie Wilson
Teldec 75277-2 (CD): "Centennial Gala Concert"

Bianca
introduced by Harold Lang in *Kiss Me Kate*

Harold Lang
Angel ZDM-64760 (CD), Angel EG-64760 (CS),
Columbia OL 4140 (LP): original cast of the
Broadway show *Kiss Me Kate* 1949

Brush Up Your Shakespeare
introduced by Harry Clark and Jack Diamond in *Kiss Me Kate*

Harry Clark/Jack Diamond
Angel ZDM-64760 (CD), Angel EG-64760 (CS),
Columbia OL 4140 (LP): original cast of the
Broadway show *Kiss Me Kate* 1949
Peter Gale/Bill Kerr/Rod McLennan
RCA LRL2-5054 (LP): "Cole"
Gogi Grant/Howard Keel/Anne Jeffreys
RCA LPM-1984 (LP): "Kiss Me Kate"
Dick Hyman
Musicmasters 5060-2-C (CD), 5060-4-C (CS): "Cole
Porter: All Through the Night"
Cybill Shepherd
MCA MCAC-25173 (CS), MCA-25173 (LP): "Cybill
Does It...To Cole Porter"
Keenan Wynn/James Whitmore
MGM E-3077 (LP), MCA MCAC-25003 (CS):
soundtrack from the film *Kiss Me Kate* 1953

I Am Ashamed That Women Are So Simple
introduced by Patricia Morison in *Kiss Me Kate*

Patricia Morison
Angel ZDM-64760 (CD), Angel EG-64760 (CS),
Columbia OL 4140 (LP): original cast of the
Broadway show *Kiss Me Kate* 1949

Mabel Mercer
Atlantic 81264-4 (CS): "Mabel Mercer Sings Cole
Porter (With Cy Walter & Stan Freeman)"

If Ever Married I'm
written for but unused in *Kiss Me Kate*

Blossom Dearie/Carmen Alvarez/Laura Kenyon
Painted Smiles P-1358 (LP): "Unpublished Cole
Porter"

We Shall Never Be Younger
written for but unused in *Kiss Me Kate*

Julia McKenzie/Kenneth Nelson
RCA LRL2-5054 (LP): "Cole"

What Does Your Servant Dream About?
written for but unused in *Kiss Me Kate*

Alice Playten/Edward Earle
Painted Smiles P-1358 (LP): "Unpublished Cole
Porter"

A Woman's Career
written for but unused in *Kiss Me Kate*

Katharine Hepburn
Painted Smiles PS-1371 (LP): "Cole Porter Revisited, Volume IV"

Works From 1949

Farewell, Amanda
  introduced by David Wayne in the film *Adam's Rib*

> **David Wayne**
>   Sony AK-47838 (CD), AT-47838 (CS): "Cole Porter
>   in Hollywood - The MGM Years"

Prologue
introduced by William Redfield in *Out of This World*

William Redfield
Sony SK-48223 (CD), ST-48223 (CS), Columbia ML
54390 (LP): original cast of the Broadway show *Out
of This World* 1950

I Jupiter, I Rex
introduced by George Jongeyans in *Out of This World*

George Jongeyans
Sony SK-48223 (CD), ST-48223 (CS), Columbia ML
54390 (LP): original cast of the Broadway show *Out
of This World* 1950

Use Your Imagination
introduced by William Redfield and Priscilla Gillette in
Out of This World

Priscilla Gillette
Sony SK-48223 (CD), ST-48223 (CS), Columbia ML
54390 (LP): original cast of the Broadway show *Out
of This World* 1950
Mabel Mercer
Atlantic 81264-4 (CS): "Mabel Mercer Sings Cole
Porter (With Cy Walter & Stan Freeman)"

Hail, Hail, Hail
introduced by Peggy Rea and William Redfield in *Out of This World*

Ensemble
Sony SK-48223 (CD), ST-48223 (CS), Columbia ML 54390 (LP): original cast of the Broadway show *Out of This World* 1950

I Got Beauty
introduced by Charlotte Greenwood in *Out of This World*

Charlotte Greenwood
Sony SK-48223 (CD), ST-48223 (CS), Columbia ML 54390 (LP): original cast of the Broadway show *Out of This World* 1950

Where, Oh Where?
introduced by Barbara Ashley in *Out of This World*

Barbara Ashley
Sony SK-48223 (CD), ST-48223 (CS), Columbia ML 54390 (LP): original cast of the Broadway show *Out of This World* 1950

Carlos Barbosa-Lima
Concord Jazz CCD-42008 (CD), CC-42008 (CS), CC-42008 (LP): "Barbosa-Lima Plays The Music of Bonfa & Porter"

George Feyer
Vanguard VSD-93/94 (LP): "Essential Cole Porter"

George Feyer
Vanguard OVC-6014 (CD): "George Feyer Plays Cole Porter"

Mabel Mercer
Atlantic 81264-4 (CS): "Mabel Mercer Sings Cole Porter (With Cy Walter & Stan Freeman)"

Marie Santell
Teldec 75277-2 (CD): "Centennial Gala Concert"

I Am Loved
introduced by Patricia Gillette in *Out of This World*

Priscilla Gillette
Sony SK-48223 (CD), ST-48223 (CS), Columbia ML 54390 (LP): original cast of the Broadway show *Out of This World* 1950

Frank Sinatra
Columbia CGK-40897 (CD), CGT-40897 (CS): "Hello Young Lovers"

Frank Sinatra
Columbia CXK-48673 (CD): "The Columbia Years (1943-1952) The Complete Recordings"

Julie Wilson
DRG CDSL-5208 (CD), SLC-5208 (CS): "Cole Porter Songbook"

They Couldn't Compare to You
introduced by William Redfield in *Out of This World*

William Redfield
Sony SK-48223 (CD), ST-48223 (CS), Columbia ML 54390 (LP): original cast of the Broadway show *Out of This World* 1950

What Do You Think About Men?
introduced by Charlotte Greenwood, Priscilla Gillette and Barbara Ashley in *Out of This World*

Charlotte Greenwood
Sony SK-48223 (CD), ST-48223 (CS), Columbia ML 54390 (LP): original cast of the Broadway show *Out of This World* 1950

I Sleep Easier Now
introduced by Charlotte Greenwood in *Out of This World*

William Bolcom/Joan Morris
Omega Record Classics OCD-3002 (CD): "Night & Day"
Charlotte Greenwood
Sony SK-48223 (CD), ST-48223 (CS), Columbia ML 54390 (LP): original cast of the Broadway show *Out of This World* 1950

Climb Up The Mountain
introduced by Charlotte Greenwood and David Burns in *Out of This World*

Charlotte Greenwood
Sony SK-48223 (CD), ST-48223 (CS), Columbia ML 54390 (LP): original cast of the Broadway show *Out of This World* 1950

No Lover For Me
introduced by Priscilla Gillette in *Out of This World*

William Bolcom/Joan Morris
Omega Record Classics OCD-3002 (CD): "Night & Day"
Priscilla Gillette
Sony SK-48223 (CD), ST-48223 (CS), Columbia ML 54390 (LP): original cast of the Broadway show *Out of This World* 1950

Cherry Pies Ought To Be You
introduced by William Redfield, Barbara Ashley, Charlotte
Greenwood and David Burns in *Out of This World*

William Redfield
Sony SK-48223 (CD), ST-48223 (CS), Columbia ML
54390 (LP): original cast of the Broadway show *Out
of This World* 1950

Frank Sinatra
Columbia CXK-48673 (CD): "The Columbia Years
(1943-1952) The Complete Recordings"

Hark To The Song Of The Night
George Jongeyans in *Out of This World*

George Jongeyans
Sony SK-48223 (CD), ST-48223 (CS), Columbia ML
54390 (LP): original cast of the Broadway show *Out
of This World* 1950

Nobody's Chasing Me
introduced by Charlotte Greenwood in *Out of This World*

William Bolcom/Joan Morris
Omega Record Classics OCD-3002 (CD): "Night &
Day"

Charlotte Greenwood
Sony SK-48223 (CD), ST-48223 (CS), Columbia ML
54390 (LP): original cast of the Broadway show *Out
of This World* 1950

From This Moment On
written for but unused in *Out of This World*
introduced by Ann Miller and Bob Fosse in the film version
of *Kiss Me Kate*

Les Brown
MCA MCAC2-4070 (CS): "Best of Les Brown"
Frankie Carle
RCA EPB-1064 (45)
Carpenters
A&M 75021-6875-2 (CD): "From the Top"
Rosemary Clooney
Concord Jazz CCD-4496 (CD), CJ-496-C (CS): "Girl
Singer"
John Coltrane
Prestige 16PCD-4405-2 (CD): "John Coltrane - The
Prestige Recordings"
Meyer Davis
Monmouth-Evergreen MES-6813 (LP): "Meyer Davis
Plays Cole Porter"
Peter Duchin
Decca 7-341158 (45)
Linda Eder
RCA 60559-2-RC (CD), 60559-4-RC (CS): "Linda
Eder"
**Lucy Fenwick/Angela Richards/Una Stubbs/Ray
Cornell/Peter Gale/Rod McLennan**
RCA LRL2-5054 (LP): "Cole"
George Feyer
Vanguard VSD-93/94 (LP): "Essential Cole Porter"
George Feyer
Vanguard OVC-6014 (CD): "George Feyer Plays Cole
Porter"
Ella Fitzgerald
Verve 821989-2/821990-2 (CD), 823278-4 (CS),
823278-1 (LP): "Cole Porter Songbook" 1956
Tiziana Ghiglioni/Lee Konitz/S. Battaglia
Philology W-45-2 (CD): "So Many Stars"

From This Moment On (cont.)

Goldie Hawkins
Atlantic 81817-2 (CD), 81817-4 (CS): "The Erteguns'
New York, New York Cabaret Music"
Lena Horne
Bulldog CBDL-2000 (CS), 2000 (LP): "20 Golden
Pieces of Lena Horne"
Lena Horne/Lennie Hayton/Marty Paich Orchestra
DRG MRSC-501 (CS), MRS-501 (LP): "Jazz Master"
Lena Horne
QWest 205-3597 (CS): "Live on Broadway (Lena
Horne: The Lady & Her Music)"
Lena Horne
DRG CDMRS-510 (CD), MRSC-510 (CS), MRS-510
(LP): "Lena Goes Latin & Sings Your Requests"
Lena Horne
RCA 66021-2 (CD), 66021-4 (CS): "At Long Last
Lena"
Lester Lanin
Epic EK-53134 (CD), ET-53134 (CS): "This Is
Society Dance Music"
Marian McPartland
Concord Jazz CCD-4086 (CD), CJ-86-C (CS): "From
This Moment On"
Mabel Mercer
Atlantic SD2-602 (LP): "Art of Mabel Mercer"
Ann Miller/Bob Fosse
MGM E-3077 (LP), MCA MCAC-25003 (CS):
soundtrack from the film *Kiss Me Kate* 1953
Ann Miller/Bob Fosse
Sony AK-47838 (CD), AT-47838 (CS): "Cole Porter
in Hollywood - The MGM Years"
Dick Noel
Decca 9-28901 (45) 1953
Anita O'Day/Billy May
Verve 849266-2 (CD), 849266-4 (CS): "Anita O'Day
Swings Cole Porter"
Shirley Scott
Prestige PRCD-24126-2 (CD): "Workin'"

From This Moment On (cont.)

    Bobby Short
        Atlantic 1214 (LP)
    Bobby Short
        Atlantic 81715-2 (CD), 81715-4 (CS): "50 By Bobby
        Short"
    Bobby Short
        Atlantic 81817-2 (CD), 81817-4 (CS): "The Erteguns'
        New York, New York Cabaret Music"
    Frank Sinatra
        Capitol EAP-1-803 (45) 1956
    Frank Sinatra
        Capitol C2-94518 (CD), C4-94518 (CS): "A Swingin'
        Affair!"
    Frank Sinatra
        Capitol C2-96611 (CD), C4-96611 (CS): "Frank
        Sinatra Sings the Select Cole Porter"
    Frank Sinatra
        Pair PDK-2-1028 (CS): "Timeless"
    Jimmy Somerville
        Chrysalis F2-21799 (CD), F4-21799 (CS): "Red Hot
        & Blue (A Tribute to Cole Porter to Benefit Aids
        Research & Relief)"
    Mal Waldron
        Prestige P-24068 (LP): "One & Two"
    Sarah Vaughan
        Pablo PACD-2405-416-2 (CD), 52405-416 (CS),
        2405-416 (LP): "The Best of Sarah Vaughan"
    Sarah Vaughan/Count Basie Orchestra
        Pablo PACD-2312-130-2 (CD), 52312-130 (CS),
        2312-130 (LP): "Send in the Clowns"
    Mal Waldron/John Coltrane
        Prestige OJCCD-671-2 (CD), OJC-5671 (CS): "Mal-
        2"
    Phil Woods Quintet
        Concord Jazz CCD-4441 (CD), CJ-441-C (CS): "All
        Bird's Children"

Why Do You Want To Hurt Me So?
written for but unused in *Out of This World*

> **Helen Gallagher**
>> Painted Smiles PS-1371 (LP): "Cole Porter Revisited, Volume IV"

Tonight I Love You More
written for but unused in *Out of This World*

> **Larry Adler**
>> Victor AGLI-37-91 (LP): "Larry Adler Plays"
> **Morton Gould Orchestra**
>> RCA LM-2986 (LP)

Oh, It Must Be Fun
written for but unused in *Out of This World*

> **Karen Morrow/Charles Rydell**
>> Painted Smiles PS-1358 (LP): "Unpublished Cole Porter"
> **Jim & Morning Nichols**
>> Kamei KR-7007CD (CD), KR-7007CS (CS): "Unconditional Love"

You Don't Remind Me
written for but unused in *Out of This World*

> **Frank Sinatra**
>> Columbia 6936 (45)
> **Frank Sinatra**
>> Columbia CXK-48673 (CD): "The Columbia Years (1943-1952) The Complete Recordings"

Maidens Typical of France
introduced by the ensemble in *Can-Can*

Chorus
Capitol SW 1301 (LP): soundtrack from the film *Can-Can* 1960

Laundresses
Capitol S-452 (LP), C2-02064 (CD), C4-92064 (CS): original cast of the Broadway show *Can-Can* 1953

Never Give Anything Away
introduced by Lilo in *Can-Can*

Lilo
Capitol S-452 (LP), C2-02064 (CD), C4-92064 (CS): original cast of the Broadway show *Can-Can* 1953

C'est Magnifique
introduced by Lilo and Peter Cookson in *Can-Can*

Ray Elis and Johnny Douglas conducting the Ray Elis Strings
RCA CAS-2522 (LP): "The Great Hits of Cole Porter"

George Feyer
Vanguard OVC-6014 (CD): "George Feyer Plays Cole Porter"

Ferrante & Teicher
Play time 4-22017 (45)

Ferrante & Teicher
Columbia CK-10073 (CD): "Broadway to Hollywood"

George Feyer
Vanguard VSD-93/94 (LP): "Essential Cole Porter"

C'est Magnifique (cont.)

Ella Fitzgerald (accompanied by Nelson Riddle and His Orchestra)
Atlantic SD-1631 (LP): "Ella Loves Cole"
Ella Fitzgerald
Pablo PACD-2310-814-2 (CD), 52310-814 (CS), 2310814 (LP): "Dream Dancing"
Forbidden Broadway, Vol. 2
DRG CDSBL-12599 (CD), SBLC-12599 (CS)
Lilo/Peter Cookson
Capitol S-452 (LP), C2-92064 (CD), C4-92064 (CS): original cast of the Broadway show *Can-Can* 1953
Lester Lanin
Epic EK-53134 (CD), ET-53134 (CS): "This Is Society Dance Music"
Gordon MacRae
Capitol F2465 (45) 1953
Hugo Montenegro & His Orchestra
Bainbridge BTC-1005 (CS), BT-1005 (LP): "Overture: American Musical Theatre, Vol. Four 1858-1966"
Charlie Shaffer
Bellaire CA-1133 (CS): "Music From Across the Way"
Charlie Shaffer
Bellaire CD-1134 (CD): "Music From Across the Way & 'Round the World"
Frank Sinatra
Capitol SW 1301 (LP): soundtrack from the film *Can-Can* 1960
Frank Sinatra
Capitol C2-96611 (CD), C4-96611 (CS): "Frank Sinatra Sings the Select Cole Porter"

Quadrille (Instrumental)
danced by Gwen Verdon and Bert May in *Can-Can*

Orchestra
Capitol S-452 (LP), C2-02064 (CD), C4-92064 (CS):
original cast of the Broadway show *Can-Can* 1953

Come Along With Me
introduced by Erik Rhodes and Hans Conreid in *Can-Can*

Jack Costanzo
Liberty LN-10202 (LP): "Themes Go Latin"
Shirley MacLaine
Capitol SW 1301 (LP): soundtrack from the film *Can-Can* 1960
Erik Rhodes/Hans Conreid
Capitol S-452 (LP), C2-02064 (CD), C4-92064 (CS):
original cast of the Broadway show *Can-Can* 1953
The Spaniels
Collectables 1429 (7" single)
Sarah Vaughan
Mercury 826320-2 (CD): "Complete Sarah Vaughan
on Mercury, Vol. 1: Great Jazz Years (1954-1956)"

Live And Let Live
introduced by Lilo in *Can-Can*

Maurice Chevalier/Louis Jourdan
Capitol SW 1301 (LP): soundtrack from the film *Can-Can* 1960
Lilo
Capitol S-452 (LP), C2-02064 (CD), C4-92064 (CS):
original cast of the Broadway show *Can-Can* 1953

I Am In Love
introduced by Peter Cookson in *Can-Can*

Ray Anthony
Capitol F3500 (45) 1960
Frankie Carle
RCA EPB-1064 (45)
Nat King Cole
Capitol F2549 (45) 1953
Nat King Cole
Capitol 4N-16034 (CS), SN-16034 (LP): "Nat King
Cole Story, Vol. 2"
Nat King Cole
Capitol C2-95129 (CD), C4-95129 (CS): "The Nat
King Cole Story"
Nat King Cole
Smithsonian Collection of Recordings, AD047, A4-
23290 (CD): "The Songs of Cole Porter"
John Colianni
Concord Jazz CCD-4309 (CD), CJ-309-C (CS): "John
Colianni"
Peter Cookson
Capitol S-452 (LP), C2-02064 (CD), C4-92064 (CS):
original cast of the Broadway show *Can-Can* 1953
Vic Damone
Pair PCD-2-1303 (CD), PDK-2-1303 (CS): "Let's
Face the Music & Sing"
Ferrante & Teicher
Columbia CK-10073 (CD): "Broadway to Hollywood"
The Five Jets
Deluxe 45-6018 (45) 1953
Ella Fitzgerald
Verve 821989-2/821990-2 (CD), 823278-4 (CS),
823278-1 (LP): "Cole Porter Songbook" 1956
Abbey Lincoln
Riverside OJCCD-205-2 (CD), OJC-205 (LP): "It's
Magic"

I Am In Love (cont.)

Shelly Manne
Contemporary OJCCD-658-2 (CD), OJC-5658 (CS): "Shelly Manne & His Men at the Black Hawk, Vol. 3"
Bobby Short
Atlantic 82474-2 (CD), 82474-4 (CS): "Moments Like This"

If You Loved Me Truly
introduced by Gwen Verdon and Hans Conreid in *Can-Can*

Gwen Verdon/Hans Conreid
Capitol S-452 (LP), C2-02064 (CD), C4-92064 (CS): original cast of the Broadway show *Can-Can* 1953

Montmart'
introduced by the ensemble in *Can-Can*

Ensemble
Capitol S-452 (LP), C2-02064 (CD), C4-92064 (CS): original cast of the Broadway show *Can-Can* 1953
Frank Sinatra/Maurice Chevalier
Capitol SW 1301 (LP): soundtrack from the film *Can-Can* 1960

The Garden Of Eden Ballet (instrumental)
danced by Gwen Verdon in *Can-Can*

Lehman Engel/Orchestra
Painted Smiles PS-1364 (LP): "Ballet On Broadway"

Allez-Vous-En
introduced by Lilo in *Can-Can*

Ferrante & Teicher
Columbia CK-10073 (CD): "Broadway To Hollywood"
George Feyer
Vanguard VSD-93-94 (LP): "Essential Cole Porter"
George Feyer
Vanguard OVC-6014 (CD): "George Feyer Plays Cole Porter"
Gordon Jenkins
Decca 9-28746 (45) 1953
Lilo
Capitol S-452 (LP), C2-92064 (CD), C4-92064 (CS): original cast of the Broadway show *Can-Can* 1953
Ohio State University Marching Band
Fidelity Sound Recordings FSRC-1315 (CS), 1315 (LP): "Hats Off to Heine"
Kay Starr
Capitol MA-1-1584 (45) 1953
Kay Starr
C2-94080 (CD): "Capitol Collectors Series"
Kay Starr
Capitol/Curb D2-77404 (CD), D4-77404 (CS): "Greatest Hits"

Never, Never Be An Artist
introduced by Hans Conreid, Phil Leeds, Richard Purdy and Pat Turner in *Can-Can*

Hans Conreid
Capitol S-452 (LP), C2-02064 (CD), C4-92064 (CS): original cast of the Broadway show *Can-Can* 1953

It's All Right With Me
introduced by Peter Cookson in *Can-Can*

Count Basie/Ella Fitzgerald
Pablo 3PACD-2625-701-2 (CD): "Jazz at the Santa
Monica Civic '72"

Tony Bennett/Torrie Zito Orchestra
DRG CDMRS-801 (CD), MRSC-801 (CS): "The
Special Magic of Tony Bennett"

Igor Bril Quartet
Mobile Fidelity Sound Lab MFCD-21-861 (CD):
"Live at the Village Gate"

Les Brown
MCA MCAC2-4070 (CS): "Best of Les Brown"

Les Brown
Pilz America 442045-2 (CD): "Giants of the Big Band
Era"

Laverne Butler
Chesky JD-91 (CD), JC-91 (CS): "No Looking Back"

Eddie Cano
RCA International 3459-2-RL (CD): "Cole Porter,
Duke Ellington & Me"

Harry Connick, Jr.
Columbia CK-46146 (CD), CT-46146 (CS), CM-
46146 (MD): "We Are In Love"

Peter Cookson
Capitol S-452 (LP), C2-02064 (CD), C4-92064 (CS):
original cast of the Broadway show *Can-Can* 1953

Billy Daniels
G.N.P. Crescendo GNPS-16 (LP): "Billy Daniels at
the Crescendo"

Meyer Davis
Monmouth-Evergreen MES-6813 (LP): "Meyer Davis
Plays Cole Porter"

Art Farmer/Benny Golson
Chess CHD-91550 (CD), CHC-91550 (CS): "Meet the
Jazztet"

Frederick Fennell/Eastman-Rochester Pops Orchestra
Mercury 43427-2 (CD): "Fennell Conducts Porter &
Gershwin"

It's All Right With Me (cont.)

George Feyer
Vanguard VSD-93/94 (LP): "Essential Cole Porter"
George Feyer
Vanguard OVC-6014 (CD): "George Feyer Plays Cole Porter"
Ella Fitzgerald
Verve 821989-2/821990-2 (CD), 823278-4 (CS), 823278-1 (LP): "Cole Porter Songbook" 1956
Ella Fitzgerald
Verve 835454-2 (CD), 835454-4 (CS), 835454-1 (LP): "Ella In Rome - The Birthday Concert"
Ella Fitzgerald
Pablo OJCCD-789-2 (CD), PACD-2310-751-2 (CD), 52310-751 (CS), 2310-751 (LP): "Montreux '75"
Ella Fitzgerald
Verve 314-515562-2 (CD), 314-515562-4 (CS): "Jazz Divas - Live"
Curtis Fuller
Savoy SJL-2239 (LP): "All-Star Sextets"
Curtis Fuller/Benny Golson
Savoy Jazz SV-0134 (CD): "The Curtis Fuller Jazztet (With Benny Golson)"
Red Garland
Muse MR-5130 (LP): "Feelin' Red"
Erroll Garner
Columbia CK-40589 (CD), CJT-40589 (CS): "Concert By the Sea"
Crystal Gayle
EMI E2-48380 (CD), L4N-10005 (CS): "We Must Believe in Magic"
Benny Goodman
Musicmasters 65093-2 (CD): "Yale Recordings, Vol. 8: Never Before Released Recordings From Benny Goodman's Private Collection"
Dolores Gray
Teldec 75277-2 (CD): "Centennial Gala Concert"

It's All Right With Me (cont.)

Johnny Griffin
Blue Note B2-46536 (CD): "Introducing Johnny
Griffin" 1987
Johnny Griffin
Blue Note B2-95591 (CD), B4-95591 (CS): "Blue
Porter"
Lionel Hampton
Atlantic 81644-2 (CD), 81644-4 (CS): "Sentimental
Journey"
Lionel Hampton
Hindsight HCD-242 (CD), HSC-242 (CS): "Live at
the Metropole Cafe (1960-1961)"
Lena Horne
RCA 47-6175 (45) 1955
Lena Horne
RCA 66021-2 (CD), 66021-4 (CS): "At Long Last
Lena"
Willis Jackson
Muse MCD-6011 (CD), MRC-5162 (CS), MR-5162
(LP): "Bar Wars"
Stan Kenton
Creative World 1025 (LP): "Adventures in Standards"
Stan Kenton
Blue Note B2-97350 (CD): "Retrospective - The
Capitol Years, Vol. 1"
Anita Kerr Singers
Bainbridge 6228 (LP): "'Round Midnight"
Barney Kessel/Shelly Manne/Ray Brown
Contemporary OJCCD-692-2 (CD): "Poll Winners
Three!"
Lester Lanin
Epic EK-53134 (CD), ET-53134 (CS): "This Is
Society Dance Music"
Peggy Lee
MCA MCAC2-4049 (CS): "The Best of Peggy Lee"
Dave Liebman Trio
Red 123236-2 (CD): "Dave Liebman Trio Plays Cole
Porter"

It's All Right With Me (cont.)

Bob Manning
Capitol F2493 (45) 1953
Warne Marsh
V.S.O.P. 8 (LP): "Music For Prancing"
Mabel Mercer
Atlantic 81264-4 (CS): "Mabel Mercer Sings Cole
Porter (With Cy Walter & Stan Freeman)"
Hugo Montenegro & His Orchestra
Bainbridge BTC-1005 (CS), BT-1005 (LP): "Overture:
American Musical Theatre, Vol. Four 1858-1966"
Marty Paich
Discovery DS-844 (LP): "New York Scene"
Marty Paich
Discovery 75005-2 (CD), 75005-4 (CS): "Malibu
Sunset"
Joe Pass/Oscar Peterson
Pablo 52625-705 (CS), 2625-705 (LP): "At Salle
Pleyel"
Ike Quebec
Blue Note B2-84098 (CD): "Blue & Sentimental" 1988
Ike Quebec
Blue Note B2-95591 (CD), B4-95591 (CS): "Blue
Porter"
Lucy Reed/Bill Evans
Fantasy OJCCD-1777-2 (CD): "Singing Reed"
Nelson Riddle & His Orchestra
Pair PCD-2-1173 (CD): "The Riddle Touch"
Sonny Rollins
Prestige P-24082 (LP): "Taking Care of Business"
Sonny Rollins
Prestige OJCCD-007-2 (CD), OJC-5007 (CS), OJC-
007 (LP): "Worktime"
Sonny Rollins
Prestige 7PCD-4407-2 (CD): "The Complete Prestige
Recordings"
Dinah Shore/Red Norvo Quintet
Capitol C2-96361 (CD), C4-96361 (CS): "Anything
Goes - Capitol Sings Cole Porter"

It's All Right With Me (cont.)

Zoot Sims/Jimmy Rowles
Pablo OJCCD-683-2 (CD): "If I'm Lucky (Zoot Sims
Meets Jimmy Rowles)"

Frank Sinatra
Capitol SW 1301 (LP): soundtrack from the film *Can-
Can* 1960

Frank Sinatra/Quincy Jones Orchestra
Qwest 25145-4 (CS): "L.A. is My Lady"

Frank Sinatra
Qwest 29139-7 (7" single)

Frank Sinatra
Capitol C2-96611 (CD), C4-96611 (CS): "Frank
Sinatra Sings the Select Cole Porter"

The Supremes
Motown 37463-5278-2 (CD), 37463-5278-4 (CS):
"Captured Live on Stage"

Mel Torme
Concord Jazz CCD-4542 (CD), CJ-542-C (CS): "Sing,
Sing, Sing - Mel Torme Live at the Fujitsu-Concord
Jazz Festival, 1992"

Warren Vache
Concord Jazz CJ-87 (LP): "Jillian"

Tom Waits
Chrysalis F2-21799 (CD), F4-21799 (CS): "Red Hot
& Blue (A Tribute to Cole Porter to Benefit Aids
Research & Relief)"

Dionne Warwick
Arista ARCD-8573 (CD), AC-8573 (CS), AL-8573
(LP): "Dionne Warwick Sings Cole Porter"

Randy Weston Trio/Cecil Payne
Riverside OJCCD-1747-2 (CD), OJC-1747 (LP): "Jazz
a la Bohemia"

Julie Wilson
DRG CDSL-5208 (CD), SLC-5208 (CS): "Cole Porter
Songbook"

Teddy Wilson
Prestige P-7696 (LP): "In Europe"

It's All Right With Me (cont.)

Teddy Wilson
Black Lion BLCD-760166 (CD): "Cole Porter
Classics"

Every Man Is A Stupid Man
introduced by Lilo in *Can-Can*

Lilo
Capitol S-452 (LP), C2-02064 (CD), C4-92064 (CS):
original cast of the Broadway show *Can-Can* 1953

I Love Paris
introduced by Lilo in *Can-Can*

Paul Anka
ABC 296 (45) 1958
Mitchell Ayres
Camden CAE-122 (45)
Les Baxter
Capitol F2479 (45) 1953
Frank Chacksfield and His Orchestra
London SP-44185 (LP): "The Music of Cole Porter"
Chorus
Capitol SW 1301 (LP): soundtrack from the film *Can-Can* 1960
Buddy Collette
Specialty OJCCD-1764-2 (CD), SPC-5002 (CS), SPS-5002 (LP): "Jazz Loves Paris"
Jesse Davis
Concord Jazz CCD-4565 (CD): "Young At Heart"
Jonathan & Darlene Edwards
Corinthian COR-103 (LP): "Jonathan Edwards &
Darlene, in Paris"
Jonathan & Darlene Edwards
Corinthian 101-CD (CD): "Jonathan & Darlene's
Greatest Hits"

I Love Paris (cont.)

Ray Elis and Johnny Douglas conducting the Ray Elis Strings
>RCA CAS-2522 (LP): "The Great Hits of Cole Porter"

Ferrante & Teicher
>Play Time 4-22017 (45)

Ferrante & Teicher
>Columbia CK-10073 (CD): "Broadway to Hollywood"

George Feyer
>Vanguard VSD-93/94 (LP): "Essential Cole Porter"

George Feyer
>Vanguard OVC-6014 (CD): "George Feyer Plays Cole Porter"

Ella Fitzgerald
>Verve 821989-2/821990-2 (CD), 823278-4 (CS), 823278-1 (LP): "Cole Porter Songbook" 1956

The Four Aces
>Decca 9-31027 (45) 1959

Georgia Gibbs
>Mercury EP-1-3176 (45)

Coleman Hawkins
>Bluebird 51059-2 (CD), 51059-4 (CS): "The Hawk In Paris"

Screamin' Jay Hawkins
>Rhino R2-70947 (CD), R4-70947 (CS): "Voodoo Jive: The Best of Screamin' Jay Hawkins"

Screamin' Jay Hawkins
>Columbia CK-3448 (CD): "At Home with Screamin' Jay Hawkins"

Screamin' Jay Hawkins
>Epic EK-47933 (CD), ET-47933 (CS): "Cow Fingers & Mosquito Pie"

Woody Herman
>Discovery DS-815 (LP): "Third Herd, Vol. 1"

Woody Herman
>Discovery DSCD-944 (CD): "Early Autumn"

I Love Paris (cont.)

Al Hirt
> RCA ANK1-1034 (CS): "The Best of Al Hirt"

Lena Horne
> Capitol/Curb D2-77616 (CD), D4-77616 (CS): "Best of Lena Horne"

Julio Iglesias
> Columbia C2K-39570 (CD), K2T-39570 (CS): "In Concert"

Etta Jones
> Prestige OJCCD-298-2 (CD), OJC-5298 (CS), OJC-298 (LP): "Don't Go to Strangers"

Stan Kenton
> Creative World ST-1044 (LP): "Stage Door Swings"

Lester Lanin
> Epic EK-53134 (CD), ET-53134 (CS): "This Is Society Dance Music"

Michel Legrand
> Columbia B-2554 (45)

Michel Legrand
> Columbia CK-10129 (CD): "Legrand Piano"

Ramsey Lewis
> Argo 5336 (45) 1959

Lilo
> Capitol S-452 (LP), C2-02064 (CD), C4-92064 (CS): original cast of the Broadway show *Can-Can* 1953

Julia Migenes-Johnson
> RCA RCD1-7034 (CD), ARL1-7034 (LP): "In Love"

Hugo Montenegro & His Orchestra
> Bainbridge BTC-1005 (CS), BT-1005 (LP): "Overture: American Musical Theatre, Vol. Four 1858-1966"

Les Negresses Vertes
> Chrysalis F2-21799 (CD), F4-21799 (CS): "Red Hot & Blue (A Tribute to Cole Porter to Benefit Aids Research & Relief)"

Jessye Norman/Boston Pops Orchestra
> Philips 412625-2 (CD), 412625-4 (CS): "With a Song in My Heart"

I Love Paris (cont.)

101 Strings Orchestra
Alshire International ALCD-7 (CD): "Love Songs"
101 Strings Orchestra
Alshire International ALCD-30 (CD), ALSC-5007
(CS): "Cole Porter"
101 Strings Orchestra
Alshire ALSC-5214 (CS): "Songs of France"
101 Strings Orchestra
Alshire International ALCD-45 (CD), ADBL-401
(CS): "The Best of the Great American Composers,
Vol. I"
Marty Paich
Discovery DS-844 (LP): "New York Scene"
Charlie Parker
Verve 827154-4 (CS), 827154-1 (LP): "Verve Years
(1952-1954)"
Charlie Parker
Verve 823250-2 (CD), 823250-4 (CS): "The Cole
Porter Songbook"
Oscar Peterson
Verve 821987-2 (CD), 821987-4 (CS): "Oscar
Peterson Plays the Cole Porter Songbook"
Esther Phillips
Rhino 90670-2 (CD), 90670-4 (CS): "Confessin' the
Blues (Jazzlore #41)"
Elizabeth Power
RCA LRL2-5054 (LP): "Cole"
Irene Reid
MGM 13158 (45) 1963
Nelson Riddle & His Orchestra
Pair PCD-2-1173 (CD): "The Riddle Touch"
Frank Sinatra/Maurice Chevalier
Capitol SW 1301 (LP): soundtrack from the film *Can-Can* 1960
Frank Sinatra
Capitol C2-48469 (CD), C4-48469 (CS): "Come Fly
With Me"

I Love Paris (cont.)

Frank Sinatra
Capitol 4N-16149 (CS): "Sinatra Sings of Love & Things"
Frank Sinatra
Capitol C2-91344 (CD): "Frank Sinatra Gift Set"
Frank Sinatra
Capitol C2-96611 (CD), C4-96611 (CS): "Frank Sinatra Sings the Select Cole Porter"
Frank Sinatra
Capitol BBX2-99956 (CD), BBX4-99956 (CS): "Concepts"
Cal Tjader
Fantasy OJCCD-642-2 (CD), OJC-5642 (CS), OJC-642 (LP): "Latin Kick"
Cal Tjader
Fantasy OJC-5278 (CS), OJC-278 (LP): "Night at the Blackhawk"
Dionne Warwick
Arista ARCD-8573 (CD), AC-8573 (CS), AL-8573 (LP): "Dionne Warwick Sings Cole Porter"

Can-Can
introduced by Lilo and Gwen Verdon in *Can-Can*

Jo Basile Orchestra/Patachou
Audiofidelity Enterprises 6135 (LP): "Folies Bergere"
Can-Can Original Cast
Capitol DW-452
George Feyer
Vanguard VSD-93/94 (LP): "Essential Cole Porter"
George Feyer
Vanguard OVC-6014 (CD): "George Feyer Plays Cole Porter"
Lilo/Ensemble
Capitol S-452 (LP), C2-02064 (CD), C4-92064 (CS): original cast of the Broadway show *Can-Can* 1953

Can-Can (cont.)

> **101 Strings Orchestra**
>> Alshire International ALCD-19 (CD): "Famous
>> Themes From Broadway Shows"
>
> **101 Strings Orchestra**
>> Alshire International ALCD-30 (CD), ALSC-5007
>> (CS): "Cole Porter"
>
> **101 Strings Orchestra**
>> Alshire ALSC-5214 (CS): "Songs of France"
>
> **101 Strings Orchestra**
>> Alshire International ALS-5395 (CS): "16 Golden
>> Hits"
>
> **Orchestra**
>> Capitol SW 1301 (LP): soundtrack from the film *Can-Can* 1960

Who Said Gay Paree?
written for but unused in *Can-Can*

> **Dolores Gray**
>> Painted Smiles PS-1371 (LP): "Cole Porter Revisited,
>> Volume IV"

Her Heart Was In Her Work
written for but unused in *Can-Can*

> **Arthur Siegel/Lynn Redgrave**
>> Painted Smiles PS-1370 (LP): "Cole Porter Revisited,
>> Volume III"

To Think That This Could Happen to Me
written for but unused in *Can-Can*

Karen Morrow
Painted Smiles PS-1358 (LP): "Unpublished Cole Porter"

When Love Comes to Call
written for but unused in *Can-Can*

Laura Kenyon
Painted Smiles PS-1358 (LP): "Unpublished Cole Porter"

Too Bad
introduced by Harry Lascoe, Leon Belasco and David Opatoshu
in *Silk Stockings*

> **Henry Lascoe/Leon Belasco/David Opatoshu**
> RCA LOC-1016, LOC/LSO-1102, CBMI-2208 (LP):
> original cast of the Broadway show *Silk Stockings*
> 1955
>
> **Fred Astaire/Peter Lorre/Joseph Buloff/Jules Munshin**
> MCA MCAD-6177 (CD), MCAC-39074 (CS), MGM
> E-3542 and MCA-39074 (LP): soundtrack from the
> film *Silk Stockings* 1957

Paris Loves Lovers
introduced by Don Ameche and Hildegarde Neff in *Silk Stockings*

> **Don Ameche/Hildegarde Neff**
> RCA LOC-1016, LOC/LSO-1102, CBMI-2208 (LP):
> original cast of the Broadway show *Silk Stockings*
> 1955
>
> **Fred Astaire/Cyd Charisse/Carol Richards**
> MCA MCAD-6177 (CD), MCAC-39074 (CS), MGM
> E-3542 and MCA-39074 (LP): soundtrack from the
> film *Silk Stockings* 1957

Stereophonic Sound
introduced by Gretchen Wyler in *Silk Stockings*

> **Fred Astaire/Janis Paige**
> MCA MCAD-6177 (CD), MCAC-39074 (CS), MGM
> E-3542 and MCA-39074 (LP): soundtrack from the
> film *Silk Stockings* 1957

Stereophonic Sound (cont.)

Gretchen Wyler
RCA LOC-1016, LOC/LSO-1102, CBMI-2208 (LP):
original cast of the Broadway show *Silk Stockings*
1955

It's a Chemical Reaction, That's All
introduced by Hildegarde Neff in *Silk Stockings*

Hildegarde Neff
RCA LOC-1016, LOC/LSO-1102, CBMI-2208 (LP):
original cast of the Broadway show *Silk Stockings*
1955

Cyd Charisse/Carol Richards
MCA MCAD-6177 (CD), MCAC-39074 (CS), MGM
E-3542 and MCA-39074 (LP): soundtrack from the
film *Silk Stockings* 1957

Carol Richards
Sony AK-47838 (CD), AT-47838 (CS): "Cole Porter
in Hollywood - The MGM Years"

All Of You
introduced by Don Ameche in *Silk Stockings*

Rance Allen Group
Stax Records MPS-8507 (LP), SCD-8507-2 (CD): "A
Soulful Experience"

Rance Allen Group
Stax SCD-8540-2 (CD), 5MPS-8540 (CS), MPS-8540
(LP): "Best of the Rance Allen Group"

Don Ameche
RCA LOC-1016, LOC/LSO-1102, CBMI-2208 (LP):
original cast of the Broadway show *Silk Stockings*
1955

All Of You (cont.)

Fred Astaire
>MCA MCAD-6177 (CD), MCAC-39074 (CS), MGM E-3542 and MCA-39074 (LP): soundtrack from the film *Silk Stockings* 1957

Fred Astaire
>MCA MCAD-31175 (CD) & MCAC-25985 (CS), MCA-25985 (LP): "Best of Fred Astaire From MGM Classic Films"

Fred Astaire
>Sony Music Special Products AK-47838 (CD), AT-47838 (CS): "Cole Porter in Hollywood - The MGM Years"

Jo Basile/Patachou
>Audiofidelity 5814 (LP): "Patachou - With Jo Basile"

Tony Bennett
>Columbia CK-57424 (CD), CT-57424 (CS): "Steppin' Out"

Kenny Burrell
>Prestige OJC019 (LP), OJCCD-019-2 (CD): "Kenny Burrell"

Kenny Burrell
>Prestige 7308 (LP): "Blue Moods"

Carpenters
>A & M 75021-6875-2 (CD): "From the Top"

John Colianni
>Concord Jazz CCD-4309 (CD) & CJ-309-C (CS): "John Colianni"

Buddy Collette/Dick Marx
>V.S.O.P. 37 (LP): "Marx Makes Broadway"

Meyer Davis
>Monmouth-Evergreen MES-6813 (LP): "Meyer Davis Plays Cole Porter"

Miles Davis
>Columbia PC-8983 (LP): "Miles Davis in Europe/Lincoln Center, 9/29/72"

Miles Davis
>Columbia PCT-9106 (CS): "My Funny Valentine/Miles in Concert"

All Of You (cont.)

Miles Davis
Columbia CK-44257 (CD) & CJT-44257 (CS): "In Person, Friday Night at the Blackhawk, Vol. I"

Miles Davis
Columbia C2S-820 (LP): "Miles in Person"

Miles Davis
Columbia PC-8649 (LP), CK-40610 (CD), CJT-40610 (CS): "Round About Midnight"

Miles Davis
Columbia PC-9106 (LP: "Funny Valentine"

Miles Davis
Columbia 4PK-48844 (CD): "Miles Davis 4 Pack"

Miles Davis
Columbia C2K-48821 (CD), C2T-48821 (CS): "The Complete Concert: 1964 (My Funny Valentine & 'Four' & More/Recorded Live in Concert) "

Sammy Davis, Jr.
Decca 9-2 9402 (45) 1955

Sammy Davis, Jr.
MCA MCAC2-4109 (CS & LP): "Hey there (It's Sammy Davis, Jr. At His Dynamite Greatest)"

Dial & Oatts
Digital Music Products, Inc. CD-495 (CD): "Dial & Oatts Play Cole Porter"

Tommy Dorsey
RCA AXK2-5573 (CS): "Complete Tommy Dorsey, Vol. 5 (1937)"

Neal Ely Quintet
Nee Nee-CD-1001 (CD), Nee-CS-1001 (CS): "Dr. Jazz"

David L. Esleck
Yes Yes SMS1000C (CS) & SMS1000 (LP): "Nocturne"

Bill Evans
Fantasy F-9618 (LP): "Eloquence"

Bill Evans
Riverside R018 (LP), 12RCD-018-2 (CD): "The Complete Riverside Recordings"

All Of You (cont.)

Bill Evans
Riverside OJC-140 (LP) & OJC-5140 (CS) & OJCCD-140-2 (CD): "Sunday at the Village Vanguard"

Bill Evans
Milestone M-9125 (LP) & 5M-9125 (CS): "More From the Vanguard"

Bill Evans
Riverside FCD-60-017 (CD): "The Bill Evans Trio at the Village Vanguard"

Mary Fettig
Concord Jazz CJ-273-C (CS): "In Good Company"

George Feyer
Vanguard VSD-93/94 (LP): "Essential Cole Porter"

George Feyer
Vanguard OVC-6014 (CD): "George Feyer Plays Cole Porter"

Ella Fitzgerald
Pablo PACD-2310-814-2 (CD), 52310-814 (CS), 2310814 (LP): "Dream Dancing"

Ella Fitzgerald (accompanied by Nelson Riddle and His Orchestra)
Atlantic SD-1631 (LP): "Ella Loves Cole"

Ella Fitzgerald
Verve 821989-2/821990-2 (CD), 823278-4 (CS), 823278-1 (LP): "Cole Porter Songbook" 1956

Scott Hamilton
Concord Jazz 197 (LP & CD) & Concord Jazz 4197 (CD): "Close Up"

John Hicks
Concord Jazz CCD-4442 (CD), CJ-442-C (CSS): "Live At Maybeck Recital Hall, Vol. 7 (John Hicks at Maybeck)"

Billie Holiday
Verve 835370-1 (LP) & 835370-2 (CD) & 835370-4 (CS): "Last Recordings"

Keith Jarrett/Gary Peacock/Jack De Johnette
ECM 847135-2 (CD), 847135-4 (CS): "Tribute"

All Of You (cont.)

Bobby Jaspar/George Wallington\Idrees Sulieman
Riverside OJCCD-1788-2 (CD): "Bobby Jaspar with
George Wallington & Idrees Sulieman"
Cleo Laine
Crescendo GNPD-9024 (CD), GNPC-9024 (CS),
GNPS-9024 (LP): "Cleo's Choice"
Mundell Lowe
Riverside OJCCD-1773-2 (CD), OJC-1773 (LP):
"Mundell Lowe Quartet"
Marian McPartland
The Jazz Alliance TJA-12004 (CD): "Marian
McPartland's Piano Jazz with Guest Bill Evans"
Shelly Manne/Shelly Manne Trio
Contemporary 5C-14018 (CS) & C-14018 (LP): "In
Zurich"
Billy May & His Orchestra
Creative World ST-1051 (LP): "Sorta May"
Mabel Mercer/Bobby Short
Atlantic 2-604 (LP), CS2-604 (CS): "At Town Hall"
Helen Merrill
Emarcy 1018 (LP): "Nearness Of You"
Helen Merrill
Mercury 826340-2 (CD): "Complete Helen Merrill on
Mercury (1954-1958)"
Modern Jazz Quartet
Prestige P-24005 (LP) & 5P-24005 (CS): "The
Modern Jazz Quartet"
Modern Jazz Quartet
Prestige OJC-002 (LP) & OJC-5002 (CS) & OJCCD-
002-2 (CD): "Concorde"
Modern Jazz Quartet
Prestige P-7421 (LP): "Modern Jazz Quartet Plays For
Lovers"
Hugo Montenegro & Orchestra
Bainbridge BTC-1005 (CS) & BT-1005 (LP):
"Overture: American Musical Theatre, Vol. Four
1958-1966"

All Of You (cont.)

Tete Montoliu Trio
Concord Jazz CCD-4493 (CD), CJ-493-C (CS): "A
Spanish Treasure"
Anita O'Day/Billy May
Verve 849266-2 (CD), 849266-4 (CS): "Anita O'Day
Swings Cole Porter"
The Pointer Sisters
Planet Records BXK1-4355 (CS): "So Excited"
Ray Price
Step One SOR-0007 (LP & CS): "Welcome to Ray
Price Country"
Annie Ross/Gerry Mulligan
EMI E2-46852 (CD): "Annie Ross Sings a Song With
Mulligan" 1988
Annie Ross/Gerry Mulligan
Capitol C2-96361 (CD), C4-96361 (CS): "Anything
Goes - Capitol Sings Cole Porter"
Stefan Scaggiari Trio
Concord Jazz CCD-4510 (CD): "That's Ska-Jar-e"
George Shearing
Capitol 2-720 (45)
George Shearing
Pair PCD-2-1302 (CD), PDK-2-1302 (CS): "The
Shearing Touch"
George Shearing
Capitol/Curb D2-77631 (CD), D4-77631 (CS): "Best
of George Shearing"
Bobby Short
Atlantic 2-609 (LP), Atlantic CS2-609 (CS), Mobile
Fidelity Sound Lab Records UDCD-589 (CD): "Bobby
Short Live At The Cafe Carlyle"
Bobby Short/Mabel Mercer
Atlantic CS2-604 (CS): "At Town Hall"
Frank Sinatra
Reprise FS-2300 (LP) & 3F5-2300 (CS) & 2300-2
(CD): "Trilogy"

All Of You (cont.)

Jack Six/Francis Thorne
Composers Recordings 585 (CD): "Porter On My Mind"

Frank Stallone
USA Music Group USACD-695 (CD), USACA-695 (CS): "Day In Day Out"

Ted Straeter
Atlantic 81817-2 (CD), 81817-4 (CS): "The Erteguns' New York, New York Cabaret Music"

Toots Thielemans
Concord Jazz CCD-4355 (CD) & CJ-355-C (CS): "Only Trust Your Heart"

Mickey Tucker
Denon DC-8552 (CD): "Sweet Lotus Lips"

McCoy Tyner
MCA 2-4126 (LP): "Great Moments With"

Pointer Sisters
Planet BXL1-4335 (LP): "So Excited"

Ted Straeter
Atlantic 81817-2 (CD) & 81817-4 (CS): "The Erteguns' New York, New York Cabaret Music"

Mel Torme
Concord Jazz CCD-4542 (CD), CJ-542-C (CS): "Sing, Sing, Sing - Mel Torme Live at the Fujitsu-Concord Jazz Festival 1992"

Sarah Vaughan
Mercury 826333-2 (CD): "Complete Sarah Vaughan on Mercury, Vol. 3: Great Show on Stage"

Dionne Warwick
Arista ARCD-8573 (CD), AC-8573 (CS), AL-8573 (LP): "Dionne Warwick Sings Cole Porter"

Julie Wilson
DRG CDSL-5208 (CD), SLC-5208 (CS): "Cole Porter Songbook"

Satin and Silk
introduced by Gretchen Wyler in *Silk Stockings*

Janis Paige
MCA MCAD-6177 (CD), MCAC-39074 (CS), MGM
E-3542 and MCA-39074 (LP): soundtrack from the
film *Silk Stockings* 1957

Janis Paige
Sony AK-47838 (CD), AT-47838 (CS): "Cole Porter
in Hollywood - The MGM Years"

Gretchen Wyler
RCA LOC-1016, LOC/LSO-1102, CBMI-2208 (LP):
original cast of the Broadway show *Silk Stockings*
1955

Without Love
introduced by Hildegarde Neff in *Silk Stockings*

Hildegarde Neff
RCA LOC-1016, LOC/LSO-1102, CBMI-2208 (LP):
original cast of the Broadway show *Silk Stockings*
1955

Cyd Charisse/Carol Richards
MCA MCAD-6177 (CD), MCAC-39074 (CS), MGM
E-3542 and MCA-39074 (LP): soundtrack from the
film *Silk Stockings* 1957

Ella Fitzgerald (accompanied by Nelson Riddle and His Orchestra)
Atlantic SD-1631 (LP): "Ella Loves Cole"

Ella Fitzgerald
Pablo PACD-2310-814-2 (CD), 52310-814 (CS),
2310814 (LP): "Dream Dancing"

Hail Bibinski
introduced by Henry Lascoe, Leon Belasco and David Opatoshu
in *Silk Stockings*

Henry Lascoe/Leon Belasco/David Opatoshu
RCA LOC-1016, LOC/LSO-1102, CBMI-2208 (LP):
original cast of the Broadway show *Silk Stockings*
1955

As On Through The Seasons We Sail
introduced by Don Ameche and Hildegarde Neff in *Silk Stockings*

Don Ameche/Hildegarde Neff
RCA LOC-1016, LOC/LSO-1102, CBMI-2208 (LP):
original cast of the Broadway show *Silk Stockings*
1955

Josephine
introduced by Gretchen Wyler in *Silk Stockings*

Janis Paige
MCA MCAD-6177 (CD), MCAC-39074 (CS), MGM
E-3542 and MCA-39074 (LP): soundtrack from the
film *Silk Stockings* 1957
Bobby Short
Atlantic 82062-2 (CD), 82062-4 (CS): "Bobby, Noel
& Cole (Bobby Short Loves Cole Porter/Bobby Short
Is Mad About Noel Coward)"
Gretchen Wyler
RCA LOC-1016, LOC/LSO-1102, CBMI-2208 (LP):
original cast of the Broadway show *Silk Stockings*
1955

Siberia
introduced by Henry Lascoe, Leon Belasco and David Opatoshu
in *Silk Stockings*

> **Henry Lascoe/Leon Belasco/David Opatoshu**
> > RCA LOC-1016, LOC/LSO-1102, CBMI-2208 (LP):
> > original cast of the Broadway show *Silk Stockings*
> > 1955
>
> **Peter Lorre/Joseph Buloff/Jules Munshin**
> > MCA MCAD-6177 (CD), MCAC-39074 (CS), MGM
> > E-3542 and MCA-39074 (LP): soundtrack from the
> > film *Silk Stockings* 1957

Silk Stockings
introduced by Don Ameche in *Silk Stockings*

> **Don Ameche**
> > RCA LOC-1016, LOC/LSO-1102, CBMI-2208 (LP):
> > original cast of the Broadway show *Silk Stockings*
> > 1955
>
> **Johnny Green**
> > MGM 12538 (45) 1957
>
> **Tommy Dorsey**
> > Bell 47 (45)
>
> **Tommy Dorsey**
> > ACD SJA-7917 (LP) "Sentimental Gentleman"
>
> **Scott Hamilton**
> > Concord Jazz CJ-165-C (LP) "Apples & Oranges"
>
> **Dave McKenna**
> > Portrait RK-44091 (CD), RJT-44091 (CS): "This is
> > the Moment"
>
> **Orchestra**
> > MCA MCAD-6177 (CD), MCAC-39074 (CS), MGM
> > E-3542 and MCA-39074 (LP): soundtrack from the
> > film *Silk Stockings* 1957

The Red Blues
introduced by the ensemble in *Silk Stockings*

Henry Lascoe/Leon Belasco/David Opatoshu
RCA LOC-1016, LOC/LSO-1102, CBMI-2208 (LP):
original cast of the Broadway show *Silk Stockings*
1955

Wim Senneveld and Chorus
MCA MCAD-6177 (CD), MCAC-39074 (CS), MGM
E-3542 and MCA-39074 (LP): soundtrack from the
film *Silk Stockings* 1957

Give Me the Land
written for but unused in *Silk Stockings*

Edward Earle
Painted Smiles PS-1358 (LP): "Unpublished Cole
Porter"

The Perfume of Love
written for but unused in *Silk Stockings*

Larry Adler
Victor AGLI-37-91 (LP): "Larry Adler Plays"

Morton Gould and His Orchestra
RCA LM-2986 (LP)

High Society Calypso
introduced by Louis Armstrong in the film *High Society*

> **Louis Armstrong**
> > Capitol F3506 (45) 1956
> **Louis Armstrong**
> > Capitol SW 750 and SW-12235 (LP): soundtrack from the film *High Society* 1956

I Love You, Samantha
introduced by Bing Crosby in the film *High Society*

> **Ray Anthony**
> > Capitol F3500 (45) 1956
> **Cal Collins**
> > Concord Jazz CJ-95 (LP): "Blues on My Mind"
> **Bing Crosby**
> > Capitol SW 750 and SW-12235 (LP): soundtrack from the film *High Society* 1956
> **Pete DeLuke Quartet**
> > Time Is TI-9809 (CD): "Mixt Bag"
> **Scott Hamilton/Jake Hanna/Dave McKenna**
> > Concord Jazz CCD-4097 (CD), CJ-97-C (CS): "No Bass Hit"
> **The King's Singers**
> > Moss Music Group CMG-1141 (CS), 1141 (LP): "By Request"
> **The King's Singers**
> > Angel CDC49118 (CD), 4XPA-32229 (CS): "This is the King's Singers"
> **Bobby Short**
> > Atlantic 81715-2 (CD), 81715-4 (CS): "50 By Bobby Short"

Little One
introduced by Bing Crosby in the film *High Society*

> **Bing Crosby**
>> Capitol SW 750 and SW-12235 (LP): soundtrack from the film *High Society* 1956

Who Wants to be a Millionaire?
introduced by Frank Sinatra and Celeste Holm in the film
High Society

> **Frank Sinatra/Celeste Holm**
>> Capitol SW 750 and SW-12235 (LP): soundtrack from the film *High Society* 1956
>
> **Thompson Twins**
>> Chrysalis F2-21799 (CD), F4-21799 (CS): "Red Hot & Blue (A Tribute to Cole Porter to Benefit Aids Research & Relief)"

True Love
introduced by Bing Crosby and Grace Kelly in the film
High Society

> **Patti Austin**
>> Qwest 25696-2 (CD), 25696-4 (CS): "The Real Me"
>
> **Tony Bagwell**
>> Starborne 2 (LP): "Romantic Moog"
>
> **Carlos Barbosa-Lima**
>> Concord Jazz CCD-42008 (CD), CC-42008 (CS), CC-42008 (LP): "Barbosa-Lima Plays The Music of Bonfa & Porter"
>
> **Pat Boone**
>> Dot DEP-1082 (45)
>
> **Richard Chamberlain**
>> MGM 13148 (45) 1963
>
> **Patsy Cline**
>> MCA 51038 (45)

True Love (cont.)

Patsy Cline
MCA Special Products MCAC-20464 (CS): "Best of Patsy Cline"

Patsy Cline
MCA MCAD-4038 (CD), MCAC2-4038 (CS), McA2-4038 (LP): "The Patsy Cline Story"

Patsy Cline/ The Jordanaires
MCA MCAD-87 (CD), MCAC-87 (CS): "Showcase"

Patsy Cline
MCA MCAD-27069 (CD), MCAC-27069 (CS): "Always"

Patsy Cline
MCA MCAC2-38015 (CS): "Sentimentally Yours/Showcase"

Ray Conniff Singers
Columbia CK-8520 (CD): "So Much In Love!"

Bing Crosby/Grace Kelly
Capitol F3507 (45) 1956

Bing Crosby/Grace Kelly
Capitol SW 750 and SW-12235 (LP): soundtrack from the film *High Society* 1956

Bing Crosby/Grace Kelly
Capitol C2-98670 (CD), C4-98670 (CS): "Memories are Made of This"

The Del Vikings
Fee Bee 902 (45) 1956

Ray Elis and Johnny Douglas conducting the Ray Elis Strings
RCA CAS-2522 (LP): "The Great Hits of Cole Porter"

George Feyer
Vanguard VSD-93/94 (LP): "Essential Cole Porter"

George Feyer
Vanguard OVC-6014 (CD): "George Feyer Plays Cole Porter"

The Four Aces
MCA Special Products MCAC-20252 (CS): "Love is a Many Splendored Thing"

True Love (cont.)

The Four Aces
MCA MCAC2-4033 (CS): "The Best of the Four Aces"
The Four Aces
MCA Special Products MCAC-20177 (CS): "The Four Aces"
Guy & Ralna
Ranwood RC-2011 (CS), RLP-2011 (LP): "Guy & Ralna"
George Harrison
Dark Horse 26612-2 (CD): "Thirty-Three & 1/3"
Julio Iglesias
Columbia C2K-39570 (CD), K2T-39570 (CS): "In Concert"
Elton John/Kiki Dee
MCA MCAD-10926 (CD), MCAC-10926 (CS): "Duets"
Jonah Jones
Capitol EAP-1-1083 (45)
Kitty Kallen
Decca 9-29959 (45) 1956
Kiri Te Kanawa/Nelson Riddle Orchestra
London 414666-2 (CD), 414666-4 (CS), 414666-1 (LP): "Kiri - Blue Skies"
Wayne King
MCA MCAD-4022 (CD), MCAC2-4022 (CS): "The Best of Wayne King"
Katherine Kovar
Accent C-5007 (CS), 5007 (LP): "Love Echoes"
Barbara Lea
Prestige OJCCD-1742-2 (CD): "Lea in Love"
Dave Liebman Trio
Red 123236-2 (CD): "Dave Liebman Trio Plays Cole Porter"
Malcolm Lockyer
Starborne 1 (LP): "In a Romantic Mood"

True Love (cont.)

Dean Martin/Nelson Riddle
> Capitol C2-96361 (CD), C4-96361 (CS): "Anything
> Goes - Capitol Sings Cole Porter"

Johnny Mathis/Henry Mancini
> Columbia CK-40372 (CD), FCT-40372 (CS):
> "Hollywood Musicals"

Anne Murray
> SBK K2-27012 (CD), K4-27012 (CS): "Croonin'"

Rick Nelson
> Imperial 155 (45)

Jane Powell
> Verve 2018 (45) 1956

Elvis Presley
> RCA EPA-1-1515 (45) 1957

Elvis Presley
> RCA 1515-2-R (CD), 1515-4-R (CS): "Loving You"

Memphis Slim
> Storyville SC-44044 (CS), SLP-4044 (LP): "Blues
> Roots, Vol. 10 - I'm So Alone"

Memphis Slim
> Muse MR-5219 (LP): "I'll Just Keep On Singin' The
> Blues"

Lawrence Welk
> Ranwood RC-8053 (CS), RLP-8053 (LP): "I Love
> You Truly"

Lawrence Welk
> Ranwood RC-6002 (CS), 6002 (LP): "Lawrence Welk
> Celebrates 50 years in Music"

Roger Whittaker
> Liberty C2-94055 (CD), C4-94055 (CS): "Best Loved
> Ballads, Vol. 2"

Roger Whittaker
> Liberty C2-98483 (CD), C4-98483 (CD): "All About
> Love"

Roger Williams
> MCA MCAC2-4178 (CS): "Music of the 1950's"

You're Sensational
introduced by Frank Sinatra in the film *High Society*

> **Ruby Braff**
> > Red Baron JK-53749 (CD), JT-53749 (CS): "Very Sinatra"
>
> **Sammy Davis, Jr.**
> > MCA MCAC2-4109 (CS & LP): "Hey there (It's Sammy Davis, Jr. At His Dynamite Greatest)"
>
> **Frank Sinatra**
> > Capitol F3469 (45) 1956
>
> **Frank Sinatra**
> > Capitol SW 750 and SW-12235 (LP): soundtrack from the film *High Society* 1956
>
> **Frank Sinatra**
> > Capitol CD-94317 (CD), C4-94317 (CS): "The Capitol Years"
>
> **Frank Sinatra**
> > Capitol C2-96611 (CD), C4-96611 (CS): "Frank Sinatra Sings the Select Cole Porter"
>
> **Frank Sinatra**
> > Capitol C2-94777 (CD), C4-94777 (CS), C1-94777 (LP): "The Capitol Years"
>
> **Jack Six/Francis Thorne**
> > Composers Recordings 585 (CD): "Porter On My Mind"

Now You Has Jazz
introduced by Bing Crosby and Louis Armstrong in the film
High Society

> **Louis Armstrong, All-Stars**
> > Storyville 4012 (LP)
>
> **Bing Crosby/Louis Armstrong**
> > Capitol F3506 (45) 1956
>
> **Bing Crosby/Louis Armstrong**
> > Capitol SW 750 and SW-12235 (LP): soundtrack from the film *High Society* 1956

Now You Has Jazz (cont.)

>**Bing Crosby/Louis Armstrong**
>>Blue Note B2-96582 (CD), B4-96582 (CS): "Blue Series: Male Vocals"

Mind If I Make Love To You?
introduced by Frank Sinatra in the film *High Society*

>**Frank Sinatra**
>>Capital SW-12235
>**Frank Sinatra**
>>Capitol SW 750 and SW-12235 (LP): soundtrack from the film *High Society* 1956
>**Frank Sinatra**
>>Capitol C2-96611 (CD), C4-96611 (CS): "Frank Sinatra Sings the Select Cole Porter"

Fated To Be Mated
introduced by Fred Astaire in the film version of
Silk Stockings

Fred Astaire/Cyd Charisse
MCA MCAD-6177 (CD), MCAC-39074 (CS), MGM
E-3542 and MCA-39074 (LP): soundtrack from the
film *Silk Stockings* 1957

Ritz Roll and Rock
introduced by Fred Astaire in the film version of
Silk Stockings

Fred Astaire
MCA MCAD-6177 (CD), MCAC-39074 (CS), MGM
E-3542 and MCA-39074 (LP): soundtrack from the
film *Silk Stockings* 1957
Fred Astaire
MCA MCAD-31175 (CD), MCAC-25985 (CS),
MCA-25985 (LP): "Best of Fred Astaire From MGM
Classic Films"

Ca, C'est L'Amour
introduced by Taina Elg in the film *Les Girls*

Tony Bennett
Columbia C4K-46843 (CD), C4T-46843 (CS): "Forty
Years: The Artistry of Tony Bennett"
Taina Elg
MCA MCAC-1426 (CS), MCA-1426 (LP): soundtrack
from the films *Les Girls/Lili* 1957

Ca, C'est L'Amour (cont.)

Taina Elg
Sony AK-47838 (CD), AT-47838 (CS): "Cole Porter in Hollywood - The MGM Years"

Les Girls
introduced by Gene Kelly in the film *Les Girls*

Gene Kelly/Mitzi Gaynor/Kay Kendall/Taina Elg
MCA MCAC-1426 (CS), MCA-1426 (LP): soundtrack from the films *Les Girls/Lili* 1957

Ladies in Waiting
introduced by Mitzi Gaynor, Kay Kendall and Taina Elg in the film *Les Girls*

Mitzi Gaynor/Kay Kendall/Taina Elg
MCA MCAC-1426 (CS), MCA-1426 (LP): soundtrack from the films *Les Girls/Lili* 1957

Why Am I So Gone About That Gal?
introduced by Gene Kelly in the film *Les Girls*

Gene Kelly
MCA MCAC-1426 (CS), MCA-1426 (LP): soundtrack from the films *Les Girls/Lili* 1957
Gene Kelly
Sony AK-47838 (CD), AT-47838 (CS): "Cole Porter in Hollywood - The MGM Years"

You're Just Too, Too!
introduced by Gene Kelly and Kay Kendall in the film
Les Girls

> **Gene Kelly/Kay Kendall**
>> MCA MCAC-1426 (CS), MCA-1426 (LP): soundtrack
>> from the films *Les Girls/Lili* 1957

I Could Kick Myself
written for but unused in the film *Les Girls*

> **Carmen Alvarez/Blossom Dearie**
>> Painted Smiles PS-1358 (LP): "Unpublished Cole
>> Porter"
> **Jim & Morning Nichols**
>> Kamei KR-7003CD (CD), KR-7003C (CS): "My
>> Flame"

Trust Your Destiny To A Star
introduced by Dennis King in the television musical
Aladdin

Dennis King
Columbia CL-1117 (LP), Sony SK-48205 (CD), ST-48205 (CS): "Aladdin"

Aladdin
introduced by Anna Maria Alberghetti in the television
musical *Aladdin*

Anna Maria Alberghetti
Columbia CL-1117 (LP), Sony SK-48205 (CD), ST-48205 (CS): "Aladdin"

Come To The Supermarket In Old Peking
introduced by Cyril Ritchard in the television musical
Aladdin

Patti LuPone
RCA 61797-2 (CD): "Patti LuPone Live"
Cyril Ritchard
Columbia CL-1117 (LP), Sony SK-48205 (CD), ST-48205 (CS): "Aladdin"
Barbra Streisand
Columbia PC-8807 (LP), CK-57374 (CD), CK-8807 (CD), CT-57374 (CS), PCT-8807 (CS): "The Barbra Streisand Album"

I Adore You
introduced by Sal Mineo and Anna Maria Alberghetti
in the television musical *Aladdin*

> **Sal Mineo**
> > Columbia CL-1117 (LP), Sony SK-48205 (CD), ST-48205 (CS): "Aladdin"
>
> **Sal Mineo/Anna Maria Alberghetti**
> > Columbia CL-1117 (LP), Sony SK-48205 (CD), ST-48205 (CS): "Aladdin"

Make Way For The Emperor
introduced by George Hall in the television musical *Aladdin*

> **George Hall**
> > Columbia CL-1117 (LP), Sony SK-48205 (CD), ST-48205 (CS): "Aladdin"

No Wonder Taxes Are High
introduced by Cyril Ritchard in the television musical *Aladdin*

> **Cyril Ritchard**
> > Columbia CL-1117 (LP), Sony SK-48205 (CD), ST-48205 (CS): "Aladdin"

Opportunity Knocks But Once
introduced by Cyril Ritchard in the television musical *Aladdin*

> **Cyril Ritchard**
> > Columbia CL-1117 (LP), Sony SK-48205 (CD), ST-48205 (CS): "Aladdin"

Wouldn't It Be Fun
introduced by Basil Rathbone in the television musical *Aladdin*

George Hall
Columbia CL-1117 (LP), Sony SK-48205 (CD), ST-48205 (CS): "Aladdin"
Kenneth Nelson
RCA LRL2-5054 (LP): "Cole"

Index of Compositions

Index of Recording Artists

Brown, Les (cont.)
191, 198, 199, 212, 213, 284,
294
Brown, Maxine, 36
Brown, Ray, 21, 47, 49, 128,
179, 180, 221, 237, 296
Brown, Roy, 48
Browne, Sam, 132
Brubeck, Dave, 22, 89, 128,
133
Bruce, Virginia, 144, 145, 153,
154
Bullock, Chick, 198, 205, 208
Buloff, Joseph, 306, 316
Burns, Karla, 262
Burrell, Kenny, 48, 173, 308
Busse, Henry, 119
Butler, Laverne, 114, 145, 294
Byas, Don, 22, 65, 133, 145
Byng, Douglas, 85
Byrd, Charlie, 15, 145, 247
Byrne, David, 255
Cahn, Sammy, 101
Calabrese, Lou, 10
Calderazzo, Joey, 22
Calloway, Blanche, 46
Calloway, Cab, 85
Campbell, John, 133, 145
Campbell, Mike, 199
Campise, Tony, 228, 238
Candido, 57
Cano, Eddie, 23, 48, 89, 186,
238, 294
Carle, Frankie, 48, 89, 145,
266, 274, 284, 291
Carlisle, Elsie, 15, 21, 23
Carlos Ramirez, 127
Carlyle, Louise, 114, 169, 186,
225, 238
Carmichael, Ian, 15, 40
Carpenters, 284, 308
Carroll, Barbara, 216

Carroll, Joan, 212, 213
Carter, Benny, 29, 48, 89
Carter, Betty, 173, 190, 247,
248
Carter, Ron, 50, 67
Casa Loma Orchestra, 23, 182,
183, 199
Causer, Bob, 89, 102
Cavallaro, Carmen, 65, 154,
166
Chacksfield, Frank, 65, 110,
119, 133, 173, 192, 209, 228,
248, 264, 299
Chamberlain, Richard, 319
Chambers, Paul, 145, 229
Charisse, Cyd, 306, 307, 314,
325
Charles, Ray, 15, 84, 209
Cherry, Neneh, 154
Chevalier, Maurice, 133, 290,
292, 302
Christy, June, 250
Cincinnati Pops Orchestra, 31,
128
Clarey, Cynthia, 173
Clark, Buddy, 179
Clark, Harry, 275
Clark, Sonny, 72
Clark, Terry, 192
Clarke, Stanley, 97
Classics, 266
Clay, Edwin, 270
Clayton Brothers, 199
Clebanoff, 65, 173
Clicquot Club Eskimos, 36, 40
Cline, Patsy, 319, 320
Clinton, Larry, 182, 183, 190,
192
Clooney, Rosemary, 80, 85, 89,
102, 106, 114, 134, 154, 166,
173, 186, 192, 199, 229, 248,
255, 256, 284

Horne, Lena (cont.)
188, 250, 285, 296, 301
Hot Club of France, 26, 72
Hot Shots, 10
Hot Shots in "Drumnasticks",
120
Hotel Pennsylvania Music (Jack
Albin), 37
Hotel St. Regis Orchestra, 182,
183
Houben, Steve, 201
Houston Symphony Orchestra,
122
Howard, Sydney, 112
Hubbard, Freddie, 97
Hunt, Pee Wee, 102
Hunter, Alberta, 86
Hutchinson, Leslie, 6, 12, 16,
26, 35
Hutton, Betty, 212, 226
Hutton, Ina Ray, 222
Hylton, Jack, 12, 20, 91, 99,
103, 107, 111, 112, 190, 193
Hyman, Dick, 16, 52, 68, 99,
122, 148, 176, 216, 222, 230,
265, 271, 275
Iglesias, Julio, 69, 122, 126,
156, 301, 321
Igoe, Sonny, 53
Igor Bril Quartet, 294
Ikeno, Shigeaki, 68, 73
Ilardi, Angeli, 118
Indios Tabajaras, 122
Innovations Orchestra, 52, 53
Ives, Burl, 117
Jackson, Jack, 86
Jackson, Milt, 132, 230, 237,
250
Jackson, Willis, 296
James, Harry, 26
Jarrett, Keith, 310
Jaspar, Bobby, 311

Jazz At The Philharmonic, 26
Jazz Group, 220
Jazz Passengers, 148
Jeanmaire, 91, 110
Jeffreys, Anne, 262, 265, 269,
271, 272, 275
Jensen, Richard, 66
John, Elton, 321
Johnson, Bill, 234, 235
Johnson, Dick, 188, 201, 222
Johnson, James P., 26, 86
Johnson, Jimmie, 26
Johnson, J. J., 26, 201
Johnson, Peggy, 86
Jones, Elvin, 67
Jones, Etta, 37, 301
Jones, Hank, 26, 66
Jones, Jonah, 321
Jones, Philly Joe, 50
Jones, Quincy, 175, 298
Jones, Thad, 52, 188
Jongeyans, George, 279, 283
Jordan, Duke, 230, 232
Jordan, Sheila, 201, 230
Jordan, Stanley, 76
Jordanaires, 320
Joseph, Irving, 69, 103, 107,
123, 148, 156, 167, 176, 188,
230
Jourdan, Louis, 38, 290
Jungle Brothers, 92
Jurgens, Dick, 69, 148, 156,
197, 201, 206, 209, 210, 211,
216
Juris, Vic, 222
Kahn, Madeline, 20, 41, 104,
131, 182, 183, 190, 208, 210
Kallen, Kitty, 193, 321
Kamuca, Richie, 201
Kaplan, Leigh, 123
Kassel, Art, 179
Kaye, Danny, 220, 221, 225,

Index of Album Titles

Index of Musicals